ADVANCE PRAISE FOR *DIGITIZING TALENT*

"Jessica Miller-Merrell has always had the rare skill of taking complex information and creating digestible chunks of information. In *Digitizing Talent*, Jessica gives thorough explanations of the digital transformation that has occurred in the talent acquisition and recruiting space. From how we have gotten here to the future of work, Jessica has written a must-read book for all responsible for the people function. The digital recruitment space is moving at a breakneck pace. Read *Digitizing Talent* to make sure you do not get left behind!"

Jackye Clayton, *VP of Talent and DEIB, Textio*

"An extremely informative guidebook that encompasses all the aspects of data and business processes digitalization. This comprehensive overview will help HR professionals revamp their overall approach to recruiting in a consistent fashion and smoothly operate the digital transformation necessary to attract and connect with the candidates they need in an era of evolving social and cultural traits as well as fast-changing business and market requirements. This book is not bluntly preceptive. Instead, Jessica takes readers through her own journey and adeptly shows how she herself was able to progressively shed the analog mindset embedded in older technologies to embrace on a professional level the digital savviness we understand and practice in our everyday lives and how more technology, not less, is crucial to resurrect the human dimensions of recruiting."

Marylene Delbourg-Delphis, *Serial Technology CEO, Board Member, and Author*

"The reality of sourcing, acquiring, and retaining talent is an essential component of every organization now and will be for the foreseeable future. Understanding how to be effective in doing this digitally can be difficult to comprehend. Jessica Miller-Merrell has done a fantastic job of making this maze of options, approaches, and directions clear in her new book. She gives depth to a topic that is critical to talent acquisition, HR, and recruiting pros in a user-friendly and tangible way. I recommend her good work as a valuable resource for every organization."

Steve Browne, *SHRM-SCP, Chief People Officer, LaRosa's*

"Candidates don't magically appear from the internet. It takes knowledge, strategy, and creativity. Jessica gives you all of that and more in this book! She did the work and the research to help you attract and land more talent."

Tim Sackett, *SHRM-SCP, SPHR, HR/Talent Technology Analyst, Influencer, and Creator*

DIGITIZING TALENT

Creative Strategies for the Digital Recruiting Age

DIGITIZING TALENT

Creative Strategies for the Digital Recruiting Age

Jessica Miller-Merrell

Society for Human Resource Management
Alexandria, Virginia I shrm.org
Society for Human Resource Management, India Office
Mumbai, India I shrmindia.org
Society for Human Resource Management, Middle East and Africa Office
Dubai, UAE I shrm.org/pages/mena.aspx

This publication is designed to provide accurate and authoritative information regarding the subject matter covered. It is sold with the understanding that neither the publisher nor the author is engaged in rendering legal or other professional service. If legal advice or other expert assistance is required, the services of a competent, licensed professional should be sought. The federal and state laws discussed in this book are subject to frequent revision and interpretation by amendments or judicial revisions that may significantly affect employer or employee right and obligations. Readers are encouraged to seek legal counsel regarding specific policies and practices in their organizations.

This book is published by the Society for Human Resource Management (SHRM). The interpretations, conclusions, and recommendations in this book are those of the author and do no necessarily represent those of the publisher.

This publication may not be reproduced, stored in a retrieval system, or transmitted in whole or in part, in any form or by any means, electronic, mechanical, photocopying, recording, or otherwise, without the prior written permission of the publisher, or authorization through payment of the appropriate per-copy fee to the Copyright Clearance Center Inc., 222 Rosewood Drive Danvers, MA 01923, 978-750-8600, fax 978-646-8600, or on the web at www.copyright.com Requests to the publisher for permission should be addressed to SHRM Book Permissions 1800 Duke Street, Alexandria, VA 22314, or online at http://www.shrm.org/about-shrm/pages/copyright--permissions.aspx.

SHRM books and products are available on most online bookstores and through the SHRMStore at www.shrmstore.org.

SHRM creates better workplaces where employers and employees thrive together. As the voice of all things work, workers and the workplace, SHRM is the foremost expert, convener, and thought leader on issues impacting today's evolving workplaces. With 300,000+ HR and business executive members in 165 countries, SHRM impacts the lives of more than 115 million workers and families globally. Learn more at SHRM.org and on Twitter @SHRM.

Library of Congress Cataloging-in-Publication Data
Names: Miller-Merrell, Jessica, author.
Title: Digitizing talent : creative strategies for the digital recruiting age /
    Jessica Miller-Merrell.
Description: Alexandria, VA : Society for Human Resource Management, [2022] | Includes
    bibliographical references and index.
Identifiers: LCCN 2022019561 (print) | LCCN 2022019562 (ebook) | ISBN
    9781586444228 (paperback) | ISBN 9781586444303 (pdf) | ISBN 9781586444358
    (epub) | ISBN 9781586444402 (kindle edition)
Subjects: LCSH: Employee selection--Technological innovations. | Employees--Recruiting--
    Technological innovations.
Classification: LCC HF5549.5.S38 M55 2022 (print) | LCC HF5549.5.S38 (ebook) | DDC
    658.3/112--dc23/eng/20220511
LC record available at https://lccn.loc.gov/2022019561
LC ebook record available at https://lccn.loc.gov/2022019562

Printed in the United States of America

FIRST EDITION

PB Publishing 10 9 8 7 6 5 4 3 2 1   61.12303

I dedicate this book to my former bosses, Tom and Mark. Thank you for doing the thing I wasn't ready to do but needed to do in order to venture out as a woman entrepreneur, teacher, and educator serving the human resources community. Your actions fueled my passion, mission, and business.

Contents

Acknowledgments

This book is a culmination of conversations, research, experiences, and support I've received and experienced throughout my professional career, which spans over 20 years. I'd like to thank my family, including my husband, Greg, and my daughter, Ryleigh, for their unwavering support.

I'd also like to thank my parents, Terry and Leigh Miller, for instilling in me my work ethic and showing me what it means to love. My work has always been a family affair with my sisters, Jamie and Julie, and their families supporting me in different ways—whether it was updating websites or offering an opinion or outside point of view.

I want to thank my mentor, Marylene Delbourg-Delphis, for many late-night conversations filled with tough but real advice even when I didn't want to hear it. I'd like to thank my friends and amazing recruiting and HR resources Jennifer Tharp and Carrie Corbin for many recruiting and life conversations that helped lead to the development of this book. Thank you to Alicia Maples for your friendship, inspiration, and guidance.

A thank you to the following HR and talent acquisition readers I interviewed for this book and those who contributed their unique perspectives:

Devin Boyle, Josh Christianson, Corinne Weible, and the amazing
teams at The Wheelhouse Group, The Partnership on Employment

& Accessible Technology (PEAT), and The Partnership on Inclusive Apprenticeship (PIA)

Zahid Mubarik, chief consultant and CEO of HR Metrics

Elizabeth Baxter, chief people officer for Torchy's Tacos

Arron Daniels, former senior recruiting sourcer for HEB, current senior talent researcher for Starbucks

Dan Ellerman, global inclusion, diversity, and equity leader

Jo Weech, founder of Exemplary Consultants

Jason Hopkins, former director of talent acquisition at Emerus Holdings and current head of global employer brand at Gopuff

Will Staney, CEO and founder of Proactive Talent

Naghi Prasad, HR technology cofounder and CEO of Astound

Beth White, founder, CEO, and chief bot at MeBeBot

Thad Price, CEO of Talroo

Ben Eubanks, chief research officer at Lighthouse Research & Advisory

Pete Weddle, COO of TA Tech

Mike "Batman" Cohen, founder and sourcer at Wayne Technologies

I'd like to thank the HR and recruiting community as well as our *Workology* community. Your curiosity, questions, and feedback pushed me to write this book and continue doing the work that I do.

A book like this cannot happen without a team behind the scenes, which includes Kelly Love Johnson, Lauren Lindemulder, Ashley Edwards, Christopher Taborda, Dayalith Hernandez, Rawnsley Chege, Irene Rondon, Martin Mureithi, Jessica Acosta, and Peter Clayton. I'm forever grateful you have chosen to be on this journey with me.

A special thank you to our book's publisher, SHRM, and Matt Davis. Your team has been great to work with.

—Jessica Miller-Merrell

Introduction

When I began writing this book, it was with all of you, the HR and talent management professionals who work so hard to keep the "human" in human resources, in mind. In HR, we're always thinking about how to be more efficient and productive and the best way to support our employees, reach top talent, find the best candidates, and deliver a superb experience. The gig economy was growing at a fairly rapid rate, some employers offered remote work as a perk, and HR technology was a natural part of our daily work lives.

As I wrapped up the final chapters and prepared for editing and reviews at the end of 2019, I had no idea what we'd be facing in the coming year. In March of 2020, the world shut down because of the COVID-19 pandemic. I've heard from a lot of people who grabbed laptops and some folders to take home when their employers sent them to work from home until . . . well, until this whole thing was over. I don't think anyone knew just how long it would last or how terrible it would be.

I vividly remember sitting in Austin traffic in March of 2020, on my way to do a final walk-through of our event space for an upcoming HRetreat that was scheduled for SXSW (these were in-person events!). My phone blew up with texts: SXSW was canceled. That's when it really hit. SXSW was founded in 1987 in Austin, and it has been THE premier destination for creatives across the globe and has grown every single year since. And it had never been canceled, not in its entire 30-plus year history. I knew we were facing something that none of us had ever had to handle.

Because of the nature of my business, I was able to quickly pivot and hold events virtually (and set up meetings, test all the virtual platforms . . .), but the world just wasn't okay. I spent weeks in virtual conferences with consulting clients and vendor partners and HR professionals wondering what would happen to their certification testing before I decided to hit pause on this book.

My people—and you know who you are because you're reading this—needed me. I could pick up where I left off when things . . . settled down. We're well into 2022, two years into a pandemic, vaccine rollout, messy politics and an election, new COVID-19 variants, and supporting our essential workers and employees working remotely (many of whom had never done so before). In short, we are on the edge of burnout and we are tired.

I want to say to each one of you: good job! Good job hanging in there and showing up to do your best. Good job being the sole support system for your employees. Good job on figuring out how to get everyone on Zoom (or Teams or Slack). You're still here. And I'm glad.

When I returned to this book, the biggest question I asked myself was "Is it still relevant?" As I scrolled through chapter after chapter, I realized that *Digitizing Talent: Creative Strategies for the Digital Recruiting Age* is even more relevant than when I began writing it. In fact, I wish I could have put it out there before the shutdown in March of 2020. Anyone who was reluctant to take recruiting and HR online before COVID-19 got a crash course in doing it by the seat of our pants. And those who were advocating for digitizing talent before the pandemic—company leadership was looking to them to implement new tech RIGHT NOW.

The most important thing I wanted to accomplish with this book was to take the mystery out of recruiting in the digital space. For most of us, HR and talent acquisition is a long-term career. If you've been in HR as long as I have, you remember when you placed help-wanted ads in a print newspaper, maybe posted a job or two on Craigslist, but as far as developing an entire digital recruiting strategy? We have a lot to keep up with already, and adding search engine optimization (SEO), best practices for online job posts, legislation around what we can and cannot ask in our online applications . . . all of this can feel really overwhelming. And many of us are working on HR teams of one or two! Know that I am here for you. I'm a real person to whom you can reach out (my contact info is at the end of this introduction). Each chapter will break a different component of digitizing talent down in easy steps and I'll be holding your hand through each one.

In addition to this book, I've created additional resources that are updated more frequently. They can be found at DigitizingTalent. com and include checklists, audio recordings of our case study interviews, and other links and helpful articles to arm you with information. You can also sign up for our 12-week supporting resource series on the site, also called Digitizing Talent, available at the book's website and at Workology.com. It's a free, 7-day, digital recruiting coaching course where I talk more about concepts and tools. Additionally, feel free to reach out on Twitter by tweeting your question using the #digitizingtalent hashtag. You can also send me and my team an email at hello@workology.com, and we will do our best to connect you to the right resource. I'd also love to hear your stories of how you are innovating the digital recruiting experience.

Thanks for being here, thanks for taking this journey with me, and thank you for reading.

Much love,
Jessica Miller-Merrell

CHAPTER 1

The Power of Digital

- The Role and Responsibility of Digital for Recruiting
- How I Got Here
- What to Expect in This Book

For most of us, living in a world without the internet is unimaginable. My 13-year-old daughter marvels at the idea of how we lived in a world without iPhones, YouTube, and Amazon's Alexa. I remember thinking and saying the same thing to my parents when they told me that television used to be black and white and people listened to records or the radio instead of cassette tapes. She's asked me too, just like I did when I was her age, if I was around when dinosaurs were alive, and sometimes I feel like I might have been with how fast technology is moving, especially when I think about the changes that are coming with artificial intelligence, blockchain, and other new technologies.

In April of 2019, 4.4 billion people were active internet users surfing the web, ordering online, reading online restaurant reviews, and booking their travel online.[1] This 4.4 billion number accounts for 58 percent of the entire world population. The average internet user, according to a Digital Trends 2019 report from social media scheduling tool Hootsuite, found that the average internet user spends 6 hours and 42 minutes a day online.[2] But many of us reading this book (including myself) remember a world without the internet. It was one where phones were tethered by cords to walls, where we took pictures with cameras on film, and where we had to wait an entire week before watching our favorite TV show episode (and we couldn't just skip the commercials).

The world I remember and grew up in has certainly changed. It's changed for all ages and demographics, whether you are from the boomer generation or are a millennial (the first generation to grow up with the internet). Just this morning, I woke up and checked my smartphone after shutting off my iPhone alarm before starting my work day, quickly scanning my calendar, email, and other social messages. And instead of driving to the office, I worked from the comfort of my makeshift office at our Airbnb, taking calls and meetings from digital communications technologies like Zoom, Google Voice, and Facebook. Then later this afternoon, I drove to Target to pick up my mobile online order, which was delivered to my car promptly as I arrived in the store's parking lot. Just now I was able to answer the doorbell to my house from another state using my iPhone and a mobile doorbell technology called Ring to find that my online Amazon order had just arrived. I'll text my neighbor later to ask her if she'll do me a favor and store my package in her garage until I head back home this weekend.

THE ROLE AND RESPONSIBILITY OF DIGITAL FOR RECRUITING

Yes, the world has changed dramatically and much of that we owe to technology. What does all of this have to do with recruiting and human resources? Well, everything. If 58 percent of your global candidate pool (and I think it's a lot more) is spending hours of their lives online, employers and recruiting and talent acquisition teams need to be heavily investing or reinvesting in being available to reach, engage, and interact with their candidates and employees online. And those numbers are still growing. That same Digital 2019 report suggests that the internet is now growing at a rate of 1 billion users every 2.7 years, and that's a conservative number. Recruiting and HR leaders should be focused on their digital efforts because the reliance, use, and expectation of being on the internet and engaging our employees and candidates digitally is going to increase.

While this book focuses primarily on the digital recruiting process and landscape, many of these same sites, principles, and technologies can be used to engage your employees. If the average American spends 6 hours and 42 minutes online every day, the digital landscape is one that every manager, leader, and business should be thinking about in terms of the entire employment life cycle, from recruiting to hiring to development to exit. They need to be thinking about digital and the internet for every aspect of how they engage each and every candidate and employee.

One thing I do know for sure is that it's okay to feel overwhelmed. By picking up this book, however, you are showing initiative and acknowledging that change is happening and that you have a willingness and a commitment to learn and grow, which I think is the hardest part. The second step is sticking with it and sharing your experience and the nuggets of wisdom and insight you've learned along the way with others.

HOW I GOT HERE

I'm a bit of an internet evangelist or enthusiast when it comes to recruitment and human resources. After just graduating from college in 2001, I was new in my HR role working as a store HR leader for Target. My store location had a quarterly budget of $250 for recruiting and job ads, and I invested all of our budget in job advertising in the classified section of the newspaper. While candidates did apply at my store location, I didn't make a single hire for the sales associate, order puller, or cashier roles that were open at my store.

Having spent our entire budget on two ads and twelve inches, I set out to find a creative and cost-effective way to reach my candidate community. I was broke and I didn't want to lose my job three months into my new role, so I looked on the internet. In 2001, the two main reasons you were on the internet were that you were looking for love or looking at NSFW websites. I decided to use the former rather than the latter in my recruiting efforts and began using free online dating websites to source candidates that fit my job openings.

I saw these online dating websites as digital rolodexes, searchable and similar to how we use LinkedIn to search by city, job title, and/or company name. Once I had my search criteria figured out and a few qualified candidates sourced, I reached out to them via private message letting them know I was a recruiter and I had a job opening they might be interested in. The response was amazing, and I quickly made hires for all types of positions at our store, from assistant manager to cashier at no cost with my creative digital sourcing.

My digital love affair (no pun intended) with the internet continued, and I expanded my internet sourcing and recruiting to forums, chat rooms, and social networking sites like MySpace. At around the same time, I created and launched a job search blog in 2005. Originally called *BloggingforJobs*, I created the blog on a free blogging platform and used it successfully to share job seeker tips and best practices while also building a candidate pipeline as HR Director at my company. I started blogging about the job search from a recruiting and hiring manager perspective, and people started writing me back and emailing me. From this, I was able to create a candidate funnel that could quickly fill my job openings.

Many of the openings I was charged with filling were what I called "evergreen jobs," meaning that I was almost always hiring for the role of sales manager, call center sales, outside sales, and other sales supervisor and sales support roles. How many of these roles I hired for, however, fluctuated based on the sales forecasts we had for the region and the division my team was responsible for. It was very common for headcounts to change dramatically. During the first quarter, our expected headcount shifted to 250 openings from 25, with the expectation that we needed to fill those roles immediately. My team wasn't prepared for the fluctuations, and we went through a painful and weekly process of explaining to our boss and the division leaders we supported via a group conference call why the roles were not being filled as fast as they wanted.

My blog and social media outreach and campaigns helped us to establish a pipeline with the understanding that headcounts would dramatically change again, and we were able to create a list of fifty to one hundred candidates who were prevetted, qualified, and waiting for offers until those headcount numbers again changed. Having worked in retail for a number of years at Target and other big-box retailers, I was no stranger to mass hiring, especially during high volume seasonal hiring times. It was a strategy that worked well for us and quickly started me down the path of sharing these experiences with other HR and recruiting leaders.

From 2007 to 2009, my internet recruiting activities accounted for 30 percent of all our hires and I discovered that candidates from social networking sites like Twitter, LinkedIn, Facebook, and MySpace had higher retention and lower turnover rates. The work I was doing was outside of the brand. I was doing it using my personal social media accounts, and *BloggingforJobs* was still relatively anonymous. My bio didn't list my employer and only included my first name and last initial.

My success in these areas was getting noticed, which was exciting, but my employer at the time wasn't excited about or impressed by my use of social media. They were fearful of the potential liabilities and risk it posed. I remember sitting down with our general counsel during a meeting about an EEOC investigation that was pending. I was the HR representative who did the initial investigation, and counsel was working on submitting the company's response. It was during that conversation he asked me about any outside activities (such as social media or blogging) and I saw the fear and concern on his face. After countless conversations with senior leaders about the benefits of social media and digital recruiting, I realized that I had a responsibility to help educate, train, and share resources and best practices with HR and recruiting leaders like our HR and recruiting leadership team. This was a new era we had entered, and digital recruiting wasn't something we should fear; it was an opportunity to reach candidates in a new and different way.

Fast forward nearly fifteen years. Since that time, I've written several books, spoken at hundreds of conferences, and published thousands of articles with the goal to educate, evangelize, and share best practices and stories of HR and recruiting practitioners. And now I'm writing this one. I think of myself as a workplace anthropologist, and my educational background happens to be in cultural anthropology. This is the branch of anthropology concerned with the study of human societies and cultures and their development. I see my role in HR as someone who studies the culture of the HR and recruiting industry as well as the human society that is the world of work. My area of interest within this microcosm is the technology that is intertwined with this human resources aspect of human society.

How I got here . . . well, it's because I made a lot of mistakes. I took a lot of chances, and I listened and talked to a lot of people. I wrote millions of words and shared what I learned with others. I read a lot of books, and most importantly, that employer I mentioned earlier in this chapter gave me the best gift I never knew I wanted. I was fired from my job. It was a blessing and it gave me the courage to go "all in"— writing, speaking, teaching, and training in HR and recruiting.

WHAT TO EXPECT IN THIS BOOK

With all of this in mind, I want to talk a bit about what you can expect from this book. In early 2010, I gave my first talk at the SHRM National Conference that discussed the use of social media and technology to drive innovation and change within the HR industry. My first love, however, has been recruiting, ever since 2001 when I found myself the HR manager at a rural Target store in Garden City, Kansas.

This book is designed for recruiting, HR, and workplace leaders at all levels. Whether you are a seasoned digital practitioner or someone who is just diving into digital recruiting for the very first time, this book is for you. I've done my best to feature case studies and success stories as well as failures to help arm you with knowledge, information, and resources to get out there, experiment, and learn how to engage your candidates using the internet and digital strategies. The key is that you learn and put the fear of the unknown aside to dive right in.

The digital recruitment space is vast and is moving very quickly, from new uses for social media and apps like Instagram and TikTok as a way to engage candidates, to new HR technologies and enhancements in messaging, automation, and supporting technologies like applicant tracking systems, recruitment marketing, and programmatic advertising platforms. I will be discussing topics like artificial intelligence, which will have its own dedicated chapter, as well as the new world of block-chain and its application in recruiting. In this book, I will do my best to give you a broad base from which to work with the focus on practical recruiting applications.

Above all, my goal is to help you educate and arm yourself with knowledge. The case studies, stories, and companies featured are of all sizes, from small startups with twenty-five employees to Fortune 10 companies. Digital recruiting is still the Wild West, and the barrier to entry is just a smartphone, an internet connection, and a willingness to talk to your candidates.

I say "Wild West" because it's still being designed, being developed, and not fully mature—meaning that you're not too late to the party if you haven't set up an online career site or a social media presence, have yet to monitor your company's brand on employee review sites, or haven't set up your Google Analytics dashboard. I'm here to say it's okay if you haven't done any of these things. I'm also here to say that if you have, congratulations! Now let's take it a step further.

The barrier to entry is low, and the expectation from job seekers is also relatively low, meaning you can set up a small digital engagement campaign and really knock their socks off, improving your recruitment brand dramatically and driving more qualified candidates to your job openings. What I really mean to tell you here is that employers, generally speaking, are doing little to nothing in terms of engagement and relationship building online. Most employers aren't sending anything beyond an automatic thank you response from an unresponsive or unmanaged email address to job candidates after they apply.

According to the *2020 North American Candidate Experience Report* from the Talent Board, 33 percent of North American candidates said that they had not heard back from employers two months after they applied.[3] This is what I mean when I say the barrier to entry is low. If a recruiting team simply commits to creating a process to respond to each candidate and giving them an update on their application within sixty days of their application, you would have a candidate and digital recruiting experience that is better than 41 percent of the rest of all employers, making you, as the employer, a shining star of the internet and your community.

Think about this for a minute: if at a retail establishment like one of the big-box retailers where I used to work, the cashier simply just thanked all shoppers for shopping at the store every single time, that cashier would be creating a better experience than forty-one out of one hundred of your competitors by doing one simple thing. Now imagine if you could automate that thank you—maybe with an automated email or a chat bot that could provide a status update and thank that same customer and/or candidate sixty days after their application or purchase, either using the ATS technology you already have or by investing under $10,000 a year for an experience improvement like this. It's possible using some of the tools and technologies we will be talking about in this book.

This book has twelve different and distinct chapters, countless case studies, and a host of digital resources for you to reference and download to help you start, grow, and focus your digital recruiting efforts. I'll also be pointing you to, and mentioning, a number of HR technology and recruiting technology companies that I believe can help enhance processes and elevate your digital recruiting efforts that I recommend.

Thank you for taking the time to pick up this book and dive in. Let's jump head first into the world of digitizing talent and getting you not just prepped but ready to make valuable and measurable change in your organization and in the fast-moving world of online and digital recruitment.

CHAPTER 2

Recruiting
Revolution or Evolution

- **The History of Talent and Recruiting**
- **Why Talent Reigns Supreme**
- **How to Measure Talent**
- **Introducing the Intellectual Capital Index**

Even in just fifteen short years, the way in which we hire and recruit has changed—and that was before the acceleration of remote and hybrid work during a global pandemic. I mentioned a number of ways in the first chapter, but I think it's worth taking a look back at the history of recruiting.

THE HISTORY OF TALENT AND RECRUITING

We use the term "talent" a lot in human resources and recruiting, but what is talent really and how important is it to our organizations?

The word "talent" is of Latin origin meaning to scale, balance, and sum. In Greek and Roman times, it was one of several ancient units of mass and was a commercial weight. The weight of a talent and its value were equivalent to naturally occurring precious metals, including gold and silver. Gold doesn't corrode and is a universal symbol of immortality and power. Gold and silver rarity was used to obtain power and demonstrate the owner's position within the larger ecosystem or culture.

If the concept of talent has its roots in measurement, power, and success, then why is evaluating and measuring talent a concept business leaders struggle with? Is it simply just the idea of having the most talent that lends to creating and growing a successful company? Unfortunately, talent isn't as simple as that. There are complexities among the layers and levels of our gold, shiny talent. It isn't just about exerting or demonstrating power. It's about performance and the impact employees or talent contribute individually and collectively for our organizations. It starts first with assessment and measurement.

I find these roots in measurement ironic because human capital is so challenging to measure. There is no financial statement or report called a Human Capital Statement. The Securities and Exchange Commission (SEC) introduced new disclosure requirements that went into effect on November 9, 2020. They now require public companies to disclose their number of employees and a description of human capital resources, along with any human capital measures or objectives—from the operating model, to talent planning, learning and innovation, employee experience, and work environment.

Despite these new requirements, the SEC has not included a definition of "human capital" or a list of required measures to disclose. In 2018, the International Organization for Standardization (ISO) published ISO 30414,[1] *Human Resource Management—Guidelines for Internal and External Human Capital Reporting*, which was the first International Standard that allows organizations to get a clear view of the actual contribution of human capital. It provides guidelines on core HR areas such as organizational culture, recruitment and turnover, productivity, health and safety, and leadership.

This challenge in measuring, managing, and organizing the concept of talent is the reason that I believe we needed a recruiting system in the first place. While I'll discuss the attempts at measuring the impact of talent with a human capital financial statement later in this chapter, I want to make sure we look at the evolution of digital recruiting from paper applications to applying online.

As the idea of recruiting and hiring became more complex and refined, the need to have a way to measure the effectiveness of the time spent hiring, not to mention the growing compliance requirements that companies have in the United States, led to the creation of the first job board in 1990 with job listings on Usenet, followed by Dice's launch of a bulletin board system (BBS). Historically, you might remember the following as an early adopter, or e-recruiter or internet recruiter, as it was called.[2]

- Monster and CareerBuilder (originally called NetStart) were founded in 1994.
- The initial steps involved the launching of Craigslist (1995) and Stepstone launching in Germany.
- Jobsonline.com became the #1 job site online in 1999, and niche sites began to appear in 2000.
- In 2002, Monster bought Jobs.com for $800,000.
- In 2003, LinkedIn launched—a new era for job boards and digital recruiting.

But before there were job boards, it was newspapers that revolutionized the recruitment industry. It was classified ads that were the catalyst that launched recruiting online. Newspapers and their advertisements began to be placed online. These sites were pre–job boards and offered a great way for companies that were hiring to elevate and expand the reach and longevity of their classified job ads in newspapers. In 1998, the first job sites appeared along with innovator Monster.com providing job seekers a mechanism for searching and applying for thousands of jobs without traveling to the company office to apply or mailing a résumé and cover letter application.

I graduated from college just as job boards were coming into their own, and yet I remember applying for jobs by completing a paper job application. My first experience with an online application process came in my first HR job where my employer encouraged job candidates to apply at the store with our application kiosks.

HR technology has significantly changed the recruiting landscape, along with how we measure success in recruiting. Back nearly before the dawn of time, HR technology was simple. We used human resource information systems (HRIS) and applicant tracking systems (ATS) that were easy to understand. Seven tabs over to add the letter H. Enter in your new hire's information. Hit enter four times. Tab over six more to enter in S for salary entering in your new hires' biweekly salary information.

My first ATS system wasn't that much different. I worked at Target where the selling features of my first HR technology were the simple breadcrumb structure I had to follow and that the hiring assessment was integrated with the application. I received the hiring assessment information via fax. I could see the basic candidate information, which I printed off and asked all my candidate interviewees to quickly sign. Interview notes were handwritten on a separate form that I attached to the application. The mailbox next to my office served as a secure repository for managers to hand off applications and their interviews, including their scores and recommended next steps.

The creation of the ATS system was out of a need for compliance, serving as online candidate application storage allowing me to organize, sort, and relatively quickly access candidate applications that were completed via a kiosk and not at the library or online. This online process was handy, especially as I navigated several HR audits by both corporate representatives and other government entities.

I think a lot of technology providers and developers don't take the time to understand or appreciate the history of the ATS. It was built as a candidate application online repository for the purposes of organizing candidate information so that companies could maintain document storage compliance. It was not a collaborative, candidate-oriented platform. It was only designed for the HR leader or recruiter. It certainly wasn't created as a talent funnel tool destined to attract candidates. Nor was it intended to handle the project management process that recruiting has now become.

I mention these things because, for those of us with ten or more years of experience working in HR and recruitment, this is the world we remember and know. It's been our reality. I remember thinking how helpful an ATS system was because it made my file room so much easier to manage. My team spent what seemed like two days a quarter working in the storage room, packing and mailing employee files and records to go to the permanent storage facility. Not all of us were as lucky as me. Since I worked for a large company, we could send our extra files to a centralized storage location.

I did work for another company, however, that had a permanent metal storage container behind our main office building that served as our long-term storage. I remember being horrified when, during my first week, I learned that the storage shed actually wasn't secure. There was no lock, and yet it was housing all our candidate applications, payroll registers, and terminated employee files, putting the employer and the employees and candidates at great risk. My first order of business was securing that building with a lock. Even fifteen years later, that potential liability makes me cringe physically, especially now when you consider the need for data and file security with cloud technology

Fast-forward to the present day. We now have integrated systems that push and pull information between HR technologies like an HRIS, sourcing technologies, job boards, and onboarding technology, as well as the ATS. I've said before that ATS systems are the selfie stick of HR. The ATS can be awkward and one note, and yet it serves an important purpose in the history of the internet and digital recruiting. With so many new innovations, features, and variables that are changing, however, it all ties into measuring our talent acquisition efforts.

Along with tools and technology like the ATS comes the necessity to understand and identify potential problem areas in your hiring process and quickly address them. Depending on the technology you have, you should spend less time developing charts and graphs for PowerPoint slides and creating Excel formulas and more time educating yourself and your leadership team on metrics and numbers that are driving results.

WHY TALENT REIGNS SUPREME

Your CEO knows talent is important. According to a 2021 Annual Global CEO survey by PwC,

> Nearly half of CEOs plan increases of 10% or more in their long-term investment in digital transformation. Today's digital focus contrasts with the situation in 2010, after the global financial crisis, when the biggest investment priority for CEOs in our survey was gaining cost efficiencies. When asked to prioritize the societal outcomes that business should help deliver, CEOs put the creation of a skilled, educated and adaptable workforce at the top of the list. At the same time, a growing number of CEOs are seeking to boost their organization's competitiveness through digital investments in the workforce; 36% aim to focus on productivity through technology and automation, which is more than double the share of CEOs who said the same in 2016.[3]

That is exactly where we, as HR leaders, fit in.

One of the most ironic things to come out of nearly two years in a global pandemic is organizational leaders shifting decision making and scenario planning around talent to company HR leaders and teams. In fact, C-level positions for HR, like Chief Human Resources Officer (CHRO) and VP of Talent are becoming more and more common. Whether a company managed essential workers or remote employees during the early days of the pandemic, empathy became a prime commodity. Company leaders looked to HR to help them understand what employees were experiencing, to find out how to keep employees safe, and to keep up with CDC guidelines and other legislation like the CARES Act. Company leaders were also looking to HR to help measure what they have historically said could not be measured.

These, my friends, are the reasons we are in the business of recruitment, or what some call "talent acquisition." We are the subject matter experts on all things talent in our organizations, but we aren't business experts in the broad sense. The truth is there is no way to effectively define and measure talent because there is simply no line on our financial statements called "Talent Impact Ratio" or "Talent Equity." We are asking for black and white concepts in the gray world of business. It's the fifty shades of talent, if you will.

HOW TO MEASURE TALENT

Recruiting and HR metrics like turnover, retention, and cost-per-hire are metrics and analytics that only look at the initial impact of talent in terms of the cost associated with the best talent that joins our organization. Unless you are an individual contributor in a revenue-generating role, the impact of talent is hard to define and measure. Metrics like revenue-per-employee are more effective at measuring the impact of great talent in your organization but don't tell us the impact of an amazing individual who works with operations. The path to their reach and impact is murky at best, and so the journey to effectively defining, evaluating, and measuring talent continues.

Books like Dave Ulrich's *Leadership Capital Index* are helping to change how we evaluate talent and the impact of leadership. It's not an easy read, but I have to remind myself that neither are financial statements or profit and loss statements (P&Ls). Understanding business is hard, and so far my biggest criticism of Ulrich's book is that it is only evaluating the benefit of leaders within the organization. His *Leadership Capital Index* doesn't go deep enough to measure the impact of talent within the entire organization. I like that it is speaking a CEO's language, but it doesn't look at the impact of frontline managers and what Seth Godin refers to as linchpins within the organization. These are employees who disrupt, transform, and impact the business in such a way that they are indispensable. Unfortunately, at present we have no real way to effectively measure the impact of those linchpins. I like the direction Ulrich is headed. I just wish it was an easier read and offered a more pragmatic perspective.

Since 2014, I've hosted the *Workology Podcast*. Some 350-plus episodes and 100,000 downloads later, I spend time every week sitting down with HR and recruiting leaders to talk about trends, tools, tech, and anything else my guests want to share with our audience. I've had some really valuable conversations, including the one I'm going to talk about here.

Granted, measuring human capital is a tough topic—which is why listening to multiple perspectives can't hurt. I had the opportunity to interview Zahid Mubarik, chief consultant and CEO of HR Metrics, for the *Workology Podcast* not too long after the SEC announced its new reporting requirements.[4] Zahid is an expert on the human capital metrics that will now be part of quarterly SEC reporting.

I asked Zahid about the driving force behind the ISO changes and why it's happening now. "In the larger context, the biggest challenge we face globally is income instability. If your people management is not in order, many aspects of the business will not work." Without sustained performance, the organization cannot maintain stability and continuity. "The reporting on what we call intangibles, the human capital factors, is becoming more and more important to the overall organization, not just in terms of headcount, but in how the company can move forward."

Zahid is also a member of an ISO committee that sets HR standards and guidelines. This is a group of people who have come together to determine what the standard should be. "The committee decides which standards are in review, then there is a process for proposal submission . . . at every stage there is an element of participation and it must be approved by the majority. These standards are meant for the global workforce, not just one country."

HR metrics introduces an element of quantification into a historically stories-based department of human resources. "The new metrics requirements are designed to take into account the needs of all stakeholders, not just those we have to convince to buy into our HR programs."

Stakeholders are anyone who has an interest in the organization—the community, the regulators, anyone who cares about employment offered by the company, anyone working for the company, company leadership, and shareholders. "The standards offer a new element of data for shareholder aspirations, but also provide information about the company to employees within the company," said Zahid.

Human capital can be such a gray area, and there has been a lot of pushback against human capital standards. Zahid said that "if the organization understands that it's important to be transparent for more reasons than minimum disclosure requirements, then from the perspective of the employee it inspires confidence in leadership and how the company is allocating resources to career development and coordinated training, hiring, and other HR efforts." When we share more and we're more up front with people, we're more profitable in our business.

"From a very basic point of view, we are gathering essential information that shouldn't be scary; it's a health check for the company that helps it determine where and on what to focus for the future."

With the new standards and SEC regulations, the spotlight will shine even brighter on HR and our ability to perform in the areas of employee development, safety, engagement, attraction, and retention.

While the SEC has not clearly defined human capital, the ISO has given us guidelines on these core HR metrics.

INTRODUCING THE INTELLECTUAL CAPITAL INDEX

One measurement I am excited about that recently launched from Talent Growth Advisors (TGA) is their Intellectual Capital Index (ICI).[5] It's part of the first-ever study to measure the specific dollar-figure contributions that talent makes to the market value of companies included in the Dow Jones Industrial Average (DJIA). Their analysis revealed that 86 percent of the average company's value is a result of the active source of intellectual capital—its talent. Employees are directly responsible for more than $4 trillion dollars of the value for companies in the DJIA alone. Their statistics research is incredible, but so far ICI is limited to the Dow Jones—those not currently listed on the stock exchange are in the same boat they were before.

However, the data and research they are providing seems promising. The top five companies listed on the ICI are the following:

- Boeing
- Pfizer
- Apple
- United Technologies
- United Health

It's not surprising these businesses are on the list. My bigger question is, what is the method behind the TGA measurement? What are they measuring, and how are they determining how talent makes a $4 trillion contribution? Is there a way to determine which departments, teams, employee types, or leaders make the most impact? At present, TGA isn't talking about it. I guess we need to buy their consulting services to really understand more about the method to their madness.

Even so, I'm excited about the progress and the movement to help define how great talent can positively impact an organization, especially those who are in supporting organizational roles. The key to measuring the talent and impact within your organization starts with educating and having a constant flow of dialogue with your leadership and management team. This becomes even more complex when you factor in not only the economic growth we are experiencing but also the new pace at which HR technology and digital recruiting is evolving.

CHAPTER 3

The Trust Economy

- **Understanding Trust Online**
- **Understanding Your Audience**
- **Your Employee Value Proposition**
- **Methods of Research: Employee Experience**
- **How Building Your Employer Brand in a Trust Economy Works**
- **Response Templates**

This new digital landscape provides dozens of options, enabling job seekers to rely on relationships and trusted online sources for recommended companies, employment, and work opportunities. The rise of employer review sites and social media puts pressure on employers to be more transparent in their recruiting and hiring processes. Employers are looking for creative ways to build relationships with candidates and tell stories that drive candidates to their career sites to apply for job opportunities. It's all part of the new candidate experience, and a new dimension in the war for talent that we've been competing in for most of our careers.

UNDERSTANDING TRUST ONLINE

Each year, global communications firm Edelman releases its Trust Barometer—a survey-driven report of how trusted governments, NGOs, businesses, and media are around the world. The *2021 Edelman Trust Barometer* draws on responses from thirty-three thousand individuals in twenty-eight countries.[1] It reveals insights about both the general population (ages 18+) and informed public (college-educated, ages 25–64, in the top 25 percent of household income in their country's age group). This year's *Edelman Trust Barometer* notably uncovered a growing distrust of government in the United States and China and increased expectations from business leaders.

After a year of unprecedented disaster and turbulence—the COVID-19 pandemic and economic crisis, the global outcry over systemic racism, and political instability—the *2021 Edelman Trust Barometer* revealed an epidemic of misinformation and widespread mistrust of societal institutions and leaders around the world. Adding to this is a failing trust ecosystem unable to confront the rampant infodemic, leaving the four institutions—business, government, NGOs, and media—in an environment of information bankruptcy and a mandate to rebuild trust and chart a new path forward.[2]

According to this year's *Trust Barometer* report, business is more trusted than government, NGOs, and media in eighteen of twenty-seven countries surveyed. Additionally, 68 percent of those surveyed believe CEOs should step in when the government does not fix societal problems, 66 percent think CEOs should take the lead on change rather than waiting for the government to impose change on them, 65 percent believe CEOs should hold themselves accountable to the public and not just to the board of directors or stockholders, and 86 percent expect CEOs to speak out publicly about one or more of these societal changes: pandemic impact, job automation, societal issues, and local community issues.

Employees are ready and willing to trust their employers, but the trust must be earned through more than "business as usual." Employees who have trust in their employer are far more likely to engage in beneficial actions on their behalf—they will advocate for the organization, be more engaged, and remain far more loyal and committed than their more skeptical counterparts.

In short, the trust economy impacts your employer brand, your organization's ability to attract talent, customer perception, employee loyalty, retention, and engagement—it hits every single part of your business.

UNDERSTANDING YOUR AUDIENCE

HR leaders are familiar with focus groups, but they are accustomed to using them as an employee experience and communication tool rather than a candidate experience research channel. Ideally, starting a dialogue with your job seeker communities that goes beyond an email survey will give you the information you need to better understand your audience, get a look into how and where you can improve the process for candidates, and what your employer brand tells candidates about your company.

In a 2020 survey from CareerPlug, 50 percent of candidates said they had a poor recruitment experience and turned down a job because of it, and 69 percent of job seekers share negative candidate experiences online or directly with friends, resulting in major reputational damage.[3] Additionally, the Talent Board reports that 73 percent of candidates were never asked for feedback on their experiences in the application process.[4] According to Career Arc, nearly 60 percent of candidates have had a poor experience, and 72 percent of them shared the experience either online or with someone directly.[5]

So how do we collect this data? Many HR departments are using surveys to collect information from candidates. Taking a page out of the marketing handbook, the Net Promoter Score (NPS) is a tool that is used to gauge customer loyalty. It serves as an alternative to traditional customer satisfaction research and claims to be correlated with revenue growth. This method can be used with candidates and in fact is being used by many companies today. It's always good to have quantitative data, but if you want to take the candidate survey a step further into advanced marketing methodologies, your next natural step is to conduct focus groups.

NPS was developed as a means to measure customer loyalty more quickly and accurately. In a *Harvard Business Review* article, the creator of the system, Frederick F. Reichheld, explained that simply measuring customer retention rates isn't enough.[6] Attracting a high number of customers is great in the short run, but loyalty is what will help your company grow exponentially in the long run. Loyal customers spread word of your business, lower new customer acquisition costs, and chose to use your services even when confronted with a cheaper option. NPS is based on survey responses to one simple question: "Would you recommend our company to a friend or colleague?"

HR teams can also use NPS to gauge employee loyalty. Employee Net Promoter Score (eNPS) is calculated in the same way, except you're asking the question, "How likely is it that you would recommend this company as a place to work?"

It's important to pulse check your eNPS regularly. Send out quarterly surveys asking your employees to rate on a scale of 1–10: "How likely is it that you would recommend this company as a place to work?"

Those employees who answer with a 9–10 out of 10 are considered net promoters. Anyone under this number is considered either a passive promoter (7–8) or a detractor (0–6). Just like your NPS, your eNPS is calculated by subtracting the number of detractors from the number of net promoters.

How eNPS Supports HR and Recruiting Efforts

Attracting and Retaining Employees. One of the top concerns of every HR department is attracting and retaining top talent. Millennials in particular have quite different demands from employers than previous generations.[7] Employees are also the best source for attracting new talent to your company, so keeping your existing team happy pays off in the future. However, Elance-oDesk found that 57 percent of millennials consider long-term company loyalty to be dead.[8] According to a survey by the American Management Association, declining employee loyalty causes low morale (84 percent), high turnover (80 percent), disengagement (80 percent), growing distrust (76 percent), and lack of team spirit (73 percent).[9] To guard your company against high turnover and the inability to attract talent, it's important to keep track of your eNPS.

Company Brand. Failing to keep on top of employee loyalty today can greatly damage your company's image. Employees are now free to air their feelings about their employer on sites like Glassdoor and Indeed. Fortune's *100 Best Companies to Work For* ranking is based on employee reviews of company culture. In what Josh Bersin of Deloitte terms the "ratings economy," scoring low on these very public channels can greatly impact public confidence in your business. Companies that make it on Fortune's list experience a 14 percent average rise in stock prices per year compared to 6 percent in the overall market.[10] If you gain your employees' loyalty, their opinion is less likely to be swayed even during difficult times that require more overtime without salary increases.

Customer Satisfaction. Employee engagement has a major impact on NPS. Your employees are your brand ambassadors, and if they don't believe in your brand, this will come across to your customers. Creating a strong company culture that helps engage and educate your employees on your company values will greatly impact brand loyalty. Surprisingly, Gallup found only 41 percent of employees actually know what their company stands for and how their brand differs from competitors.[11]

YOUR EMPLOYEE VALUE PROPOSITION

At its heart, an employee value proposition (EVP) is the unique set of benefits an employee receives in return for the skills, capabilities, and experience they bring to a company. An EVP is about defining the essence of your company—how it is unique and what it stands for.

An EVP describes the mix of characteristics, benefits, and ways of working in an organization. It's the deal struck between company and employee in return for their contribution and performance. This "deal" characterizes an employer and differentiates it from its competition.

Developing a strong EVP is a key element of any recruiting and retention effort. At its most basic level, an EVP represents everything of value that an employer provides to its employees—pay, benefits, training, career development opportunities, and so on—and it is then "marketed" to the workforce. EVPs matter because they should be the foundation on which your brand and all your internal retention efforts, as well as your external recruiting efforts, are established. I'll go into depth about EVPs in Chapter 5.

METHODS OF RESEARCH: EMPLOYEE EXPERIENCE

Focus groups can be a valuable source of qualitative market research, which can be leveraged to achieve key business goals such as improving customer service, developing products, and increasing brand awareness. With job seeker focus groups, the goal is the same, but you'll use this research opportunity to understand the candidate experience, the impact of your employer brand, the audience of candidates you are attracting, the types of information about your company job seekers want, and answers to questions they have in the hiring process.

Using traditional marketing as a model, we can identify best practices for focus group market research. Here are six best practices when setting up your candidate experience focus group.

1: Identify Your Target Audience. That should be job seekers and candidates, right? Selecting an accurate representation takes a little more forethought and there's a balancing act at play. You'll want to exclude people who don't represent your actual prospective candidates, but you need to include everyone who does. This is where your candidate personas can help. You can use your survey to help identify a cross section of applicants by adding a few questions that exclude or include your typical job applicant.

You don't want to ask arbitrary questions such as whether or not candidates are currently employed, about their marital status, or other personal or demographic characteristics. However, the survey can help identify potential focus group members by engagement. Your qualification criteria should take this into account.

2: Filter Your Sample Size into Suitable Focus Group Participants. Factors that can be used to filter unsuitable from potentially suitable candidates include topic, industry, persona, geographic area (applicants applying outside of your local area will have vastly different responses than local candidates), and past participation or engagement. If your candidate took your survey, they're slightly more engaged than those who didn't and are also willing to offer an opinion about your process.

3: Map Out the Process Your Focus Group Will Follow to Complete the Research. When you're reaching out to candidates to build your focus group, you'll want to set some time aside as part of your planning process to ensure your process is as efficient as possible. Yes, this is where you're going to make sure your focus group participants have an amazing candidate experience so they can talk to you about improving candidate experience. It doesn't get more meta than that, but understand that you're asking for something so valuable that you'll need to identify anything in your focus group process that could annoy participants to a point that you could skew the results of your research. Gather all the information you need on the initial call and have a time and day, along with details, prepared. Make sure your focus group participants aren't bombarded with calls or emails from multiple members of your team. Finally, make sure you know the demographic—whether you're reaching out to candidates who abandoned the application process, have been rejected for a position with your company, or who were offered and declined a position. The short version: handle with care.

4: Set a Budget and Timeline That Allows for Adjustment during Focus Group Selection. Remember that you're doing research because you don't know the answer. Once you've committed to holding a focus group, the next step is to immediately begin reaching out to potential focus group members so that you have time to use real data from the call outcomes to make adjustments if necessary. During the first interaction (either online or on the phone), specify what they can expect in terms of follow up. When that recruitment process is communicated and followed, people will actually show up and be more willing to share their opinions openly.

5: Finalize Your Discussion Guide and Identify Ranking and Response Rate. Unlike surveys, focus groups are going to give you discussion and dialogue, so ranking responses is more difficult and your guidelines will be broader. Using a "discussion guide" rather than a specific list of yes and no response questions will give you rich information and feedback. With your HR team, you should identify topics and map out note-taking, questions related to your topic, and key points you'd like to report on. Collect the information you need to consider in recruiting them the first time you talk to them. You'll only want to go back to them if it is critical to your research.

6: Give Participants a Reason to Attend, and Consider Incentives. A focus group session is a lot more to ask from job seekers than an email survey. Especially considering that some of these job seekers may have been previously rejected for positions at your company, you'll need to offer them a reason to attend other than "we'd like to hear your opinion," and that reason can't be "you might have a better chance of scoring a job with our company." Any indication of favoritism based on focus group attendance will skew your results. Schedule the focus group at an off-site location, offer lunch or coffee, and depending on your industry (if your company is a retailer or offers other services relevant to candidates), you might even offer a gift card or certificate to redeem with your company or another popular local retailer.

It might seem obvious, but one of the biggest mistakes marketers make is organizing and holding focus groups and then not putting the same effort into the results. Decide what to do with your data. Don't sit on it; act on it. Holding a focus group takes a lot of effort from your team and the participants. It will be wasted effort if you're not focused on the end goal—improving your candidate experience and making your team better at recruitment.

We've been trying to learn what makes a great candidate experience for years. In this labor market, it is increasingly difficult to persuade a passive candidate to participate in a recruitment process, and it's more important than ever to create the best candidate experience possible. In order to do that, we need data. Your focus group feedback might just be the best source for improving all aspects of your recruiting process, from candidate experience to employer brand.

Employee surveys give you an opportunity to measure employee satisfaction in ways that are unique to your industry, company, and how you do business. Depending on the size of your company, this is where you're going to want to work with stakeholders and hiring managers from each department. Setting these questions up with the help of managers who will be responsible for supervising your new employees not only gets to the heart of what they want to learn about engagement, but also guarantees buy-in on making changes based on survey data. To achieve a truly successful employee survey, it is necessary to write survey questions that speak to the experiences and needs of employees at different levels of the corporate hierarchy.

Each department's leadership can choose from standardized questions or write new questions that pertain to the business and the tasks performed by employees. Managers can also allow for multiple choice, multiple selection, single selection, or other forms of questions that result in quantified data, or choose those that require a short essay answer for gathering qualitative data, if preferred. Employees respond best to quantifiable questions that have a rating scale of agreement. It is also important to keep the questions as straightforward as possible so additional research is not needed to understand the survey data.

Expected action should be built into your survey results. Your company leadership must be invested in taking action on common citations and responses to these surveys, from your onboarding program to new hire training to benefits and team experience.

If your company conducts exit interviews or surveys but hasn't set up a process to collect employee feedback as soon as onboarding begins, a huge piece of the employee satisfaction puzzle is missing. While exit surveys are common, the tightening labor market means that it's imperative to capture your company's areas of weakness well before an employee decides to leave. In fact, some employers are beginning to conduct "stay surveys" as a proactive talent strategy. Consider early surveys the remedy to attempting to recoup losses when a good employee quits.

Measuring Your Candidate Experience

Candidate experience is defined as how job seekers perceive and react to employers' sourcing, recruiting, interviewing, hiring, and onboarding processes. It has proven to be directly tied to recruiting performance, making it one of the most highly regarded talent acquisition topics today.

If a job seeker had a poor experience during an interview a decade ago, they would be less likely to apply again in the future, accept a job offer, or buy that company's products or services. They would also probably tell their inner circle about their poor experience.

That all still happens today, although the ubiquity of social media and employer review sites have dramatically expanded the dynamic and size of our inner circles. As a consequence, news of a poor candidate experience can travel much faster and further. Research shows that candidates who had a poor experience are far more likely to tell others not to apply to a company and may even write a negative Glassdoor review. This brings me back to the statistic I shared earlier in this chapter from CareerPlug's 2020 survey: 69 percent of job seekers share negative candidate experiences online or directly with friends.

The Talent Board is a nonprofit organization focused on the elevation and promotion of a quality candidate experience.[12] The organization, its Candidate Experience Awards program, and its sponsors are dedicated to recognizing the candidate experience offered by companies throughout the entire recruitment cycle and to forever changing the manner in which job candidates are treated. Each year, participating companies send surveys to hundreds of thousands employment candidates (both successful and not) to assess their experience during the recruiting process. This rigorous, scientifically supported data enables companies to see how they're doing, both internally and relative to the rest of the industry.

Measuring the experiences of 152,000 candidates across 133 companies in North America, the *2020 Talent Board Research Report* found that great candidate experience increased from 25 percent to 31 percent since last year, an increase of 24 percent from 2019.[13] Interestingly, the resentment rate fell from 14 percent to 8 percent. So what caused positive associations to climb in 2020 while negative impressions plummeted?

The Talent Board began tracking candidate experience in 2011, following the 2008 recession. Since then, it has only tracked candidate experience in a growth market. According to the 2020 report,

> The pandemic-driven recession and social and racial inequity have changed how candidates and employers interact, and those changes have had a positive impact on the candidate experience. When the COVID-19 shutdown occurred, organizations across the United States came to a full stop almost overnight. With hiring on hold, employers were forced to adopt a much higher level of transparency than under normal circumstances. Employers had to inform candidates in their pipeline that hiring was on hold, or communicate new protocols for virtual hiring. Many organizations posted more empathetic language than usual on their career sites to the same effect, as well as ongoing candidate communications. The overall impact of this transparency? Candidates appreciated the empathetic communication and adopted a more forgiving attitude than we've seen in recent years.

What do other companies get out of these awards and research? They get benchmarks and a strong sense of the importance of candidate experience for recruiting success. Because the Talent Board has been conducting this research for nearly a decade, we can track what matters to candidates in various economic and social contexts, which helps us direct our efforts into what translates as most meaningful to the talent we want to attract.

According to the Talent Board, its research up to and including 2020 finds five consistent hallmarks of an excellent candidate experience. Organizations that provide an excellent candidate experience are differentiated by these practices.

Have Consistent Communication. Communication should be consistent across your hiring process, from pre-application to onboarding. You can use a mix of automated tools (usually on the front end) and human interaction (especially in later stages). Communication is the primary differentiator of a good candidate experience.

Set Expectations. Don't leave candidates hanging at any stage. Set expectations for when they can expect to hear back from you and what's coming next in the process. Following through on what you tell them is crucial, so set expectations that are realistic on your end.

Ask for and Provide Feedback. Incorporating feedback opportunities makes the process more engaging and personal. The feedback candidates give you may be negative, but the fact that you ask for it increases their positive impressions. On the flip side, providing feedback to final stage candidates is essential, too. Let them know why you aren't going to pursue them any further.

Embrace Transparency and Accountability. The more transparent and accountable you are with candidates, the better their experience will be. They'd rather hear you say that you've put hiring on hold than not hear back at all.

Ensure a Fair Process. Candidates don't have to feel happy with your decision (after all, most won't land a job at your organization). But they should leave feeling like they were treated fairly in your decision-making process.

HOW BUILDING YOUR EMPLOYER BRAND IN A TRUST ECONOMY WORKS

Traditional marketing teams are familiar with funnel engagement, and recruiting teams have adopted many of the same practices for candidate marketing. Developing personas, mapping out how you're reaching them and where, and reporting on the results are inherently useful to the hiring process. Your talent funnel (see Figure 3.1), or pipeline, allows you to recruit not only for the positions you have open now but also for those you may need to fill in the future. For high-volume hiring, a talent pipeline is a necessity.

A talent pipeline can improve the candidate experience and the company-candidate relationship. When you are recruiting for future opportunities, you have to work much harder to build trust with potential candidates. You are engaging in more meaningful conversations to gain perspective on the career goals of talents in your industry. Talent pipelining also allows you to better personalize your messages, answer questions, build relationships, and most importantly, automate your job postings. Your candidate database and social media platforms become more than sourcing tools; they become relationship-building platforms.

Developing Candidate Personas

Marketers begin the process of messaging by creating marketing personas, or profiles of the wants, desires, and interests of the people most likely to buy the product or service they are promoting. Once personas are created, research and messaging are focused on these specific groups of people identified as target audiences. Based on target personas, customized experiences are designed to lead these individuals through a customer journey—beginning with awareness and ending with conversion.

Once you have identified your ideal candidate(s), you can create a hiring funnel for recruitment marketing. This is how recruiters can create a compelling employee journey for their target job candidates. By creating personas based on the types of diverse personalities or skills sets you're looking for, you can more effectively recruit and build messaging to attract a specific type of person. Start with your company's EVP and the skills and experience you value most, including soft skills like work ethic and culture fit.

Employer Review Sites: What Do We Do with Them?

While your career website is your company's most important recruitment channel and the top resource candidates access during their

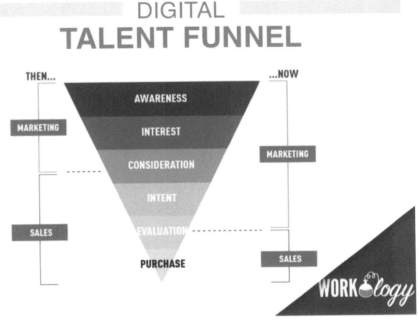

Figure 3.1   The digital talent funnel

research process, employer review sites have grown significantly in popularity over the past decade. A 2017 report from LinkedIn discovered that the company website is the first destination for research (53 percent of candidates), followed by LinkedIn (38 percent) and search engines (35 percent).[14] Candidates are looking for company values, what current employees have to say about working for your company, transparency (especially in job descriptions), and what makes your company stand out in your industry—all of the factors identified as crucial for candidate experience by the Talent Board's research.

Many companies choose to ignore reviews, either because they don't think it's necessary or because they dismiss negative reviews as coming from disgruntled former employees (or disgruntled current employees). And that's the heart of it. Every company has at least one disgruntled employee, some have many, and many employees are disgruntled for a reason.

However, candidates will still read your reviews on employer review sites. According to Talent Tech Labs' (TTL) trends report on candidate engagement, 80–90 percent of candidates say that a positive or negative interview experience can change their mind about a role or a company.[15] More than 60 percent of job seekers read company reviews and ratings before making a decision to apply for a job.

You can't scrub negative reviews from the internet. You can dispute reviews making certain accusations through a tedious process on some sites.[16] What you can control is how you and your company respond to reviews, both positive and negative, on employer review sites by developing a review response strategy.

The five most common perspectives companies take on review sites are as follows:

- We don't respond to any reviews. Instead, we focus on amplifying the positive via updates, photos, awards, and company content.
- We only respond to correct misinformation with facts. For example, a former employee complains about the lack of PTO, and the company responds highlighting PTO, sick leave, holidays, and floating holidays to paint a more accurate picture.
- We only care about the truly egregious. And we will request that Glassdoor remove reviews that use profanity, refer to an employee by name, or can be legally upheld as damaging to the business.
- We will respond, but with general templates. This shows that we acknowledge the review; we then provide a general HR number or email address if the person wants to elaborate.
- Our CEO responds. This shows that our leadership is listening and responds with the level of information deemed appropriate.

Creating a Response Strategy for Candidate and Employee Reviews

When creating a response strategy, you'll want to consider both positive and negative reviews. Your response can amplify positive messaging on review sites and show candidates that your company is genuinely paying attention to what employees say about working for your company, even if what they have to say is negative.

I never recommend not responding as an option. Why? According to the same TTL report cited previously, 69 percent of job seekers are likely to apply to a job if an employer actively manages its brand (responds to reviews, updates profiles, and shares info on culture and work environment).

My recommendation is to roll out a review response strategy in stages. For example, you could begin by developing a response to 4- and 5-star reviews with a "thank you for taking the time to tell us about your experience" and, in some form, "we appreciate you."

As you move deeper into responding to reviews with 3 stars or fewer, these phrases are also appropriate, with the addition of information that indicates you and your company hear the feedback and will communicate to the appropriate company leaders. While your recruitment strategy for reviews and comments should include responses and situational scenarios on how recruiters and you, as the employer, will respond and engage, they should be customized so you don't sound like you're copying from a template.

Your responses will be seen online below the candidate or employee review, and they are what potential candidates are going to read and make a decision about when applying for a role at your company. Your response should reflect your company culture and show that you listen to constructive feedback.

While we tend to want to dismiss anonymous reviews, and there are some that may be about not getting a position the candidate applied for, try to evaluate these reviews as constructive criticism and create responses that address them in a positive way. For example, if a candidate review states that they never heard back from a recruiter with your company or had issues with your application technology, the best strategy is to respond quickly and offer a method of contact (email or phone) so you and your team can get more information.

These types of responses show that you care about your candidate experience and (whether the reviewer chooses to get in touch or not) indicates to potential applicants that you're open to hearing about areas where you can improve. Thank the reviewer, offer a method of communication, and state that you appreciate the time they took to bring the issue to your attention. In short, communicate that your company is listening.

Review sites are becoming a more important and trusted part of not just the job offer and interview process, but the entire candidate engagement process that starts the moment the prospective candidate begins to consider your company as an employment option. Above all, it's important to be consistent in your process regarding your responses to employee reviews, both negative and positive.

Profiles on sites like Indeed and Glassdoor should be claimed, which requires a fee but means you can verify the profile as an employer and add updated photos, descriptions, awards, relevant links, and other information. There are over 20 million unique monthly users on Glassdoor, with the majority in the United States, college educated, and age 18–44.

Companies can help positively build their brand on these sites with an internal strategy. Start by requesting that all members of the HR team and marketing write reviews before you ask your employees to leave a Glassdoor (or other employer site) rating, then encourage your current employees to leave reviews.

Consider the potential candidate researching your company on a review site. They're reading horror stories and snarky comments. How likely do you think they are to apply to a job with your company? Consider the same candidate reading the same reviews, except with your thoughtful, unbiased, and kind responses. This changes the game: the candidate sees that your company genuinely listens, and is therefore more inclined to apply. Any positive policy change within your company, such as adding perks like additional PTO or fully paid health insurance, is an opportunity to return to review sites and respond to reviews that mention "restrictive PTO" or "terrible health coverage" and let the reviewer (and readers) know that you heard their feedback and tell them about the new policy or perk.

Here's a top-level list of review sites your company should consider listening and monitoring on an ongoing basis.

- **Glassdoor:** Offers an anonymous review site as well as a job-search resource for job seekers and web visitors.
- **FairyGodBoss:** Employer review site for women. Lots of great opportunities for employers to engage women in the workplace.
- **Google Reviews:** Google manages consumer reviews. These reviews are powered by the most popular search engine and are worth monitoring.
- **Indeed:** Offers an anonymous review section of their website in addition to a forum, job postings, and the ability for job seekers to upload their résumé.
- **Yelp:** This site is most known for customer reviews. However, it is important for employers to monitor for reviews and feedback.
- **JobCase:** Very active hourly work community, forum, and employee reviews by location.
- **RateMyEmployer:** Canada employer review site that has over forty-five thousand candidate and employee reviews.
- **Kununu.com:** This international review site has its roots in Germany and has recently launched in the United States.
- **TheJobCrowd:** Employer reviews for recent college graduates. Includes salary information, graduate career information, and employer lists and resources.
- **Vault.com:** Company ranking and review site. Includes rankings for colleges, internships, and schools too.
- **Comparably:** Free for employers to set up pages. Includes compensation, company review, and culture.
- **InHerSight:** Employer review site for women. Scorecards for employers on how female-friendly their organization is.
- **CareerBliss:** Review site for compensation, job search, and company review information.
- **Xing.com:** Company review site that offers job search information. Focused primarily in Germany and European markets.
- **LinkedIn:** Reviews and ratings as part of company LinkedIn pages.

RESPONSE TEMPLATES

This includes samples of responses to both positive and negative reviews. Make sure those responding understand they should customize their responses and call back to anything specific the reviewer mentioned.

Positive/Neutral

[past employee]
Thank you for taking the time to leave us a review! We are glad you enjoyed your experience at COMPANY and wish you the best success in the future.

[current employee]
Thank you for taking the time to leave us a review! We are glad you are happy with your job and cheers to your future success at COMPANY.

Thank you for your thoughtful review! We appreciate hearing about your personal experience at COMPANY and are glad to learn that you are passionate about serving our customers.

Thank you for taking the time to write a thoughtful review! We appreciate hearing about your experience at COMPANY and are glad to learn that you are passionate about serving our customers and enjoy working with your team members. We appreciate your feedback and will share your comments with our leadership team.

Negative/Specific

[past employee]
Thank you for taking the time to write a review. We strive to provide extensive development opportunities that allow our employees to advance their career and we're sorry that your experience was unfavor-

able. We will share your feedback with our leadership team and we wish you well in your future endeavors.

Thank you for your review. We strive to provide competitive compensation plans and extensive development opportunities for our employees so they may deliver a great customer experience. We sincerely appreciate your feedback and will share it with our leadership team.

Thank you for providing feedback on your experience working at COMPANY. We strive to provide competitive salary packages. We will share your comments with our leadership team.

[current employee]
Thank you for sharing your concerns. Please know our management team is focused on ensuring all employees are treated fairly and that their opinions are heard. We understand that training and development opportunities are important, along with competitive salary packages. We would like to get more information on your specific experience in order to improve. Would you mind emailing us at HR@company. com?

Thank you for sharing your concerns. Your feedback is important to us and we would like to get more information on your specific experience. Would you mind emailing us at HR@company.com?

The end game for all recruiting is driving candidates to an action, which is applying for a job or joining your talent community. In an online world, your recruiting funnel is likely to be 99 percent digital (with exceptions in some industries). Each stage of the funnel moves your ideal candidate towards conversion activity from other digital properties, like social media, covered more in the next chapter.

CHAPTER 4

Demystifying Digital

- **What Is Digital Recruiting?**
- **Who's on Social Media in 2022**
- **Which Social Media Channels Should We Use?**
- **All the Social Media Channels**
- **Secret Weapons for Sourcing Candidates**
- **Your Company Career Website**
- **Career Site Navigation Best Practices**
- **Career Site Landing Pages**

Social media isn't just for teenagers sending Snapchats or posting pics to Instagram. The audience for social media spans baby boomers to Gen Z—and these are your target candidates. The business case for digital recruitment goes far beyond your social channels and posting jobs on LinkedIn. This chapter focuses on dispelling myths, and explains how digital can help you reach hidden talent communities, including diverse and passive candidates, in new ways.

WHAT IS DIGITAL RECRUITING?

Digital recruiting is a multifaceted strategy to engage job candidates and push them to your ultimate career destination, which is your company career site. Your digital recruiting strategy is as unique as your fingerprint. No single strategy or group of tools can be 100 percent duplicated and applied to another company. It just doesn't work that way. And I think that's where we get lost. Recruiters and talent acquisition leaders need to step back and ask questions. They need to fully understand the business, the industry, and specific markets in the location, as well as understanding expectations of candidates. So before we implement a new applicant tracking system (ATS), add a text recruiting campaign, embrace social media, or invest in artificial intelligence, we need to back up and start at the beginning.

Your employer brand is the common thread that runs through all of your recruiting marketing efforts, and it's also the first place to begin when reviewing your current processes to determine what you can do better and more efficiently. Is your reach limited to your company site, or do you have a brand presence on social channels like LinkedIn, Facebook, Instagram, and Twitter? Two out of four? All four, but only when you have time?

Social channels can be low-cost channels for amplifying your brand. Your recruitment marketing strategy can drive a strong presence on social media by cross-posting customer and employee stories to engage new customers and drive quality candidates to your career site to apply.

Figure 4.1 The social recruiting universe

WHO'S ON SOCIAL MEDIA IN 2022

Roughly seven out of ten Americans say they use some kind of social media site—a share that has remained relatively stable over the past five years, according to a new Pew Research Center survey of US adults. When Pew Research Center began tracking social media adoption in 2005, just 5 percent of American adults used at least one of these platforms. By 2011, that share had risen to half of all Americans, and today 72 percent of the public uses some type of social media.

For many users, social media is part of their daily routine. Seven out of ten Facebook users—and around six out of ten Instagram and Snapchat users—visit these sites at least once a day. YouTube and Facebook continue to dominate the online landscape, with 73 percent and 69 percent of American adults, respectively, reporting using the platform. And

YouTube and Reddit were the only two platforms measured that saw statistically significant growth since 2019.[1]

When it comes to the other platforms in the survey, 37 percent of adults say they ever use Instagram and about three out of ten report using Pinterest or LinkedIn. About one quarter say they use Snapchat, and similar shares report being users of Twitter or WhatsApp. A Pew Research Center report from 2021 revealed that TikTok, an app for sharing short videos, is used by 21 percent of Americans, while 13 percent say they use the neighborhood-focused platform Nextdoor.

Even as other platforms do not match the overall reach of YouTube or Facebook, there are certain sites or apps, most notably Instagram, Snapchat, and TikTok, that have an especially strong following among young adults.[2]

With more than 6.5 million jobs posted and 500 million members, nearly 90 percent of recruiters use LinkedIn to attract and source candidates. Regular content, cobranded profiles, and featured (paid) jobs on LinkedIn could go a long way to provide candidates information about your company and drive qualified traffic back to your career site.

Facebook, especially Facebook videos, and Instagram stories can also give potential candidates insight on what it's like to work for your company. Ask questions to engage candidates, create a unique Instagram hashtag and encourage current employees to use it when sharing workplace photos, and tap your existing talent to share their expertise in articles on LinkedIn showcase pages.

WHICH SOCIAL MEDIA CHANNELS SHOULD WE USE?

The success of recruiters depends heavily on their ability to build relationships with a large talent pool, foster and nurture those relationships, and reach a broader pool of qualified candidates. There's no one social media channel that businesses should be using, but recruiters should definitely use LinkedIn.

The number of users on LinkedIn has grown from 78 million in 2010 to 774 million in 2021. And by "users," I mean candidates. There are also 58 million businesses on LinkedIn. Many are your competitors, and their employees are your target candidate audience. Additionally, in October 2020, there were 14 million jobs listed on LinkedIn.[3]

If you love statistics like I do, a good place to start is LinkedIn's Economic Graph—a digital representation of the global economy.[4] In April 2017, the social network for businesses and job seekers launched the LinkedIn Economic Graph Research Program (EGRP) to pair academic researchers with LinkedIn engineers to investigate ways to understand the global economy, create economic opportunity, and help companies be more productive and successful.

So yes, if you had to pick one social network, LinkedIn should be part of any company's recruiting strategy.

ALL THE SOCIAL MEDIA CHANNELS

Social media is a powerful marketing tool and critical to amplifying any message. Once you commit to these channels, recruitment marketers must be able to "listen" to social messaging just as well as they communicate. If you're broadcasting job postings on company social media channels, including Twitter, LinkedIn, and Facebook, consider it the entry point to a strategy.

From there, monitor your social channels, and include Glassdoor, Yelp, and Google to make sure your company reviews don't go unanswered. I discussed this at length in Chapter 3: The Trust Economy, but the most important thing to know about social listening is that response can drastically counter any negative messaging if done with sincerity. This is also when you'll want to be proactive posting photos of your company culture, allowing your employees to share their experiences, and highlighting the perks your employees love.

When it comes to having a presence on social media channels, consider your target candidate personas and where they spend their time. The majority of 18- to 29-year-olds say they use Instagram or Snapchat and about half say they use TikTok, with those on the younger end of this cohort—ages 18 to 24—being especially likely to report using Instagram (76 percent), Snapchat (75 percent), or TikTok (55 percent). A vast majority of adults under the age of 65 say they use YouTube. Fully 95 percent of those 18 to 29 say they use the platform, along with 91 percent of those 30 to 49 and 83 percent of adults 50 to 64.[5]

For example, if one of your candidate personas is a seasonal, hourly retail employee around college age, investing time into a social channel like Instagram or Snapchat could help you reach that persona in a highly targeted way. I'll mention some examples of how companies are using different channels for hiring based on target candidate personas as well as company culture and needs assessment (such as the need for more diversity in hiring).

Instagram is one of the best social channels for promoting your company's culture. You can take a page from AT&T's book; they created a #lifeatatt hashtag that any employee, from corporate to retail, can use to show what a day at AT&T looks like on the company's Instagram story.[6] Turning your employees into company champions is an excellent way to promote ownership and investment. Snag a "LifeAt___" Instagram hashtag and put someone in charge of reposting photos. Time investment: minimal. Cost: free.

Facebook is still a thing. I know this because I'm in it for the better part of my workday. I have Facebook groups for HR professionals who are studying for their HR certification exams (Ace the HR Exam) and for those who want to get recertification credits and professional development opportunities (Upskill HR).

Consider that the candidates you really want to reach already have jobs. In this tight talent market, most candidates are currently employed and not all of them are actively looking. You can focus on recruiting passive candidates, or the top talent currently employed by your competitors, by holding live events online. Not only will you stand out from your competitors, you're offering potential future employees the opportunity to get to know your company in real time and without having to be physically present.

If you have robust social channels, you can promote "virtual open houses" or "meet the hiring manager" events. If you're still in the early stages of growing your social presence, a small advertising budget for an event via social media can bring new followers and interested candidates.

Using Facebook for recruiting is a very effective way to reach candidates that are "passive," or not searching for a job but open to the right opportunities. Using Facebook posts and ad targeting features, you can connect with these hard-to-reach candidates.

There is so much competition on Facebook, it's difficult to get traditional posts out there without putting a lot of budget behind them. But the word is that Facebook has been giving video posts a lot of love in the feed, showing them more often than other posts. So video content should be part of your efforts. There are standard videos that companies can make to give job seekers an idea of what it's like to work for a specific company.

Tips for Making a Recruiting Video

- Use a mobile phone made in the last few years.
- Have good lighting on the faces of your subjects (avoid backlighting).
- Hold your phone in the landscape (horizontal) position.
- Try to limit background noise.
- Start fast with a video of employees talking about why they like the company.[7]

Take it to the next level with live video. What if you could connect with potential candidates live and real time via video? This is possible right in your Facebook feed with Facebook Live. You could show them what a few minutes on the job are like, introduce some coworkers, or do a question and answer session about a job opening.

How to Use Facebook Live for Recruiting

- Start promoting the day and time of the live session on social media a week before.

- When you're ready for the event, open the Facebook app on your phone.
- Navigate to the Facebook page you're posting to, and tap "Publish."
- Tap "Live Video."
- Tap the blue "Go Live" button.
- Let visitors know you're answering employment questions.
- Watch for questions and comments to appear below the video feed and be ready to answer them.

Large companies that are on top of their social recruiting game, like UPS, Target, and Spectrum have already started using this tool. Live video feels more personal and has the added bonus of reaching candidates who would not have noticed or seen a standard job post.

SECRET WEAPONS FOR SOURCING CANDIDATES

Consider that every recruiter searching for candidates already knows how to use Boolean searches. What's your secret weapon when it comes to sourcing? For this, we're going to look at the lesser-known tactics used by a smaller percentage of creative sourcers. I like to compare this to my own sourcing efforts in 2001. As store HR leader for a large big-box chain, I used dating websites to source, recruit, and hire candidates.

As our need for employment branding and recruitment marketing grows, it's important to have a presence in a variety of online communities and audiences to engage the qualified candidates we all want to attract. This means looking outside of traditional social channels like LinkedIn, Twitter, and Facebook and turning to platforms where the candidates in your industry, with the tenure and experience you're looking for, spend their time.

Here, we'll take a look at some other social communities through which recruiters can engage and build relationships beyond the standard big three of social media.

Quora

People come to Quora to find answers to their questions. The easiest way to get started is to set up and build your own professional profile and include all the credentials that make you an expert on industry-specific topics like technology, recruiting, human resources, hiring, and so on. Follow other "Quorans" who have large followings and engage by upvoting and commenting on their responses. Recruiting on Quora is more hands-on than other social communities, as you only get noticed the more you engage and answer questions from other users. Eventually, Quora will send you alerts when relevant questions that you can likely answer are submitted, but in the beginning you'll need to find those questions.

Your expert profile is just the first step. Once established, you can begin looking for experts that fit your talent profiles. For example, if you're on the hunt for full-stack developers, search for questions under that topic and see who the experts answering the questions are. You can then reach out to the expert Quoran to get an idea of their interest in open positions. Introduce yourself and see if they would be open to a quick conversation. Then you can informally talk to them about your company and your open positions.

Reddit

You may know the popular online forum reddit.com as a place to get answers to your questions or find news stories—and memes (see r/gameofthrones for some laughs). You might not know that it's the fourth largest website online today. Just as I used what was popular online in 2001 (dating sites) to find candidates, Reddit can be a secret weapon in your sourcing toolbelt.

If you haven't used Reddit before, you can start by setting up an account. If you plan on using Rddit for recruiting, it's a good idea to be transparent about it in your bio (by identifying your job title, company, or agency). Next, you'll want to read the Reddit FAQ.[8] The Reddit platform is different from others in a lot of ways, so you will want to make sure you are using it properly. Additionally, the acronyms might be confusing, and there's an extensive glossary available.[9]

Then take a look at subreddits (these are "folders" on Reddit by topic) like r/forhire to see what is currently being posted for job openings. For example, a subreddit called r/recruitinghell might initially seem like an interesting place to share stories with fellow recruiters. It's not. It might, however, be a great place to learn what *not* to do as a recruiter. The subreddit description is "This subreddit is for all of those recruiters and candidates who really don't get it. Post your horror stories and show us those amazing job offers!"

There are subreddits for you, like r/humanresources, described as, "A subreddit for Human Resources professionals: answering difficult questions, plugging you into appropriate resources, and monitoring your own development." Feel free to hop on there and share or respond.

When you're using Reddit for recruiting and sourcing, it's important to be familiar with the site and understand how its users communicate. User profiles vary widely, and each subreddit has its own rules (and if you don't follow them, you can get banned quickly), which makes searching for user profile information difficult. There are over four hundred thousand subreddits, and each one is governed by its own set of moderators who volunteer their time to remove spam, create community guidelines, interact with users, and answer questions.

The communities (subreddits) are going to be key to finding talent and understanding the profile of the type of candidate you're trying to find. For example, if you're looking for specific tech talent like developers, there are hundreds of developer subreddits, but it's important to get familiar with how they're used, what the purpose is, and whether or not the redditors in that subreddit might be receptive to outreach from a recruiter.

One thing that's consistent with other social media channels on Reddit is that no one likes to be spammed and they hate clickbait (or deceptive advertising).

Knowledge sharing is important for engagement. You can participate in industry-specific subreddit threads on topics where you are genuinely able to offer advice or assistance. For example, if you're sourcing for front-end web developers, but you don't speak the language, stick to the hiring or résumé subreddits, not the tech threads. Look for career guidance subreddits, résumé subreddits, city-specific subreddits, or subreddits that are topical for you and what you do in your work life.

Every post or comment you create will be available on your profile page, and redditors will check the profile pages of other users to see if they're legitimate and have the experience they claim to have. It's important to provide value to the Reddit community in a consistent and sincere way so that when you do reach out to potential candidates, you will already have established credibility.

Finally, I mentioned Boolean strings and x-ray searches in the previous section. You can use the same techniques to find what you're looking for on Reddit.

Meetup. You can set up your own Meetup account to host local events. You can also connect your Meetup account to your company Facebook page, so if you host events on Facebook, they'll be on Meetup as well. Members of Meetup can find your group via preference suggestions based on locations and topics of interest, so you'll want to write an engaging bio that identifies the purpose of your account and the groups you'll set up. For example, if you want to target industry groups on your local Meetup site, add those topics to your interests list and take the time to join other groups in the same general interest area. Plan a small event that focuses on a specific topic, like best practices in UX (source the passion projects of your team leaders for ideas), and cast a wide net for attendees. You can also offer to be a guest speaker for other relevant local Meetup groups.

How does this translate to relationship building and adding new candidates to your hiring funnel? At your event, have a sign-in station for attendees and capture email addresses to add to a list for follow-up communication. If you're speaking at another group's Meetup, make sure you're prepared with your direct contact information or to get contact information from attendees (without hijacking someone else's event).

Facebook Groups. While still part of Facebook, the future of social is private and these groups offer a great way to engage the community, offer up advice, and build on those relationships. I've seen this used effectively by companies such as Whole Foods to reach a small but effective technology group of job seekers by offering up their offices to host a meetup group. A member of their recruiting team swooped in to offer their meetings as a location, thereby building trust and potentially engaging a very sought-after group of technical talent in the highly competitive Austin talent market.

No matter which online community you dive into, knowledge sharing is important for candidate engagement. Participate in industry-specific community threads on topics where you are genuinely able to offer advice or assistance. For example, if you're sourcing for front-end web developers, but you don't speak the language, stick to hiring or résumé communities, not the tech threads. Look for career guidance topics, résumé topics, city-specific topics, or other threads that are topical for you and what you do in your work life.

While it remains increasingly important to be visual digitally in your recruiting efforts, it is also important to watch, share, and build relationships in these more private communities and become acquainted with their respective linguistic and behavioral characteristics. Before you ask people to adopt you, adapt to them!

YOUR COMPANY CAREER WEBSITE

As a recruiter, your career site is one of the most important tools for branding and attracting candidates to your job postings. However, simply setting up a page with job listings means that you might be missing out on opportunities for moving candidates into your recruitment funnel. Consider the following when you're conducting an audit of your career site.

1: Ease of Search
Have you searched for postings on your own site? Your search parameters should be easy to understand (by location, by job type, by job

title) and the results should be accurate. If a candidate puts in "New York, NY" and "marketing," they shouldn't get results for retail jobs in California. Your development team can optimize your careers page search to ensure your search is highly targeted and accurate.

2: Mobile Friendly

According to a 2021 Appcast report, mobile applies surpassed desktop applies for the first time in 2020; 60.7 percent of job applications were completed on mobile devices compared to 39.3 percent on desktop.[10] Your career site should be responsive. Visit your own job listings from your phone. Is the search and application process as good on mobile as it is on a desktop? If not, it's time for an overhaul. The same goes for the sites where you post jobs that redirect to your careers page. Are the job listings you're paying for easy to use on mobile?

3: Know Your Numbers

When it comes to metrics, Google Analytics (GA) is going to be your best friend. Not only will it show you how many site visits you have to your careers page, it also shows entry pages, length of visit, bounce rates (people who quickly visit and leave your site, which indicates that you may need to tweak your content for SEO), and where they go next. GA can also break your audience down by device so you can get specific numbers on how many visits you have from desktop or mobile devices, including what type of mobile device.

4: Ease of Use

Similar to ease of search, your careers site should be user-friendly. Walk through the steps for searching for and applying to jobs you've listed on your own page. Is anything unclear? Confusing? Think like the candidate. Do you know that your résumé has been submitted? Is there a confirmation page or email that follows submission? These are two more opportunities not just to engage candidates, but to reassure them that their résumé didn't just get sucked into the black hole of the internet.

5: Mixing Mediums

Rather than simply listing jobs on your careers page, consider mixing different types of content to engage a diverse audience—including photos, video, and written content. Is your company active on social media? Choose the most active channel and create a widget that streams content from Instagram, for example, where you show off your brand or what it looks like to work for or with your company. Create a short video touting the benefits of your brand. Not only does it give visitors a reason to stick around, it gives them more memorable information and an inside look at your brand.

6: Search Engine Optimization

You don't have to be an SEO expert to optimize your site. Adding landing pages and frequently updated content in the form of a blog will boost your SEO. Search engines love fresh content, including videos; a static site won't rank as high in searches. Make yours dynamic and you'll stand out from the rest. Consider what job seekers will search for to find your site and use that content (sparingly—loading posts with keywords doesn't do the trick) in your blog posts or on your landing page.

7: Prominent Placement on Your Company Site

If job seekers can find your company site, but not your careers page, you're missing an opportunity to engage candidates. Most candidates will visit a company page to do research. If your careers page isn't prominently linked—in a sidebar, a top navigation menu, or a pop-up—they'll head for the nearest job search engine instead.

Bonus: Make It Easy

Make it easy for your job seekers to apply for jobs. Add multiple "apply now" buttons on your job posting or career posting at the top and bottom of your posting to increase your candidate conversion rates.

If you use these seven tips and apply them to your careers page, you can measure the success with Google Analytics. Is your bounce rate getting lower over time? Are people sticking around longer and visiting other pages on your site? Like I said above, GA can be your best friend when you employ new strategies on your careers page. And one more tip: consider adding a feedback form. Everyone likes to offer an opinion; if you give your users the opportunity to critique your application process, you will have "beta" testers who give you quality assurance feedback that can help you further improve your site.

CAREER SITE NAVIGATION BEST PRACTICES

Your company career site is the center of your digital recruitment marketing universe. When I conduct talent brand audits, the career site and its user experience is one of the top elements I focus on to make recommendations for improvement. I've gone into detail about landing page best practices, but here we'll focus on the most common area that many companies skip when building an online presence: career site navigation.

Simply setting up a page with job listings and a list of benefits means that you might be missing out on opportunities for moving candidates into your recruitment funnel. Not every company has the luxury of having an in-house user experience (UX) or dedicated development team. While your website developer or agency are likely able to make recommendations, expertise specific to the candidate experience falls on you and your team. The person or team working on your site is going to want to know what you expect from their efforts and your preferences for how your career site should look and respond.

One of my favorite local restaurants here in Austin is Torchy's Tacos. It's great food, but their branding is next level. I had the opportunity to interview Elizabeth Baxter, Chief People Officer with Torchy's, and I asked about their website.[11]

Elizabeth told me about "My Torchy's," the company's new human resource information system (HRIS) program:

It was several years in the making and it's actually Ultipro that built it for us. And we've been very happy with the result. So it's a one-stop shop. That's our HR info system that the team now uses. And prior to that, we were using eight different systems for HR functions, which is crazy. And a lot of different companies are in that same situation. So when we moved it over to that, though, we really spent the time with our hiring process to make sure that it's in one system and it's as seamless as possible. So we completely overhauled and made sure that our questions make sense for the position that they're applying to. We also added some screening questions, like I mentioned before, that help us really quickly determine if they're a good fit for Torchy's and then what role they'd be a good fit for based on what they're interested in, naturally. And then the third element of it is that in-person interview. So we've done a lot of things, even with the hiring button, and invested some money in some easier hiring buttons with Indeed. So everything's auto connected. And if you click that easy hire button, within minutes you're already applied with Torchy's versus having to go into our website and do everything separately. And so we've gotten some really great feedback about that.

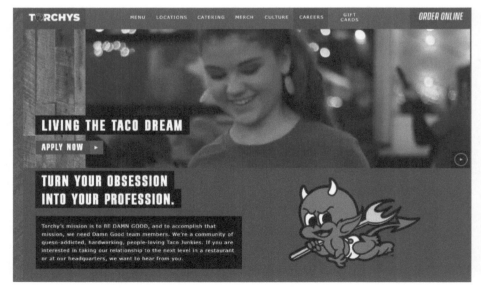

Figure 4.2 Torchy's career website (torchystacos.com/careers/)

How to Improve Your Career Site Candidate Experience

There are several things to take into consideration to optimize your career site user experience that require minimal effort and budget, and they all relate directly or indirectly to site navigation. When you're auditing your own site, think like your candidate will think and start where they are most likely to begin their search (and how they find your career site).

Start with the Search Engine. Consider what job seekers will search for to find your site and use that content (sparingly—loading posts with keywords doesn't do the trick) on your top-level careers page. Consider subnavigation (subnav) pages and landing pages that include high-value search terms for jobs in your industry and create content with these terms in mind. Make sure each page has a headline (H1), title (SEO title), and a meta description that includes a call to action. The latter two are what show up when your site comes up in Google, as the example below shows.

The SEO title (Careers | Join the Un-carrier Today| T-Mobile) tells job seekers that they've found the right page when they searched for "t mobile jobs." The meta description is a strong call to action and includes the company's brand statement. You can see that this career site has subnav pages because they show up as "extensions" below the search result. This indicates that the company has given a lot of thought on the information it presents to potential applicants.

Placement on Your Company's Site. This might seem like a no-brainer, but many companies still only link to their career site in the footer of their company home page. Given that most candidates will visit a company page to do research, if your careers page isn't prominently linked—in a sidebar, a top navigation menu, or a pop-up—they'll head for the nearest job search engine instead.

Accessibility for Persons with a Disability. Ease of use must also take accessibility into consideration. According to a 2015 survey of people with disabilities conducted by The Partnership for Employment and Accessible Technology (PEAT), 46 percent of respondents rated their last experience applying for a job online as "difficult to impossible."[12] If your career site user experience doesn't take accessibility into account, including using alt tags on images and video captions and passing design contrast tests for low-vision and color blindness, it will limit your pool of applicants. (For more on accessibility, see Chapter 8: Making Digital Recruiting Accessible and Inclusive.)

Diversity. Don't underestimate the impact of having targeted content and landing pages on your career site that are intended to reach diverse candidates, such as people of color, women in STEM fields, and veterans. Landing pages that highlight your company's diversity and inclusion programs are an excellent way to reach diverse groups of candidates. While the purpose of your career site is to appeal to job seekers by highlighting your employment brand and defining what makes your

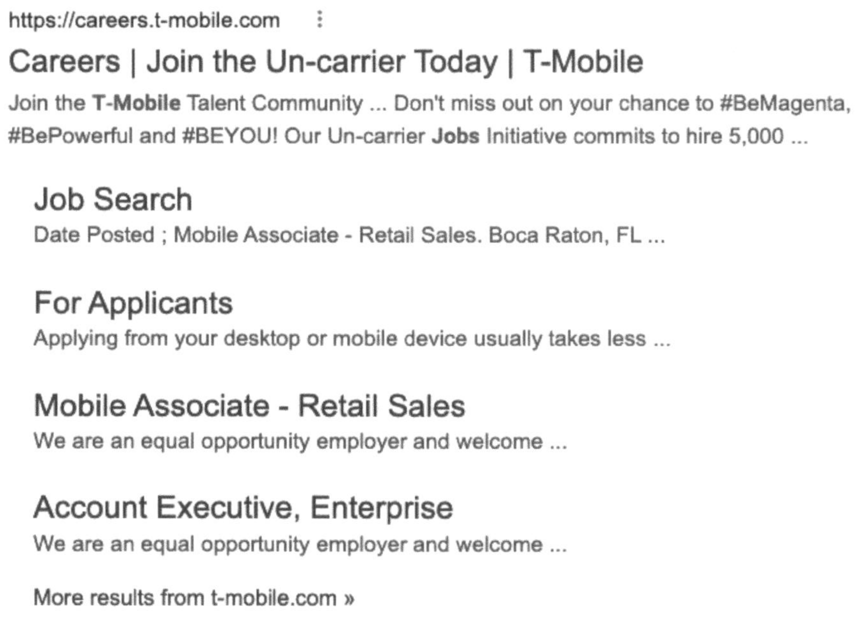

https://careers.t-mobile.com ⋮

Careers | Join the Un-carrier Today | T-Mobile

Join the **T-Mobile** Talent Community ... Don't miss out on your chance to #BeMagenta, #BePowerful and #BEYOU! Our Un-carrier **Jobs** Initiative commits to hire 5,000 ...

Job Search
Date Posted ; Mobile Associate - Retail Sales. Boca Raton, FL ...

For Applicants
Applying from your desktop or mobile device usually takes less ...

Mobile Associate - Retail Sales
We are an equal opportunity employer and welcome ...

Account Executive, Enterprise
We are an equal opportunity employer and welcome ...

More results from t-mobile.com »

Figure 4.3   The structure of search results in Google

company stand out from your competitors, landing pages are inten-tional platforms used for building talent funnels with a specific conver-sion goal (for example, applications from female tech candidates).

Calls to Action. The text on your call to action (CTA) buttons matters. If "See More" or "Learn More" is your default button text, those are both relatively passive requests. "Apply Now" is a stronger CTA and makes the next action clear. It's fine to include "Learn More" links to keep candidates on your site to see more information about your company, but "Apply Now" or "Why Work for Us" are more compelling. It's also important to include CTA buttons in multiple places on your job list-ing and subnav pages. If a candidate is returning to your site to apply, having a button at the top is perfect. For new candidates who will scroll through the content for a job posting, a button at the bottom is an easy next step.

Video. Search engines love videos and so do candidates. Even if your career site only includes an office tour video, it gives a candidate a look into what it's like to work for your company. Taking it a step further and including short videos from specific teams or lines of business can make the experience even better.

What Does Best Practice Navigation Look Like?

Airbnb's career site is an excellent example of navigation best practic-es.[13] It's clean, has clear messaging, and doesn't muddy the user experi-ence with too many calls-to-action. The top module on the page allows candidates to quickly navigate to open positions.

Scroll down the page and you can see the company's mission state-ment in a short, three-paragraph format, and the module that follows showcases Airbnb's benefits and employee value proposition (EVP) fol-lowed by a link to tour the company's offices.

One of the features many companies don't always include on a career site is questions candidates may have. Including a frequently asked questions (FAQs) page in your navigation can save your HR team and potential applicants a lot of time, and it's relatively easy to put together based on the questions your team gets from candidates. Airbnb also put a lot of thought into its mobile application process.

Want more examples? Ongig has a nice list of career sites that follow these best practices.[14]

CAREER SITE LANDING PAGES

It's important to understand that there is a difference between your career site and your recruitment landing pages. Landing pages are a tool for marketers, in this case, recruitment marketers. While the purpose of your career site is to appeal to job seekers by highlighting your employment brand and defining what makes your company stand out from your competitors, landing pages are intentional platforms used for building and nurturing talent funnels with a specific conversion goal (for example, applications from qualified candidates). A recruitment landing page is designed with one very intentional conversion goal—to find the right talent for your business and increase job applicants.

Landing pages are optimized, meaning that they follow good content and SEO practices for organic traffic and are targeted for paid campaign traffic. They can be extremely powerful for a one-off position, as

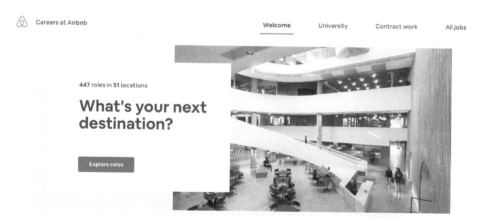

Figure 4.4   Airbnb's career site home page

BENEFITS

Live your best life

There's life at work and life outside of work. We want everyone to be healthy, travel often, get time to give back, and have the financial resources and support they need.

Comprehensive health plans

Paid volunteer time

Healthy food and snacks

Generous parental and family leave

Learning and development

Annual travel and experiences credit

Figure 4.5   Airbnb benefits snapshot from its career website

Questions about joining Airbnb?

Learn more about our interview process on our frequently asked questions page.

Figure 4.6   Airbnb FAQ for candidates

well as for ongoing or evergreen positions and in your diversity recruiting and hiring efforts.

How to Optimize Your Recruitment Landing Pages

Now that we've established the difference between your (very important) career site and landing pages, here are five best practices to boost engagement and conversions on your recruitment landing pages.

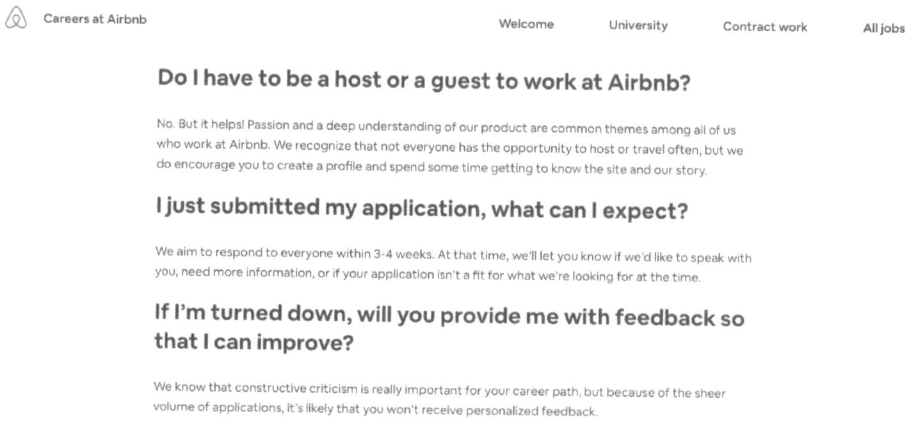

Careers at Airbnb   Welcome   University   Contract work   All jobs

Do I have to be a host or a guest to work at Airbnb?

No. But it helps! Passion and a deep understanding of our product are common themes among all of us who work at Airbnb. We recognize that not everyone has the opportunity to host or travel often, but we do encourage you to create a profile and spend some time getting to know the site and our story.

I just submitted my application, what can I expect?

We aim to respond to everyone within 3-4 weeks. At that time, we'll let you know if we'd like to speak with you, need more information, or if your application isn't a fit for what we're looking for at the time.

If I'm turned down, will you provide me with feedback so that I can improve?

We know that constructive criticism is really important for your career path, but because of the sheer volume of applications, it's likely that you won't receive personalized feedback.

Figure 4.7   Examples of Airbnb FAQs

Careers at Airbnb   ≡

447 roles in 51 locations

What's your next destination?

Explore roles

Figure 4.8   Airbnb mobile application process

I: Social Engagement. Your landing pages should be easy to share on social media. Many people searching online for jobs know people who are doing the same, or are in Facebook or LinkedIn groups for your industry. Even if the person visiting your page isn't interested in the position, it's likely they know people who are. Making these pages easy to share through social media or email with click-to-share buttons can help broaden the reach for the job listing. You can even include the embed codes for career description videos so they can be used on blog posts and other sites.

2: Clear Call to Action. Visitors need to be compelled to stay on your landing page and take a specific action. Too many CTAs could confuse your visitors, resulting in fewer conversations. When faced with too many choices or too much information at once, people tend to freeze up and decide to do nothing. Stick with one or two significant calls to action. As you're developing your pages, it's good practice to test your CTAs by adding one at a time and monitoring the results as you go, or if you're using marketing automation software, set up an A/B page conversion test.

You should also consider the button text, or the text on your CTA. While "next" might prompt an action, it isn't clear to the user where "next" will take them. "Apply Now" is always a solid CTA. "Learn More" seems to be an intuitive next step, and it would be fine on your career site, but your landing page should have all of the information a candidate needs about the position. "Learn More" buttons or links are fine at the bottom of the page to make the page "sticky" and keep a candidate on your site to see other open positions, more details about your perks and benefits, or a specific benefit like a training and development program. "Learn More" should not be a primary CTA.

3: Responsive. It's worth taking the time to create an exceptional mobile experience. An Aberdeen Group study found that responsive design on landing pages resulted in a 10.9 percent increase in conversions per year, compared to nonresponsive design that only had 2.7 percent yearly growth.[15]

4: Optimized. You can use your Google Adwords planner tool or a Chrome plugin like Keywords Everywhere to identify high-volume search keywords and strings (long tail phrases) that can help your landing pages rank higher in searches.[16]

Bonus Tip. Don't forget to upload your videos on other video sharing sites to help drive passive traffic to your career site. Sites like Vimeo, Facebook, YouTube, Instagram, and Pinterest help increase the likelihood that qualified job seekers will view your video and complete the ultimate candidate conversion act of applying for your job.

Career Page Content Improves Candidate Application Rates

Finally, your landing pages are crucial to engaging next-generation candidates, improving your candidate nurturing in a tight talent marketplace, and are no longer a "nice to have" part of your recruitment marketing strategy. If you want to be competitive in this marketplace, recruiting like a marketer is one of the most important things you can do to keep up with your competitors. Strategic landing pages are used by 68 percent of businesses to acquire leads.[17] If your company is competing with any of those in that 68 percent, you're going to get benched before the game starts. Without them, your talent funnel could shrink considerably once you get past the awareness and consideration stage.

CHAPTER 5

Employer Brand Basics

- Why Do I Need an EVP?

- Creating Your EVP

- Examples of EVP Statements

- The Role of Employer Branding in Digital Recruiting

- How to Get Started with Marketing Your Employer Brand

- The Talent Funnel

- Shifting the Focus of Your EVP from Company to Employee

At its heart, an employee value proposition (EVP) is the unique set of benefits an employee receives in return for the skills, capabilities, and experience they bring to a company. An EVP is about defining the essence of your company—how it is unique and what it stands for.

An EVP describes the mix of characteristics, benefits, and ways of working in an organization. It's the deal struck between company and employee in return for their contribution and performance. This "deal" characterizes an employer and differentiates it from its competition and transforms employees or potential employees into champions.

WHY DO I NEED AN EVP?

Developing a strong EVP is a key element of any recruiting and retention effort as part of the larger employer brand. At its most basic, an EVP represents everything of value that an employer provides to its employees—pay, benefits, training, career development opportunities, and so on—and it is then "marketed" to the workforce.

EVPs matter because they should be the foundation on which your brand and all your internal retention efforts as well as your external recruiting efforts are established. One of the mistakes companies make when creating an EVP is focusing on the leadership of their company rather than making an employee-focused EVP. For recruiting and retention, your EVP statement must reflect the value to the employee, not the value to company leadership or the bottom line (while those are both nice side effects of a solid "talk-the-talk" and "walk-the-walk" EVP).

You'll want to make an effort to develop your EVP in the words of your employees and potential candidates via the following:

- Executive interviews and workshops with key stakeholders to understand talent priorities from a strategic perspective.
- Qualitative focus groups that enrich your understanding of employee values and perceptions.
- Branding and marketing support, including optimal and differentiated messaging, tested internally.

CREATING YOUR EVP

It's easy to throw a few value propositions into a statement and put it on your careers site or have it stenciled on a wall. However, it's key to create an EVP that reflects the current values of your workplace, and that means starting internally. How is your company morale? Honestly, how is it? If your EVP talks about how much your employees love working for your organization and why, but your current employees would roll their eyes at the statement, you have two options: (1) Rewrite your EVP or (2) Focus on improving morale for your current employees before you start marketing a value proposition to potential employees.

"Improving morale" seems like a never-ending, broad, "depends on who you talk to" kind of task. As an HR professional, your employees are not only the best advocates for your brand, they can sniff out a false statement from a mile away. You're never going to make 100 percent of your employees happy 100 percent of the time, but what you can do is find out if there are one or two common threads that may be impacting employee morale negatively. Consider anonymous surveys (and understand that, depending on the state of your company morale, many employees will not believe the surveys are anonymous), establish trust between human resources and employees of the company, and use surveys not only to try and uncover negatives, but also to isolate the positives. Start with the positives.

Your current employees and what they love about your company are going to be the best resource for crafting a strong EVP statement. If you discover that most employees rate the CEO negatively (pro tip: take a look at your company's Glassdoor reviews), but they love their own autonomy and they're not micromanaged, your EVP could focus on the fact that your employees are empowered to make their own decisions, to take risks without consequences, that they feel their creativity is rewarded, and so on.[1]

According to research by Gartner, organizations that effectively deliver on their EVP can decrease their annual employee turnover as much as 69 percent.[2]

An employee survey can also help you identify what you could easily fix from a human resources perspective. Some years ago, I consulted for a company CEO who loved to promote the fact that he met one-on-one with every single employee every quarter. However, employees didn't exactly see these meetings as a benefit. Perhaps because the company had a large millennial employee base, employees felt that these one-on-ones with their CEO was akin to being "called to the principal's office." They took every suggestion or comment during these meetings as criticism. When asked what they preferred, the answer was more communication with their direct supervisors.

Did they care whether or not the CEO knew them personally or understood what they did at the company? No. They cared about whether or not the CEO was equipped to steer the company in a positive direction that would make an impact on the company's bottom line. The result? No more one-on-one meetings and more regular and transparent updates from the CEO on the financial health of the company.

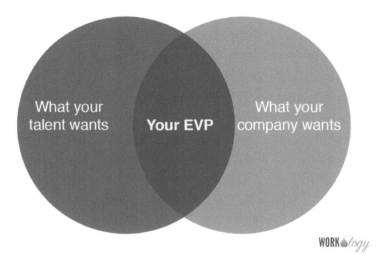

Figure 5.1 What is an EVP?

Knowing what employees want and value is the foundation of a successful EVP. However, employers cannot assume that they know which parts of the employment package employees view as the most significant. A perception gap can result in a weak EVP. If employers assume incorrectly, they could be missing critical opportunities to emphasize how the organization provides what employees prize most.

EXAMPLES OF EVP STATEMENTS

When building your EVP, consider that the most significant contributors to retention are development and career opportunities together with the relationships and respect that the employee builds within your organization, particularly those with managers and with peers.

The most important question to ask when creating your company's EVP is "What do we currently offer to our employees in exchange for their time and effort?"

Company EVP Examples

When I conduct EVP coaching, I usually mention examples showing how companies try to portray their uniqueness and differences. Here are some of them:

HubSpot. "We're building a company people love. A company that will stand the test of time, so we invest in our people and optimize for your long-term happiness."

Yelp. "We work hard, throw Nerf darts even harder, and have a whole lot of fun."

Goldman Sachs. "At Goldman Sachs, you will make an impact."

Google. "Do cool things that matter."

PwC. "From empowering mentorships to customized coaching, PwC provides you with the support you need to help you develop your career. You'll work with people from diverse backgrounds and industries to solve important problems. Are you ready to grow?"

Shopify. "We're Shopify. Our mission is to make commerce better for everyone—but we're not the workplace for everyone. We thrive on change, operate on trust, and leverage the diverse perspectives of people on our team in everything we do. We solve problems at a rapid pace. In short, we get shit done."

Honeywell. "You can make a difference by helping to build a smarter, safer and more sustainable world."

L'Oreal. "Lead the future of Beauty. When you love your work and the people you work with, amazing things can happen."

Nike. "We lead. We invent. We deliver. We use the power of sport to move the world."

Bark. "Be the person your dog thinks you are."

What to Do with Your EVP

Once you've developed a clear and descriptive employee value proposition statement, share it with your employees, candidates, and new hires. Having an EVP statement allows you to easily communicate the value your company offers.

Finally, SHRM recommends that employers review their EVPs regularly to make sure they remain relevant. Asking EVP-related questions when employees join or leave the company, during performance reviews, and in employee surveys can provide ongoing data about how employees perceive the EVP. Recruitment and retention metrics can also indicate how well the EVP fits with employee needs and expectations.

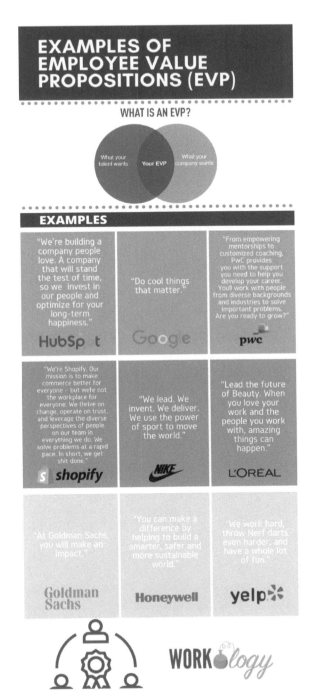

Figure 5.2 Examples of employee value propositions

THE ROLE OF EMPLOYER BRANDING IN DIGITAL RECRUITING

An employer brand describes an employer's reputation as a place to work, and its employee value proposition, as opposed to the more general corporate brand reputation and value proposition to customers. The term was first used in the early 1990s and has since become widely adopted by the global management community. The art and science of employer branding is concerned with the attraction, engagement, and retention initiatives targeted at enhancing your company's employer brand.

A candidate's market, combined with new consumer behavior, has led to the rise in importance of employer branding as a human resources and marketing discipline. Since the Great Recession, the market has shifted in favor of candidates given low unemployment. This means that employers are fighting over the same small pool of candidates to fill their open roles, especially in hard-to-fill areas like developers, engineers, and other STEM-based roles.

Consumer behavior has also changed the way that people look for jobs. The candidate journey isn't simply a job seeker finding your job and applying. This is especially true of the best candidates—they want to research a company and build a relationship with it over months before applying for a job. This creates a dynamic where companies who invest in employer branding are seeing lower cost-per-hire and time-to-fill.

The simplest ways of measuring a return on employer branding investment are as follows:

- Increased awareness that leads to more applicants, and tracking how these applicants translate to hires.
- Increased conversion rates of interested applicants after implementing employer branding tactics.
- Decreases in time-to-fill and the progress this allows a business to make.
- Decreases in third-party recruiter spending.

There is now an emerging group of tools that can assist HR and marketing teams in their employer branding efforts. Some of these tools were originally designed for marketing purposes. Others are existing HR technologies that have evolved to have employer branding capabilities such as the newer generation of applicant tracking systems (ATS) and job boards.

HOW TO GET STARTED WITH MARKETING YOUR EMPLOYER BRAND

Traditional marketing strategies are becoming commonplace in recruitment. The war for talent is on and recruiters must start thinking like marketers to streamline processes and compete for the best talent in a tight labor market. We should be familiar with campaign-based marketing, nurturing, omnichannel engagement, and each stage of the recruiting funnel.

Where to Start? The Talent Brand Audit

Your employer brand is the common thread that runs through all of your recruiting marketing efforts, and it's also the first place to begin when reviewing your current processes to determine what you can do better and more efficiently. Often called a talent brand or employment brand audit, this comprehensive analysis looks at all aspects of your digital brand and candidate experience. It focuses on many areas, but specifically, the top four are as follows.

Your Recruiting Technology. Your applicant tracking system (ATS) is the heart of your recruiting and application process. Your ATS can enhance the candidate experience with customization, including social media job posting, sharing, and applying buttons that make it easier for qualified candidates to apply quickly and easily for the jobs they want. You can also set up messaging automation with an FAQ for candidates and use your apply bounce-back email to direct candidates to questions most asked by them during the interview and hiring process, as well as use the opportunity to re-engage previous applicants with content marketing.

Technology can help you move more quickly to secure a strong candidate. As the time these candidates are on the market gets shorter, taking the time at the outset to establish a clear process and plan for all those involved in the hiring process with your recruiting technology gives you the freedom to move quickly when it counts. A speedy process will help you lock in a great candidate before they move on to another opportunity.

Your Social Media Channels. With seven in ten Americans on social media, and 92 percent of employers using social media, social channels are low-cost and necessary channels for amplifying your brand.[3] Work with your marketing team and collaborate on a dual strategy to drive a strong presence on social media by cross-posting customer and employee stories to engage new customers and drive quality candidates to your career site to apply.

Employee testimonials are a powerful way to share what makes your organization unique and a great place to work. Don't forget about leveraging videos as a way to share these testimonials and on all social media platforms. Companies such as Twilio combine video with testimonials that complement their employment branding and social media efforts. Beyond research and employee testimonials, visual media helps to set employers apart from one another. This includes photography, videos, and other digital assets that complement your job posting. For similar examples, check out AT&T's career site, T-Mobile's career "tours," and careers at Airbnb.

Your Job Descriptions. The best job postings provide information on the qualifications and skill sets needed to be successful in the role. The single most important part of your job posting is the title. Like an email subject line, it is the first piece of information your candidate will read. It should accurately describe the job, provide information about the skill sets required, and encourage the candidate to either explore or move along to another opportunity. A poor job posting headline can keep you from reaching the best talent and draw out the hiring process possibly indefinitely.

An effective job description should include key responsibilities for the position as succinctly as possible. You might consider a short version for posting to job boards and elsewhere online with a link to the longer description on your career site. The second most important feature of a job posting is a call to action (CTA) that drives candidates to apply. Keep your CTA short and to the point. It could be as simple as, "Apply here," but you want your call to action to stand out from those of your competitors. Take a look at your competitors' job postings and consider conducting A/B tests with different CTAs to see which drives better results.

Your Career Site. I've mentioned before that your career site is your company's most important recruitment channel and the top resource candidates access during their research process. Your talent brand includes the perceptions of prospective, current, and previous employees and influences whether or not people choose to apply, accept offers, and stay at your company. A talent brand audit is an excellent way to measure this information with regards to where you are now, set goals and define where you would like to be, and implement or change processes based on the information gathered via your audit. This is how you control (most of) the information that is out there about your company, your messaging, and the perception of your company for the long term. It's dynamic by its nature, which means that a long-term candidate marketing strategy that supports your employer brand must be maintained and audited frequently.

THE TALENT FUNNEL

Marketing teams are familiar with funnel engagement; if you haven't already, consider adapting the same process for your candidate marketing. Developing personas, mapping out how you're reaching them and where, and reporting on the results are inherently useful to the hiring process. Your talent funnel, or pipeline, allows you to not only recruit for the positions you have open now, but for those you may need to fill in the future. For high-volume hiring, a talent pipeline is a necessity.

Content Marketing

In the simplest terms, content marketing is a strategic marketing approach focused on creating and distributing valuable, relevant, and consistent content to attract and retain a clearly defined audience—and, ultimately, to drive profitable customer action. For recruiters, this means candidate engagement and supporting a robust talent pipeline.

Content marketing is important for candidate nurturing in the mid-to-lower hiring funnel. All candidates should get a list of resources to help them in their job search, whether it's with your organization or with someone else. The key is to create a referral source that continues to drive high-quality job seekers to expand and grow your employment brand in far-reaching ways. This can be in the form of an FAQ along with other candidate assets that can help provide information about your company, unique qualities, and custom content and resources targeted to your job candidate personas.

Candidate Nurturing

Customization and candidate nurturing are key to maintaining a positive candidate experience from job application to interview to acceptance or rejection. Once you have personas and data, customization falls into place and you can focus on nurturing candidates through your hiring funnel.

Consider sending surveys to a select group of candidates (for example, those you have an interest in after the initial application). This could be a four- or five-question survey asking the candidates to share their goals, interests, or even something like a hobby or some other more personal aspect unrelated to work. I touched on surveys and focus groups in Chapter 3. That said, be clear in the survey that responses will not be factored into the hiring decision. With such additional information, you can get a better idea of what your candidates' interests are and use this information to better personalize the interview experience.

Measuring Success

Every marketer knows it's impossible to scale new programs and processes without data. Data is at the heart of many of the decisions we make, but it's also the key to improving in the three key areas of time, cost, and quality. It's nearly impossible to separate time from quality from cost, as the crossover effect is inherent in these recruiting metrics when it comes to analytics.

Data and predictive analytics will allow you and your recruiting team to make informed decisions about what to automate, where to spend time on high-touch tasks, how to reach candidates more quickly and in a targeted way, and manage costs. For specific nurturing and candidate marketing efforts, you'll want to identify the key performance indicators that align with your company goals, such as open and click-through rates for email campaigns, engagement rates for digital or social advertising, and so on. Additionally, there are a few key metrics you'll want to focus on as you get started building your recruitment marketing strategies. I'll discuss metrics and reporting in more detail in Chapters 10 and 11.

- **Time-to-fill:** The average number of days the position is posted to the time a candidate accepts a job offer.
- **Time-to-start:** The average time between when a candidate accepts an offer to their first day as an employee.
- **Candidate-to-hire ratio:** These ratios can vary from the number of applications, to hires, to the applicant-to-interview ratios for initial interviews as well as final interviews.
- **Source-of-hire:** What applicant sources are performing the best across the board by position and among recruiters? Candidate engagement is one of the most powerful metrics for analyzing your employment brand. Drilling down to engagement per

source of hire gives you the information you need to make modifications to your brand's public perception on various channels, whether it be your career site or social channels.

- **Quality of hire:** Recruiting metrics that measure which source of hire produces the best-performing candidates or those with the longest tenure.
- **Lost productivity per open requisition, per day:** Determining a lost productivity metric for *all* positions as well as specific ones per day can help establish how recruiting impacts the bottom line.

Finally, when recruiters adopt a marketing approach for building talent pipelines, significant changes happen in your company's employer branding, prospect attrition, and scale of candidate outreach. The benefits of recruitment marketing include a reduction in your low-impact recruiting tasks while allowing you to focus on recruiting top-quality hires and innovators who are difficult to attract using standard approaches for hiring.

SHIFTING THE FOCUS OF YOUR EVP FROM COMPANY TO EMPLOYEE

Your EVP is not about what your recruiting team or senior leadership wants, but how your employees perceive your company's value and what resonates with them. It's important to find the right balance between supporting company expectations and what candidates want from your company.

An EVP may not be a requirement to start in recruitment marketing, but it is a great way to ensure that your recruitment efforts align with the culture of the organization and also correlates with better retention. If you recruit the right people that fit with your EVP, you can reduce turnover rates because you're reaching and engaging candidates that have a culture fit that's better in tune with your organization.

CHAPTER 6

Mobile, Mobile Everywhere

- **Why Mobile Matters in HR and Recruiting**
- **Three Pillars of Mobile Recruiting**
- **How We Use Mobile as Consumers versus Candidates: The Case for Mobile-First Development**
- **Texting as a Recruitment Marketing Channel**
- **Other Mobile Recruiting Applications and Technologies That Are Driving Adoption**
- **Mobile and Gamification of the Apply Process**

In this chapter, we'll take a look at the move towards mobile in recruiting, whether it's candidate communication, social media, or our expectation for instant access to resources and people. We have evolved as a society to an "always connected" default. In a relatively short period of time, we have gone from shutting down our workstations at the end of a day to enjoy a blissfully work-free evening, to a workforce of constant connectivity through these little screens that fit in our pockets and go with us everywhere, twenty-four hours a day, seven days a week. To be competitive (and therefore successful), we have to be available when and where our candidates are. This shift isn't unique to recruiting, but it is meaningful in the sense that our customers, the job seekers and employees we serve, have also evolved into an "always on" marketplace. Just as consumers are now accustomed to picking up their smartphones and making a purchase from Amazon at three o'clock in the morning, our customers expect to be able to apply for jobs, access work schedules, and get answers to questions at any time of the day or night.

WHY MOBILE MATTERS IN HR AND RECRUITING

You may find it strange that I'm dedicating an entire chapter to mobile. I'm doing so because I think it is the most important part of the candidate experience and one that, as talent acquisition leaders, we are missing out on. The mobile experience matters as increasingly more candidates rely on their smartphones as their sole computer for themselves and their entire family.

Mobile is the single most important change in the world since the invention of the internet. According to Pew Research Center, the vast majority of Americans—97 percent—now own a cell phone of some kind.[1] The share of Americans who own a smartphone is now 85 percent, up from just 35 percent in Pew Research Center's first survey of smartphone ownership conducted in 2011. The same survey reports that 15 percent of American adults are "smartphone-only" internet users—meaning they own a smartphone but do not have traditional home broadband service. Reliance on smartphones for online access is especially common among younger adults, lower-income Americans, and those with a high school education or less.

Mobile allows for individuals to be connected in real time, on the fly, and literally from the palm of their hand. They have the world and its resources at their fingertips, making for some of the most empowered buyers and consumers we've experienced to date. Mobile users are empowered to learn, engage, and research for themselves without having to wait.

A large percentage of these mobile users are in the market for a job. These job seekers conduct personal and professional business from their piece of technology that is more important than all others. And that technology comes in the form of their mobile device.

Mobile allows for instant connection, which in the recruiting world can allow for a distinct competitive advantage in engaging top talent first, especially in the contingent labor, health care, and information technology markets. Text messaging in particular is the most unobtrusive and effective form of communication from your mobile device, especially considering that 99 percent of text messages are read within ninety seconds, compared with in-app push notifications averaging 50–80 percent open rates. Email open rates are the least engaging at 18 percent industry-wide, according to eMarketer (but we're not going to discount them from our mobile strategy).[2]

Why is mobile-first technology a recruiter's secret weapon in the war for talent? Mobile allows for instant engagement and connectedness, which is especially important in the candidate experience as well as for placing qualified talent quickly and easily.

Mobile Usage Statistics in the United States in 2021

- Over 80 percent of internet users use mobile devices to surf the web.
- 83 percent of mobile users expect a flawless experience whenever they visit a website with any mobile device.

- Up to 70 percent of web traffic comes from mobile devices.
- 95.1 percent of active Facebook traffic comes from mobile devices.
- 57 percent of LinkedIn traffic comes from mobile.
- Mobile devices are responsible for more than 70 percent of watch time happening on YouTube.
- 90 percent of Twitter views happen on mobile.
- Google is responsible for 96 percent of search traffic coming from mobile.
- 80 percent of Alexa's top-ranked websites are mobile-friendly.[3]

Here's one from Cisco's Global Mobile Data Traffic Forecast that might surprise you: the average smartphone user checks their smartphone 150 times a day.[4] If this seems high, you can check your own usage in your smartphone settings—how long you've spent on your phone, which apps you spend the most time using, and how many times you check your phone on average. It's not just Pavlovian. It's completely integrated into our lives.

Our dependence on devices isn't a bad thing. We have access to literally anything with a tap on a browser app. We can check on our friends, professional and personal, on dozens of social platforms. We text more than we talk. We have email, calendar apps, videos, learning platforms, notes apps, reminders, and we can have a meal or a grocery order delivered in under an hour via an ever-growing number of personal services apps. Remember how you did all of these things in 1994? It definitely took a lot more time. Recruiters depended on paper files, phone calls, open houses, and newspaper job ads, and the internet was still spelled with a capital "I." Many of us remember the screeching sound of dial-up and your AOL screen name. I'm dating myself, but in my early days of HR, email was an interoffice method of communication.

While the first handheld cell phone for consumer use was sold in March of 1984, the Motorola DynaTAC 8000X cost $3,995. In 1996, mobile phones became a little more defined and better looking than how they were before. Antennas were shortened and the designs modified; the features were also upgraded. Smartphones have existed since the early to mid–1990s (with the advent of the IBM Simon) and gained some traction during the early 2000s with phones such as the Danger Hiptop and Blackberry devices, but they didn't become popular until much later.

The first generation iPhone (known as the iPhone 2G after 2008) is the first smartphone designed and marketed by Apple Inc. After years of rumors and speculation, it was officially announced on January 9, 2007, and was released in the United States on June 29, 2007. The iPhone debuted at $499 for the 4GB and $599 for the 8GB model on contract. Those prices weren't unheard of at the time—early Motorola RAZR flip phones were incredibly expensive as well—but it meant Apple couldn't penetrate the mainstream market, at least initially. The Blackberry held onto its position as the leader of the smartphone world for a few years, but it was eventually overtaken by the iPhone and then wiped completely out of existence. The iPhone 3G model was released in 2008, and after Apple started seeing some competition, they released a 3GS model in 2009. Ten years later, 81 percent of the population of the United States had a smartphone, and we can't remember what we did without them.

Mobile devices, smartphones in particular, make us more productive than we ever imagined we could be. We see articles in our news feeds every day about "breaking our smartphone addiction," but how many of us really want to do it? We're doing better than 90 percent of the population if we can put them away while we're on vacation. Bottom line? Mobile isn't going anywhere. It's booming.

THREE PILLARS OF MOBILE RECRUITING

My mobile phone goes with me everywhere. It's my preferred method of communication and the device I use most to shop, search, and connect with friends, colleagues, and family. At present count, I have 125 mobile apps on my iPhone (some that I use more than others). Mobile is quickly replacing not just our landlines and desktop computers, but also our televisions, cameras, and radios. This technology I liken to a new age Swiss Army knife, which serves as a source of information, resources, and connectivity in every aspect of our daily lives. Mobile provides us freedom to choose the way in which we live our life.

For a growing number of candidates, the mobile device is their preferred method of internet access and communication, which means employers must consider mobile to engage talent. It's no longer a luxury for employers. It's a necessity. The challenge? Mobile can be complicated. It's not simply having a mobile application process, a career site, or a social media strategy. It's all of the above.

Like any recruiting strategy or plan, a mobile strategy should be unique to the organization; however, there are some mobile basics which are true regardless of the industry, company size or location. I call them the three pillars of mobile recruiting.

Social Media

According to the most recent Pew Research study on social media use in 2021, 84 percent of adults ages 18 to 29 say they ever use any social media sites, which is similar to the share of those ages 30 to 49 who say this (81 percent).[5] By comparison, a somewhat smaller share of those ages 50 to 64 (73 percent) say they use social media sites, while fewer than half of those 65 and older (45 percent) report doing this. These age differences generally extend to use of specific platforms, with younger Americans being more likely than their older counterparts to use these sites—though the gaps between younger and older Americans vary across platforms.

Social media is a platform to connect with friends, stay up-to-date on news and current events, and research, which increasingly includes the job search. Social media platforms like YouTube, Twitter, Facebook, LinkedIn, Instagram, Pinterest, and TikTok offer a great way to engage prospective job seekers in real time. Job seekers can connect directly with employers and recruiters versus a job board or agency recruiter who serves as a go-between. Job seekers feel more connected on social media, and since a large percentage of activities via social media happen

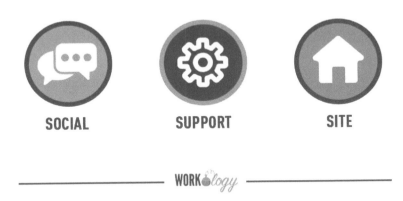

Figure 6.1 Three pillars of mobile recruiting

on a mobile device, employers must assume candidates are accessing these sites on multiple platforms and should prepare accordingly.

Social media can be a multichannel strategy. With an active and engaged presence on social media, you're building a subset of your candidate funnel, as well as supporting and broadcasting your employment brand. Social media can be many things, but at the end of the day, it's a method by which you engage candidates and drive quality talent to your career site to apply for open positions or sign up for your content marketing efforts, like your talent email newsletter.

The Original Electronic Mobile Activity: Email. This brings me to the original electronic mobile activity—email. Even with the rise of social media, email is the best and most personal way to engage a candidate. And yet, as recruiters, we often treat email automation and messaging as secondary sources of engagement and trust-building. It's important to understand that we couldn't do our jobs without email. Hubspot reports that more than 50 percent of US respondents check their personal email account more than 10 times a day, and it is by far their preferred way to receive updates from brands.[6] The number of active email accounts is expected to hit 5.6 billion this year.

Despite the growth and prominence of mobile messengers and chat apps, email is an integral part of daily online life. In 2020, the number of global email users amounted to 4 billion and is set to grow to 4.6 billion users in 2025. In 2020, approximately 306 billion emails were sent and received every day worldwide.[7] This figure is projected to increase to over 376 billion daily emails by 2025. Recent industry data shows that the trend towards mobile also holds true for email: in December 2018, 43 percent of email opens were via mobile.[8] Desktop email clients' open share had declined to 18 percent, and webmail accounted for 39 percent of opens. Based on the dominance of mobile, it is no surprise that the iPhone email app was the most popular email client, accounting for 29 percent of email opens. Gmail was ranked second with a 27 percent open share.[9]

Support

Supporting efforts include recruitment marketing, messaging, and branding. They also can include supplementary career site applications and technology, including a mobile app. Support functions and technologies are essential to the mobile apply process. This means having buy-in from your company stakeholders to support not just your mobile recruitment marketing but also the mobile functionality on your career site or campaign landing pages. For example, if job seekers can find your company site, but not your careers page, you're missing an opportunity to engage candidates. Most candidates will visit a company page to do research. If your careers page isn't prominently linked—in a sidebar, a top navigation menu, or a pop-up—they'll head for the nearest job search engine instead.

Also, do your company brand and employer brand align in your digital efforts? Do your recruitment campaigns, job postings, and display ads look like they are from two different companies? You want job seekers to recognize both your consumer and employer brand, not make them wonder if the job description they're reading on their smartphone is from the same company by the same name.

And that's why I'm sharing examples and samples in this book. These might seem like small actions, but they help support and elevate your hiring process and help your employer stand out from the competition, which is essential in this talent market that essentially has zero unemployment.

Site

As I have said before, your career site is the heart of your online employer presence. As the employer, you are fully in control of the platform, the message, the engagement, and the interaction. All other platforms, engagement, and candidate interactions have one key mission: drive the candidate to the career site to apply for a job, or join a talent network or job alert. This is the candidate's official notice telling the employer that they are interested in the company and a specific job opening. Candidates, wherever they are and whatever device they choose to show their interest, should be able to access and enjoy the career site, especially on a mobile device.

Job applications submitted via mobile devices last year surpassed those submitted via desktop, according to an Appcast analysis of some 7 million applications to nearly 1,300 US employers. Mobile applications made up roughly 61 percent of all applications in the recruiting technology firm's analysis.[10] When examining how apply rates compare on mobile and desktop devices, the report also reveals the following:

- Desktop apply rates decreased 6.7 percent in 2020 compared to 2019.
- In contrast, there was a 21.2 percent increase in mobile apply rates in comparison to last year.

What this means for recruiters is that your mobile apply experience must be fast and flawless.

Search engine optimization (SEO) is critical to the mobile career site experience. In 2016, Google began testing mobile-first indexing.[11]

Google explained that it sees more mobile searches than desktop searches on a daily basis.[12] At the time, when Google evaluated a page's ranking, it looked at the desktop version of the site. To fix this, Google began looking at the content, links, and structured data of the mobile version of your site if one was available. The key part of that sentence is "if one is available." If you're not optimizing your site for mobile search, you could be losing half of the traffic your optimized competitors are getting to their career pages.

While Google isn't very transparent about its algorithms, we can assume mobile-first indexing is in place. In early 2017, in its Webmasters Tools Search Console, Google added a "Mobile Usability" report under the Search Traffic heading. This can help you identify how your pages rank in mobile interactivity. For example, elements that are too close together or wider than the screen on a mobile device will cause errors. These pages with issues should be addressed immediately if you want to continue scoring well in SEO.

Those of us without an analytics or development team standing at the ready can use tools like Google's Mobile-Friendly Test that scans your site for flaws when it comes to mobile search engine optimization.[13] It will display any errors the site may have while being indexed by Google's site crawler, and you can modify them in your website CMS or collect a list to hand off to your team's web developers.

According to Google, responsive design is more appealing than a separate mobile version of a website.[14] This is because it eliminates a wide range of issues people are now having trying to maintain both desktop and mobile aspects. And a bonus is, instead of having two completely separate URLs for content, you only use one. One of the biggest problems this eliminates is making sure both desktop and mobile sites have the same content. Now that many of us are part-time junior developers (i.e., we understand how to use Wordpress or Drupal content management system), the time we spend changing content on our career site pages is reduced and our opportunity to attract more targeted search traffic is raised.

HOW WE USE MOBILE AS CONSUMERS VERSUS CANDIDATES: THE CASE FOR MOBILE-FIRST DEVELOPMENT

Deloitte's 2021 *Connectivity and Mobile Trends Survey* identifies emerging smartphone consumer behaviors that happened before and during the global pandemic.[15] Consumer use of mobile technology greatly increased during the pandemic, with activities like using a mobile app or website to order food growing from 36 to 56 percent, curbside pickup growing from 31 to 51 percent, and contactless payments increasing by similar numbers. Of those who started using smartphones for retail purposes, 70 percent said they'll continue to do so.

Even before the pandemic, Deloitte's 2019 *Global Mobile Consumer Survey: US Edition* reported that consumer use of mobile had nearly reached market saturation. Some highlights from the report:[16]

- Smartphones easily remained the most favored mobile device among US consumers, growing by 3 percent and reaching 85 percent penetration overall.
- Smartphone growth was strongest among older age groups at over 10 percent, reflecting already strong adoption among younger generations.
- Americans are viewing their smartphones more often than ever before, on an average of 52 times per day.
- Smartphones are the preferred mobile device for most online activities.
- More than a third of adults report using their smartphones "very/fairly often" for business purposes outside normal working hours. Fifty-nine percent use their personal smartphone during normal working hours "very/fairly often."

As consumer mobile use expands, so does mobile use for candidates. According to Appcast's 2021 *Recruitment Marketing Benchmark Report*, mobile applications surpassed desktop applications for the first time in 2020; 60.7 percent of job applications were completed on mobile devices compared to 39.3 percent on desktop.[17] The industries hiring large numbers of workers for select job functions are partly responsible for the significant jump in mobile apply rates—many of these jobs were for hourly roles, essential workers, retail, and other high-volume hiring based on demand—and candidates applying for many of those types of jobs prefer mobile. However, better mobile apply processes are also a factor.

Glassdoor's 2019 report *The Rise of Mobile Devices in Job Search: Challenges and Opportunities for Employers* found that the application process is significantly more difficult for mobile job seekers.[18] Mobile job seekers, on average, successfully complete 53 percent fewer applications and take 80 percent longer to complete each application, hindering workers who rely on their phones to search for jobs.

The Glassdoor report also indicates that reducing the time needed to complete an online job application by 10 percent is associated with a 2.3 percent increase in job applications from mobile job seekers and a 1.5 percent increase in applications from desktop job seekers. Employers with difficult mobile job application processes are likely deterring many potential applicants.

Promoting a job opening as mobile-friendly can increase the number of job applicants by 11.6 percent at the expense of jobs from other employers that aren't mobile-friendly. In a tight labor market, having a mobile-friendly job application process can be a powerful way for employers to compete for talent.

We're not pushing mobile as a "next-generation" marketing tool. The next generation is already here. Mobile adoption for job seekers is actually highest for workers aged 35–44 years old in the prime of their careers. As such, mobile usage should not be dismissed as a unique characteristic of younger job seekers. A significant share of workers in all age groups in the American workforce rely on mobile devices as a core tool to connect with employers online. Glassdoor's report shows that the use of mobile devices in job searches, including phones and tablets, actually peaks among the 35–44 year old age group at 55 percent, trailing off to a low of 44 percent on both ends of the age spectrum—18–24 and over 65. Gen Z and millennial workers use their phones less than their Gen X counterparts when it comes to searching for jobs.

Making your career site mobile accessible (and mobile optimized) should be an integral part of omnichannel marketing. It is your company's most important recruitment channel and the top resource candidates access during their research process.

Need a case for updating your HR technology? Mobile job seekers successfully complete applications 53 percent less often and each completed application takes 80 percent longer than for desktop job seekers. Given the inherent difficulty of using mobile devices for tasks such as responding to questions or attaching documents, coupled with the lackluster mobile optimization of some ATSs, it is no surprise that mobile job seekers face a much more difficult time applying to jobs than desktop users.

Using Google Analytics to Understand Where to Invest in Digital

Industry reports aside, you can find out how many users access your career site or landing pages using Google Analytics. With a device category report, you can get data on device type. This includes desktop, mobile, and tablets, providing insight into how many candidates are accessing your site with a mobile device. If you can see that a significant percentage of site visits are from a mobile device, you'll want to focus development of your career site on improving user experience on mobile, beginning with a responsive website that works just as well on mobile as on desktop.

I haven't mentioned mobile apps, although they have been important over the years. In recent history, companies like AT&T and PepsiCo have developed mobile-specific recruiting apps. These are often expensive to maintain; however, for app-focused sites or brands like Taco Bell and Papa Johns (which have mobile delivery options), I recommend working with your marketing team to make room to use an app as an opportunity in some form to recruit candidates.

Figure 6.2   Google Analytics dashboard

TEXTING AS A RECRUITMENT MARKETING CHANNEL

Recruiters who specialize in an industry that has a small social circle care about not just the candidate experience, but relationships and engaging their network. The same holds true for business leaders and HR who are looking at a way to engage their new hires or current employee population. Mobile can do that, especially when a candidate is ready to pull the trigger and jump into a red hot job seeker market. Text messaging can be a candidate engagement and recruiting game changer.

Four Ways Recruiters and HR Can Use Text Messaging

- **Updating your candidate relationship manager (CRM) and candidate contact information:** There's nothing worse than being interrupted by a call from an unknown number or from a recruiter you aren't quite ready to engage. By texting them, you can check in, but more importantly, update your CRM and make sure it's up to date. With applicant tracking interfaces (APIs) between a texting vendor and your applicant tracking system (ATS) or CRM, this is an absolute possibility.
- **Confirming appointments, phone calls, meetings, and interviews:** Texts provide candidates a quick reminder or an opportunity to quickly check their schedule to make sure they are able to attend their interview.

- **Quick check-ins:** These are fast, nonintrusive ways to check in with a candidate. The messages can be personalized, scheduled, and even automated to help your recruiters maintain productivity but still make time for engagement.
- **Enhancing your current process:** Maybe it's following up with a candidate whom you are eagerly waiting on to complete their new hire paperwork or assessment that is keeping them from moving ahead in the process. Sometimes we all need a little reminder or nudge in the right direction. Texting can be a great way to do this.

There are so many advantages of using text messaging as a recruiting tool, including a higher quality of hire, less bias, a lower cost-per-hire as a result of lower travel costs, an improved candidate experience, and a shorter time-to-fill open positions.

For my own business, I have taken the dive into marketing via text for the past seven years with a SHRM Annual Conference text group on *Workology* to drive awareness and information to achieve a specific goal (in this case, information about after-hours events and parties at HR and recruiting conferences). For the SHRM 2019 Annual Conference, it looked like this:[19]

> Welcome to the 2019 SHRM Unofficial Party, Reception, Meet-up, Cocktail, and Activities List. This list is password protected for 24 hours exclusively for VIPs. As parties and events are added or updated, they will be notated with a ★New★ or ★Updated★ tag at the beginning of the event. To receive this information immediately, text "SHRM" to 55678.

Conference attendees can opt-in via an SMS short code, which allows me to communicate with a larger audience than traditional marketing methods like email when events are added or with other updates. If you're not familiar with the technology, an SMS short code is a five to six digit phone number that is used by businesses to opt-in consumers to their SMS programs and then used to send text message coupons, offers, promotions, and more to customers who have previously opted in. It's a relatively low-cost method of communication. The cost of a short code varies by what type of short code you're looking to lease. If you're interested in leasing a dedicated short code, you can either lease a vanity short code for $1,000 per month, or lease a nonvanity short code for $500 per month.

You can set up your automated text message or SMS system and advertise that candidates can apply by texting a simple word to a short number. Include the short code on your print materials so potential candidates can opt in to your job listings and events. Want to see how it works for yourself? Text JMM to 55678 to see what I mean.

These shortcodes work as digital "business cards"—an easy code to remember when you're meeting people face-to-face at events or using display advertising. Companies like Gap Inc. and Target use them effectively to reach a broad talent pool. I recently saw a sign at a Burger King while making a pit stop with my family as we traveled cross country over the summer: "We're Hiring," followed by "text the word JOBS to 242424." I think this is a perfect tactic for anyone, but it especially works well for companies that hire at a high volume.

Once candidates use your text code, it's important to take advantage of the short time frame when you are on the candidate's mind by asking the right questions, providing the right incentives, and knocking down any barriers to applying. Consider adding customized questions like zip code and email address to qualify job candidates before encouraging them to apply for a location, suggesting that they attend a job fair, or directing them to specific job openings.

In recruiting, traditional texting (without a short code) is also effective. Research indicates that 90 percent of text messages get read.[20] Text messages are very likely to be viewed by the recipient, but if the recipient is redirected to a website, for example, they are much less likely to respond. A text platform that allows the candidate to respond directly can be the beginning of a conversation rather than a dead end. This is an opportunity for recruiters to begin a dialogue with candidates, engage them, and move them from text to phone call or text to email.

Consider the example of restaurant reservation company OpenTable. It has been on the cutting edge for SMS and email for its restaurant customers, who in turn benefit from the technology for its dining reservations. OpenTable is an early adopter of Canvas, a text-based interview platform that launched in 2017 that allows recruiters to start text conversations with candidates. Starting in 2018, OpenTable replaced its initial phone interview entirely with text screening for hiring its sales team. The text responses are reviewed by a human recruiter, and the platform also uses machine learning to recommend responses to questions from candidates—or might automatically generate a link to the company's benefits page, for example.

You can also use texting technology to confirm job interviews, inform candidates about next steps, prescreen candidates with programmed text questions, and direct potential hires to your company career site via a mobile apply process. No more wasted time leaving voicemail messages, playing phone tag, or sitting in your office sending and responding to emails. Texting with multiple people at once is more efficient and allows recruiters to juggle 20–30 conversations on a text dashboard at the same time.

Additionally, unlike a traditional phone conversation, a transcript of a text conversation provides insight into what questions a candidate takes longer to respond to and if at any point a candidate seems to have lost interest. This allows you to modify your text outreach strategy in real time to optimize based on candidate experience.

Setting Up Text Messaging for Candidate Outreach

I set up a texting communication platform at the staffing company I worked with, and it was a great way to engage candidates in every stage of the hiring process. Email has become a "passive" form of communication, especially considering that text messaging provides an opportunity to engage a candidate since 90 percent of text messages are read within 30 minutes. This is a great way to keep the conversation and engagement levels going with your candidates. This really puts a personal stamp on your candidate engagement levels, and depending on the platform you use, there are a number of ways to automate the levels of outreach and conversation.

"Cold" Candidates. You can use text messaging to text directly to candidates you don't have a relationship with. It's quick and easy to determine their interest in a role and, most importantly, determine if they are an active candidate who is interested in learning more. This is where further qualifying in the form of a phone call can help expedite your efforts. In many cases, the response is immediate, improving your time-to-fill and lower recruiting costs per candidate.

Follow Up. Candidates, regardless of their role, experience level, or candidate quality, need to know where they stand in the recruiting process. Recruiting is a mix of the long and the short game. Going back to employment branding and the candidate experience, the text message can be a great way to give a candidate a quick status update or follow up on where they are in the hiring process without having to answer their phone calls or send an email that probably won't be seen.

Interview Confirmation. While candidates have the best intentions, most don't go to such lengths to keep physical addresses, including office numbers, at their fingertips. Not every person is like me and makes sure to include notes in calendar and meeting requests. Use text messaging to make it easy for candidates. Confirm their interview twenty-four hours before the scheduled time via text. Include the address of the interview location including suite or office number so they can easily put it into their Google or Apple maps.

Opening a Closed Door. Unfortunately, most applicant tracking systems aren't built like a CRM tool allowing recruiters to source talent in their own databases and leave notes for themselves or others, like one would do with traditional CRM technology like SalesForce. Text messaging services within a CRM can make it easier for recruiters to stay engaged with candidates or re-establish contact with a candidate who interviewed or applied for roles previously but wasn't offered the job. Whether you use a CRM or not, text messaging is a quick way to engage a candidate who you've had a previous relationship with, one that allows you to customize the message for a personal touch.

Posthire. Using text messaging to drive candidates through the hiring process, including onboarding, employment testing, and assessments, is a great way to gently remind them to complete a task so that we can push through the hiring process. Companies like AT&T use text messaging as a way to do just that. Texting isn't their only source of communication. They use texting as a way to follow up on conversations with many of these text messages being automated, especially in those hard-to-fill roles like STEM or physicians, where high-quality candidates are in demand with the competition.

Seasonal Hiring with Text Messaging

The very nature of seasonal hiring is what I like to call "fast and loose." You certainly do your due diligence, but it happens very quickly, so you need a technology that can keep up with that pace. This is where text messaging and SMS can change your world. (At least your world from October to December!)

You've set up your automated text message or SMS system and advertised that candidates can apply by texting a simple word to a short number. The important part now is that you take advantage of the short time frame when you are on the candidate's mind by asking the right questions, providing the right incentive, and knocking down any barriers to them applying. Use these tips to help make a good impression:

Keep It Short and Sweet. Don't ask three questions when one will suffice. How about zip code? And even better, follow up with asking them to select one of four job titles to target them specifically.

Brag a Little. Does your company offer an employee discount, an incentive for working the whole holiday season, a higher-than-average wage, or a fun environment? Tell them about it!

Don't Make It Complicated. Make it as easy as possible to apply. If they can apply through text, don't direct them to an online application. If they can read about the job through a text, don't ask them to visit your website for a job description. I would love someone to allow for a candidate to apply via text message. We're not there yet, so I'll settle for directing them to a website or store kiosk where they can apply and interview immediately.

Seasonal Hiring by Text and Your Recruiting Funnel

I'm always amazed at how companies put an incredible amount of time and effort into their seasonal recruiting, only to turn around next year and start back at square one. When you use text messaging and SMS, you then have an entire database of candidates (both those you hired this season and those you didn't) whom you can reach personally with just the push of a button. You don't have to be top of mind all year because you can reach them personally when you're ready to hire next season. Additionally, most retail environments consistently have positions open, so utilize the pipeline you developed for those positions as well.

Think beyond what most retailers do every October, November, or whatever your busy season happens to be, which is reactive recruiting, and instead use text messaging and SMS. By proactively using the opportunity to engage an audience of prospects for multiple holiday seasons, you'll engage candidates for years as they gain more experience and education and their work availability or times change.

Texting Can Improve Candidate Experience

We know how important it is to maintain communication with a candidate during the hiring process, but I'd bet that sometimes you feel like throwing your hands up and saying, "Who has the time?!" One of the advantages of using text and SMS is that you can set up automated messages to let candidates know you received their application, where you are in the selection process, if they qualify for an interview, and how even to set up an interview. If you're concerned about this method being too impersonal, the good news is that today's workforce is generally very comfortable with this technology as an accepted form of communication. Additionally, you can customize your messages so they don't feel so stiff.

We've all been in the position where we apply for a job and are disappointed and confused when we never hear back from the company. Use this technology to make sure that none of your candidates have to be in that situation. This can be the difference between never speaking with the candidate again and being able to reach out to them next season, and even the difference between someone who now has a tainted view of your company and someone who continues to be engaged, shop there, and maybe even reapply next year. When letting someone know they didn't get the job, be tactful, give them a reason if possible (such as availability), encourage them to reach out to you next year (if you want them to), and if you'd like, go a step further and let them know you'll reach out next holiday season.

Job Postings via Text

In 2008, job board Beyond (now Nexxt.com) added a checkbox to its job seeker registration form without knowing exactly how it would use the functionality in the future. The box asked for permission to text users about job opportunities. Mobile marketing was fairly new in 2008, and regulations were in place that penalized advertisers who messaged people who didn't expressly opt in to those communications.

Nexxt made a smart bet that text messaging would be a part of its business, and getting permission ahead of actually knowing how texting would be a part of business made sense. Years later, TextRecruit introduced them to the opportunity and Text2Hire was born, letting employers blast job opportunities to Nexxt job seekers.

Announced in 2018, the next moneymaking opportunity for these two channels turned out to be sourcing. TextRecruit calls it TextTalent.

The company says it's a new way to quickly search, screen, and schedule time with candidates from the best third-party networks. When companies import candidates in TextRecruit, they can now select candidates in Nexxt's database of some seven million job seekers who have opted in to its text messages. Recruiters can then search for candidates by job title, location, and industry.

OTHER MOBILE RECRUITING APPLICATIONS AND TECHNOLOGIES THAT ARE DRIVING ADOPTION

Using video in your marketing strategy is both a mobile and social solution to digital recruitment. ComScore reports that the two activities that account for the most digital time spent are social media and video viewing.[21] Together the two account for more than one-third of all internet time spent. Since we know most internet time takes place on mobile, reaching candidates where they spend the most time on their mobile device is imperative to the success of a digital recruitment strategy.

Whether your applicants come to your site via mobile or desktop, job postings with videos are viewed 12 percent more than postings without video. On average, employers receive a 34 percent greater candidate application rate when they add video to their job postings. They are a powerful way to relate and resonate with your candidate in a way the written word does not.[22]

There is so much competition on social channels that it's difficult to get traditional posts out there without putting a lot of budget behind them. However, if you look at Facebook as an example, video ranks higher in its algorithms than a text or photo post. And making it easier to share them from your social feed and career site can organically boost the reach and engagement.

Videos add value, and they don't have to be viral. According to Cisco, 82 percent of all internet traffic will be video before the end of this decade.[23] Don't make it harder than it has to be. A hiring manager can do a quick and simple video for your job posting or your recruiting team can film an office tour with a smartphone. It's inexpensive and it's personal, which is great for your employer and your job brand. If you have a video on your job posting, engagement increases exponentially.

Remember earlier in this chapter when I mentioned being available to your candidates 24/7? It doesn't have to be (and shouldn't be) literal. Consider responsive channels like social, email, website chatbots, and messaging to create an exceptional candidate experience and a reputation that you respond to messages from candidates in less than twenty-four hours.

MOBILE AND GAMIFICATION OF THE APPLY PROCESS

Here's a little secret that most adults won't necessarily share. We use our mobile devices to play games. I do it. You do it. I don't have to look at your phone to know that you have Two Dots or Candy Crush or another of the thousands of popular app-based games.

According to a 2018 study by Electronic Entertainment Design and Research (EEDAR), about 67 percent of Americans, or roughly 211 million people, play video games on at least one type of device, with more than half of those playing on multiple platforms.[24] The study, which is based on an online survey of five thousand people, also showed that 90 percent of those play games on their smartphones, tablets, or both.

There is no judgment here! Games, in general, have influenced our society positively in different ways. Gaming makes us more competitive and better problem-solvers. It enhances critical thinking and it helps us make friends with similar interests. What does this have to do with recruiting on mobile? Elements of gamification can be used to improve your talent acquisition and applicant screening.

I attended a March 2019 SHRM webinar sponsored by Talroo called "Gamification in the Talent Acquisition Space," in which Jamie Winter (vice president of consulting and hiring and promotion practice leader at APTMetrics) and Ren Nygren (chief consulting officer at APTMetrics) explained how gamification techniques can be used in HR assessments and provide valuable data into cultural fit.[25]

In the last several years, there has been an explosion in game-based assessments. There are four basic types:

Recruitment games are located outside the recruitment funnel that are typically used for employer branding and candidate attraction. (See Heineken's "The Interview" for an excellent example.[26]) The pros of these games is that they're engaging and can be an excellent tool to attract candidates. They can also convey your company brand. The con is that the data is not intended for actually screening candidates. It's marketing, not high-stakes assessments.

Noncontextualized games function more like assessments and place the applicant in a fantasy-based environment that doesn't look anything like the job they're applying for—think Angry Birds but for hiring. The pro is that these games can be fun and engaging, but the con is that predictive validity is questionable with these games. They're also based on shelf content and there's limited ability to convey your brand.

Game-based assessments (trait-based games) are built as games to assess candidate traits. These have more promise in terms of screening candidates. What we're seeing in the market are games that measure cognitive ability and personality. These measures tend to have the most promise in terms of predictive validity. While intended to be fun, they may also have issues with fairness and may have been originally created to measure neurological deficits, so you could put your company at risk with the ADA with these.

Gamified assessments are psychometric assessments that apply game mechanics, like a narrative or storyline that offers flexibility of choice in terms of how they complete the assessments, as well as allowing candidates to offer feedback. (For an example, see *Viceroy Energy Leadership Identification.*[27]) They're engaging, people tend to have less test anxiety, and the results are similar to what you'd gather from a conversation. You get a highly predictive assessment and candidates really get immersed in them. These are also valuable for conveying your employer brand.

The con is that they can be expensive due to the level of customization they offer.

When it comes to what you should focus on for your company's future game-based assessment programs, these are the key points to use for evaluation:

- Predictive validity and reliability are key.
- Fairness and efficiency trumps fun; mobile is a must.
- Face validity is critical—no cartoons or avatars.
- Customize to reinforce your brand.
- Gamify to address a problem (e.g., boredom or engagement issues).

The advent of technology and AI is certain to change what game-based assessments look like today, opening up new opportunities for measurement. Much research needs to be done around these approaches as they emerge. Winter and Nygren recommend using the above checklist to evaluate new assessment technology. The best assessments will be the ones that are the most valid predictors of a candidate's potential.

CHAPTER 7

Job Seeker and Candidate Targeting

Digital isn't just about social media. There are paid and unpaid ways to engage active and passive candidates that go beyond traditional job boards, paid ads on social media, and programmatic and pay-per-click campaigns. In this chapter, I'll cover these methods and the logic for each. I'll also discuss brand ambassadors and other programs that can increase your candidate reach using digital tools and technologies.

PROACTIVE VERSUS REACTIVE RECRUITING

To be successful in a near-zero unemployment economy, reactive recruiting (or filling specific openings) relies on reducing time-to-hire. Once you've opened a position, posted a job, interviewed candidates, and are ready to make an offer, chances are that your top candidate is also the top candidate for multiple other companies. Unfortunately, reducing time-to-hire happens to be one of the most difficult tasks for companies. In our current market, it's nearly impossible (emphasis on "nearly"). One way recruiters can pivot and focus on improving this key performance indicator (KPI) is by streamlining processes, using technology, and investing fully in proactive recruiting. Does this mean that reactive recruiting is a thing of the past? Not exactly, but your focus on proactive efforts that will keep your talent funnel active, along with using technology to speed up time-to-hire, means that your reactive recruiting strategy is now rolled into your proactive strategy.

As the window of opportunity for recruiters in this strong economic market continues to shrink, we have to be proactive, not just in our efforts to fill specific positions but in building our talent pipeline for future openings. Recruitment marketing hinges on campaigns designed to drive targeted traffic to engage with your talent community or apply for specific job openings. The key is to attract, engage, and nurture candidates who haven't yet applied for a job and convert them into applicants by communicating your employer brand and value starting with the tried and true job description.

When developing job postings and position descriptions, think about what makes your company attractive and the top skills you're seeing in candidates, and then focus your messaging on those specific items. The job description is your marketing asset. It's your way to communicate what you're looking for and who would be a good fit. Think back on your target candidate personas and tailor your content to emphasize what's most important to your company in terms of skills and experience. Whittle down your laundry list to descriptive and engaging terms. You want people to be inspired and excited to join your company, not just checking keywords against their résumé. Do not start with the overarching blanket organizational statement. Begin telling them what makes the job unique and exactly the problem they will help solve and the learning they will experience.

How candidates are engaging companies and applying for jobs is changing. I've already mentioned the digital recruiting universe. In this vast space, the number of candidate options and platforms in which to engage, learn about jobs, and apply for roles has changed—from newspapers in the 1980s, to job boards and applicant tracking systems (ATSs) in the 1990s to 2000s, and expanding to a host of other platforms in the present and what's to come. This extraordinary expansion is one of the reasons I wanted to write this book. How we market and engage our present and future job candidates has become vast and incredibly complex. In this chapter, I hope to make it less complicated for you and your team.

THE JOB BOARDS OF YESTERDAY AND TODAY

You're familiar with the standard definition of job boards. In the simplest terms, a job board is a website that facilitates job hunting and ranges from large-scale generalist sites to niche job boards for job categories such as engineering, legal, insurance, social work, teaching, and mobile app development, as well as cross-sector categories such as green jobs, ethical jobs, and seasonal jobs. If you're still unsure, take a look at the *Workology* job board at https://jobs.workology.com where I post HR and recruiting jobs. Users on my board, as well as most job boards, typically upload résumés and submit them to potential employers and recruiters for review while employers and recruiters can post job ads and search for potential employees.

The term "job search engine" might refer to a job board with a search engine style interface or to a website that actually indexes and searches other websites. This is how job boards are defined now.

To understand the job boards we work with today, I'll run through a brief and abbreviated history. The first official launch of job board sites was in 1992 when Bill Warren introduced "Online Career Center." Initially, it was a BBS (or bulletin board system), which eventually merged with Monster in 1995. In 1994, Robert J. McGovern began NetStart Inc. as software sold to companies for listing job openings on their websites and managing the incoming emails those listings generated. NetStart Inc. changed its name in 1998 to operate under the name of their software, CareerBuilder.

In the early years, job boards had a generalist approach. Recruiters could find employees from across the world and vice versa. While newspapers had a limited reach and geographical constraints, job board websites could reach out to innumerable people at one go. Six major newspapers joined forces in 1995 to list their classified sections online. The service was called CareerPath.com and featured help wanted listings from the *Los Angeles Times*, the *Boston Globe*, the *Chicago Tribune*, the *New York Times*, the *Mercury News*, and the *Washington Post*.

The new online promotional model imitated the classified ad model on the web. Affordable and cost effective, there were no geographical constraints and recruiters could get coverage for multiple job listings across industry verticals. These features made job board sites popular in the recruitment world. With the generalist approach marking the beginning of this online job search revolution, new ways and ideas followed suit. Creative sourcing techniques like Boolean searches and online communities began to gain a footing.

For my own sourcing efforts in 2001, I was a store HR leader for a large big-box chain that had high-volume hiring needs. Because the job boards of that time were saturated with recruiters and candidates, I looked for nontraditional channels. I also didn't have a lot of cash to spend. And yes, I used dating websites to source, recruit, and hire candidates. It sounds strange, but I wasn't the only one looking in every corner of these new online spaces. In a 2016 *Workology Podcast* episode with Arron Daniels, sourcer for HEB careers, he confessed he used a site called Farmersonly.com (a dating site for farmers) to find and source candidates.[1]

During the early 2000s, the job board space evolved into four types of websites:

- **Niche boards:** Like *Workology*'s job board, these offer more personalized approaches to job search and recruitment. Niche boards focused on specific job roles, titles, job descriptions, and opportunities within a particular geographical region.
- **Network sites:** Network sites have multiple listings. Recruiters and employers could hire for multiple vacancies, different job roles, and posts from the same vendor.
- **Job aggregators:** Indeed is the perfect example of a job aggregator site. Sites like Indeed collect and collate information from multiple listings where potential candidates can land their dream jobs through a single search.
- **Social networking:** Social job sites like LinkedIn completely changed the way recruitment took place. Candidates have the opportunity to showcase their skills in an open database, and recruiters can easily take their pick. Even TikTok launched a jobs feature in 2021. Unfortunately it wasn't well received.

Around 2008, a recession hit the service sectors and human resource management. Low budgets led to limited hiring, which created a void in the recruitment world. Some of the job board sites completely stepped out of the business arena, and those who managed to survive tried to revamp their existing models. The majority of job board sites had to rethink their strategies.

Social recruitment gained momentum (we'll talk more about this later in this chapter), and companies began using social recruitment channels. Compared with the conventional sites, these platforms offered direct opportunities to both employers and potential candidates. Sites like Indeed still outperform traditional job boards, but the face of online recruiting is very different today than when Indeed was a top source of hire.

In brief, source of hire is the metric that shows what percentage of your overall hires entered your pipeline from each recruiting channel or source (e.g., job boards, referrals, direct sourcing). It answers the question "Where do my hires come from?" Source of hire is split into two categories:

- **Internal source of hire:** This term refers to any candidate hired from within an organization. Examples include promotion, transfer, and referrals.
- **External source of hire:** This term refers to any candidate sought and hired from outside an organization. Examples include job boards, social media platforms, or thirty-party recruiting agencies.

At one time, a wanted ad in the back of the newspaper was the cutting edge of recruitment tech. Then online job boards were all the rage. Today we're swimming in a vast digital space and searching for any data that tells us how to best spend our recruiting budget. There's no single answer, but there are ways to use the data that we do have to determine what channels to test, how to optimize the efforts, and where we should invest our recruiting time and money. This chaos and change is the reason I began writing *Digitizing Talent* to help demystify and make sense of the changing digital recruiting landscape.

WHAT SOCIAL MEDIA HAS BECOME TO RECRUITERS AND CANDIDATES

With a seemingly endless list of recruiting channels, determining the most effective strategy for sourcing candidates can be a formidable task. You could put a large budget into a job board and hope you're targeting the right candidate base, but when it comes to choosing what will work best for your company, it's imperative that you first assess where the candidates are that you want to reach. There's a good chance you'll land on a social media channel.

It's no longer enough to have a presence on social media or have a social media channel that is only monitored during traditional working hours. Customer response management on digital channels is imperative for brands, and Facebook is more blunt about the fact that marketers are going to have to pay for reach.[2]

Organic reach on social media simply isn't enough to get your brand and message in front of the audience you want to cultivate. In a December 2013 article titled "Generating Business Results on Facebook" (since deleted, but we have an archived version in Figure 7.1), the paragraph in which the impending drop-off in organic reach is revealed concludes with an ad pitch from Facebook: marketers are told they should consider paid distribution "to maximize delivery of your message in news feed." This is a nice way of saying that the primary reason a brand should grow its presence on digital channels like Facebook is NOT to create a free (or earned media) method of reaching consumers. Your brand's fan base is designed to make future Facebook ads work better.

Facebook ads are paid messages from businesses that are written in their voice and help reach the people who matter most to them. Advertisers create campaigns that have specific goals, or advertising objectives, and they create ads within those campaigns to help them reach those objectives. For example, a business may create a campaign because they want to get more people to visit their website. When they create ads within that campaign, they'll choose images,

How has marketing on Facebook evolved?

Since we introduced the Like button in 2010, fans have been key to marketing on Facebook. At first, brands needed fans in order to share their messages in News Feed, where people spend more than 50% of their time on the platform. In 2012, to increase the effectiveness of marketing on Facebook, we enabled marketers to reach all of their existing and potential customers—not just fans—in News Feed on desktop and mobile.

How can your brand's messages appear in News Feed?

Brands have always been able to reach some of their fans in News Feed without using paid media and can continue to do so. But content that is eligible to be shown in News Feed is increasing at a faster rate than people's ability to consume it. People are connecting to more Pages and individuals every day. And each day, more brands and organizations are posting on Facebook. As a result, we expect organic distribution of an individual Page's posts to gradually decline over time as we continually work to make sure people have a meaningful experience on the site. Your post has a better chance of appearing organically to your fans and their friends if it's relevant to them and if their friends interact with it (see "Creating a personalized newspaper" below). But to maximize delivery of your message in News Feed, your brand should consider using paid distribution, as it enables you to reach people beyond your fan base and move beyond the organic competition.

Creating a personalized newspaper

To make peoples' News Feeds read like personalized newspapers curated by the family, friends and businesses they care about, we continually prioritize content based on a variety of factors, including (but not limited to):

- The number of times they engage with that friend or brand Page posting a piece of content
- The number of likes, shares and comments a post has received

Reaching all of the people who matter to you

Your ability on Facebook to reach everyone who matters to your brand—not just your fans—can add significant value to your business.

70% higher return on investment on campaigns that maximize reach

Maximize impressions, not just clicks

99% of ad-exposed consumers who purchase in stores don't click on ads

[Source: A Datalogix study of over 50 digital campaigns on Facebook, Oct. 2012, looking at campaigns in the top half of reach efficiency versus the bottom half of reach efficiency.]

Figure 7.1 "Generating Business Results on Facebook" archived version

text, and an audience that they think will help them get that increase in visitors.

A boosted post is a post to your Facebook page's timeline to which you can apply money to boost it to an audience of your choosing. This is the simplest way to advertise on Facebook. Boosted posts differ from Facebook ads because they are not created in Ads Manager and don't have the same customization features.

To optimize paid advertising on Facebook, consider the following tips.

Choose different ad placements: When you boost a post, you'll be able to check or uncheck whether or not you want to place your ad on Instagram in addition to the Facebook mobile and desktop news feed. With Facebook ads, you get the added benefit of choosing placements in Facebook news feed side ads, Messenger ads, Instagram stories, instant articles, and audience network.

Use specific ad objectives: Choosing an ad objective early on will help you to focus on which campaign type best aligns with your current business goals. Boosted posts allow you to focus on website clicks, page engagement, and local business promotions, but the full ad system in Ads Manager lets you choose objectives like store traffic, conversions, and lead generation. You can also create and manage ads through the Ads Manager mobile app.

Maintain creative control: With Facebook ads created through Ads Manager, you can design an ad that fits your goals. Create carousel ads, add specific descriptions, and add a call-to-action button that'll drive more of your audience to take action. These are only a few of the creative and formatting options available in Ads Manager that aren't available when boosting a post from your page.

Use advanced targeting capabilities: Boosting posts lets you decide on interests, age, and gender for your ad targeting. This helps you reach people who most likely care about your business. With Facebook ads, you can use more advanced tools to create overlapping audience types, lookalike audiences, and more.

It's important for any business to identify exactly what they're hoping to achieve with an ad. For example, if you want audience engagement on your page or to develop your brand awareness, boosting a post is a great way to maximize visibility and grow your audience. To create more advanced ad types and campaigns, use Ads Manager.

FACEBOOK JOB POSTINGS

In 2017, Facebook rolled out a new feature allowing companies to create and promote job postings on their business page. Paying to promote these new job postings is drastically cheaper than LinkedIn job slots and ideal for an audience that is not on that platform.

You can create job posts for open positions at your company and post them on your company's page. Note that the Pages Manager app in Facebook is now called Meta Business Suite Mobile.

To create a job post, follow these steps:

1. From your news feed, click "Pages" in the left menu.
2. Go to your page.
3. Below "Create Post" at the top of your page's timeline, click "Job."
4. Upload a photo, enter a job title, thoroughly describe the position, and add other details to your post (example: location of your company, job salary). You can also click "+ Add Question" if you want to ask applicants more questions.
5. If you'd like to receive job applications by email instead of your page messages inbox, scroll down to the bottom and enter your email address below "Receive Applications by Email." When you have filled out the required info, click "Next" at the bottom.
6. Click "Post."

To see all job applications that have been submitted, click Manage Jobs at the top of your page or check your email if you chose to receive applications by email. To manage the job posts you've created, click "Jobs" in the left column of your page.

Keep in mind that job posts automatically expire after 30 days. After 30 days, page visitors won't be able to see the job post on your page. However, page admins and editors will still be able to see the job post and renew it. You can also boost your job posts to reach more applicants.

The applications come through your Messages tab and the value of the information provided really varies. The upside is that it's easy to communicate and engage with the applicant. If you receive many applicants, keeping track of them can be challenging. Facebook tried to alleviate this by allowing the option of labels and notes. If boosted correctly, these postings would be great for smaller companies without an applicant tracking system (ATS) or compliance standards. For larger companies, I recommend regular Facebook ads that take the seeker to a landing page sharing your culture. These landing pages can direct the seeker to apply through the ATS, which is better for tracking and compliance purposes.

CAN WE STILL GET SOMETHING FOR NOTHING?

As recruiters, we focus so much on paid distribution through job boards that we sometimes forget about the channels that cost nothing for job postings. Sometimes going back to what we did before we had a budget is the solution for reaching top talent. We also should consider what's trending in our respective industries and job searches in general.

YouTube: Beyond Google's search engine, video is a powerful medium. YouTube is currently the second most popular website in the world with over 800 million unique users visiting each month, making it the perfect place to find a new and more engaged audience.[3] Consider including testimonials from current employees, a snapshot of your company's culture, and an engaging job description. One-minute videos can include more information than you'd think, plus you can use the budget that you'd planned on spending on CPC advertising for video production.

Bonus: Videos on your career site (and shared via social media) are good for your employer brand. Employer brand videos are a great way to engage prospective applicants and communicate your company's story, brand, culture, and mission in a way that words and images simply cannot. Include your social links and an email alert subscription call-to-action or candidate sign up, and your career site can be a way to fill your hiring funnel even when you're not actively trying to fill open positions.

Note: If you have a standard business YouTube channel that's connected to a single Google login, consider moving it to a brand account. It's free, and YouTube provides easy instructions to do so at support. google.com. A brand account allows you to have multiple users managing your channel, which is a must when using videos for recruiting.

Twitter: Twitter remains the third most popular search engine and is the go-to platform for breaking news and information. You can set up an RSS feed of job postings from your own career site or you can use free tools like Hootsuite to set up free scheduled postings featuring your jobs. With the right hashtags including city, position title, and industry, you can drive passive traffic to your job postings.

There's also the added benefit of having a presence on a very active social channel. When people are actively searching for a job, their friends and family know about it. Putting your job postings on your Twitter channel with hashtags increases the likelihood that your posting will reach qualified candidates who are also actively searching.

Do you think that Twitter is past its prime? An annual study by Pew Research Center reports that Twitter is a popular social network for two specific groups that recruiters covet:[4]

- College graduates and those age 18 to 29 to fill entry-level roles.
- Urbanites that make over $75,000 a year for more senior positions.

There are other active ways to use Twitter in your recruiting strategy. To find people based on occupation or location, you can use Twitter's search bar. Twitter also has a useful advanced search option where you can do a more detailed search. This is useful to find influencers to follow as well as potential candidates.

Aggregated jobs appear in Indeed's organic, or free, search results, and Indeed recommends the following best practices to ensure your jobs appear on its site and help you maximize hiring results:

- Provide an individual web page for each job on your career site. Indeed search results link to a specific web page for each job. This ensures that each job listing has a unique URL. Check that your jobs are posted in HTML on individual web pages and avoid posting your jobs on your website as a PDF or Word document.
- Include essential job information. Your jobs are more likely to appear in search results if each job listing on your site contains separate fields for job title and location as well as a detailed job description. Your job listings must also include a prominent link or button to apply online or an email address. Including a location specifying an address is best, but city, state, or zip code is a must.

- Set up automated source tracking. Automated source tracking provides the most reliable data about candidate sources. Your ATS provider can help you set up source tracking so you can tell exactly where your candidates are coming from and measure the performance of your recruitment advertising channels. Another option is to use a connected ATS that already integrates with Indeed.
- Provide an XML job feed. This is the fastest way to include your jobs on Indeed. It should include the details of all the jobs on your site and be updated each time new jobs are added.
- Follow Indeed's search quality guidelines. Job listings that don't meet Indeed's standards for organic inclusion may be subject to review before appearing in Indeed search. Job listings that are misleading or compromise the job seeker experience may be subject to restrictions or even removal from search results altogether.

HOW WE FIND CANDIDATES IN A CROWDED DIGITAL MARKETPLACE

When we look at the talent acquisition (TA) process, one of the most important pieces of TA is sourcing, a form of proactive recruitment. Instead of relying on candidates to find us, we use the internet and find them.

In a crowded job market with high demand for employees, especially employees with specialized skills, sourcing candidates can be extremely difficult. A 2021 Recruiter Nation Report from Jobvite demonstrates the difficulties of attracting and hiring talent in a candidate-driven job market, especially in the midst of a global health crisis.[5] The report found that 60 percent of recruiters surveyed believe organizations will lose high-quality employees if they do not transition to remote-first working, while 40 percent said candidates have turned down an interview or job offer due to a lack of diversity in an organization. The report also highlights the channels that recruiters find most effective for growing employer brands that have seen drastic increases over the past year, with company career sites at 48 percent (up from 22 percent in 2020) and social networks at 64 percent (up from 47 percent in 2020).

We can optimize our career sites, improve our employer brand, raise the stakes when it comes to benefits and perks, and improve our candidate experience. But none of these things will make sourcing new candidates easier. Sourcing involves a great deal of research, parsing information on search engines, browsing social media profiles, and searching for specific candidate skill sets on LinkedIn. It's a continuous loop for talent sourcers, as the search for top talent is never put on hold.

Search Engines and Boolean Strings

As HR leaders, we've had to get creative in our sourcing methods as the unemployment rate has declined and the job market has shifted in favor of candidates. Many of us already use some form of Boolean search, which has been an internet sourcing and recruiting staple for years, allowing recruiters to search for databases, member lists, and candidate profiles. If you're not familiar with Boolean searches, Google X-Ray is a great place to start.

A search engine x-ray (Google or Bing) effectively allows you to search web pages for specific keyword combinations and information. A Google X-Ray is the most basic of Boolean logic. By using Boolean, you can target your results without having to comb through thousands of pages of search results. It is an effective way to source for candidates who have specialized skills and keywords listed on social networks, websites, and online databases.

Step 1: Select a Search Engine You Wish to X-Ray. Using a search engine such as Google, you x-ray the site using the "site:" command, for example, "site: twitter.com (HR pro OR "human resources professional")."

For the purposes of this example, we will be looking for results on Twitter. This command works with most sites where you can access information that is not behind a password-protected network such as

Facebook and LinkedIn. Facebook and LinkedIn are not always search engine x-ray friendly.

You can see from my string that I searched not just for common HR job titles, but also words that my candidate target might include in their profiles. The "OR" in this signifies to the search engine that you are looking for a number of different words in the profile. If you choose to use "AND" it would tell the search engine you need these words in combination. The longer and more defined your Boolean string is, the shorter and more refined your search engine result lists will be.

Step 2: Type the "Site:" Command Followed by the URL of the Website You Are Wishing to Search. Omit the "www." and the "http(s)". One of the things that makes Boolean great is that it can search almost any site. For example, if you are looking for programming talent or someone with "ruby on rails" experience, you don't have to rely on sourcing technology or résumé databases. You can search sites like Meetup.com, Quora, and Github for prospective candidate profiles. The challenge, is that these candidates aren't necessarily interested in your opportunity, meaning that you will spend some time tracking down their phone number or email to get in contact with them while uncertain if they are actively interested in the position you are hiring for.

Step 3: Add Keywords and Location. Next, add your keywords and a location if you wish to be specific in your search. It is best to make your search as broad as possible and narrow your search strings over time. As I mentioned earlier, the more parameters you set, the more specific the search results that come back will be. If you are looking for candidates in a certain city or nearby metro area to a location, you can search for those very specific profiles.

Step 4: Further Narrow Your Results. To further narrow down your search, use those keywords we talked about earlier. For a tech position you would include "RoR" or "rubyist" or "rails." For HR you might include certifications like SPHR, PHR, or SHRM-CP.

The key when it comes to Boolean search is finding URL patterns that will help establish profiles. This is extremely helpful in x-raying sites and locating the contact data of qualified candidates in membership communities. You can set up a Google X-ray on Indeed sourcing for profiles and your requirements, too. On a basic level, this is what sourcing technologies do in the market today. However, they are sourcing and crawling information on multiple social sites, collecting and displaying that data for you on a nice and easy-to-use dashboard without having to use Boolean logic.

You can use the same technique to find what you're looking for on Reddit. Reddit search supports the Boolean operators AND, OR, and NOT (case sensitive) as well as parentheses:

- By default, search queries use the AND operator.
  (For example, hedgehogs AND porcupines and hedgehogs porcupines are equivalent)
- You can use the OR operator when you want to match submissions that contain either term.
  (For example, hedgehogs OR porcupines)
- You can exclude terms with NOT.
  (For example, hedgehogs NOT porcupines)
- You can use parentheses ( ) to group parts of a search together.
  (For example, (hedgehogs OR porcupines) NOT sonic)

You can search for subreddits from the subreddits page at r/subreddits/search. Subreddit results also appear at the top of the main search page at r/search.

WHAT IS PROGRAMMATIC ADVERTISING AND WHY SHOULD IT MATTER?

Programmatic advertising allows HR and talent acquisition professionals to make buying decisions in a split second based on a pre-established site:twitter.com (SPHR AND Dallas AND "HR Pro")   ✕ 🎤 🔍

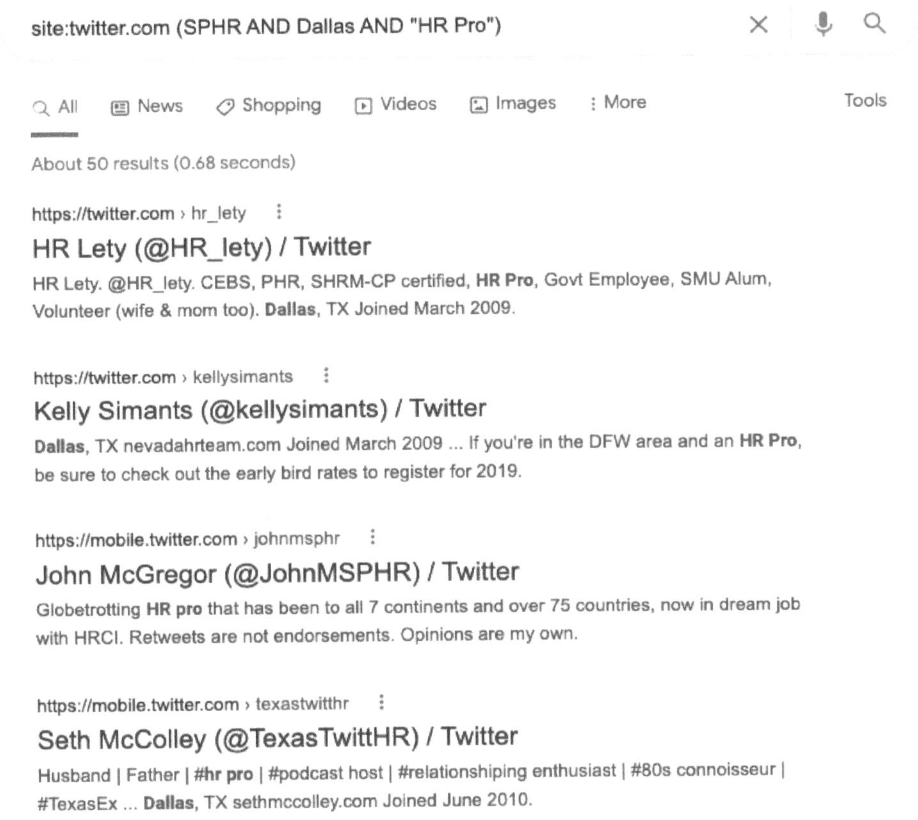

🔍 All   📰 News   🏷 Shopping   ▶ Videos   🖾 Images   ⋮ More   Tools

About 50 results (0.68 seconds)

https://twitter.com › hr_lety   ⋮
HR Lety (@HR_lety) / Twitter
HR Lety. @HR_lety. CEBS, PHR, SHRM-CP certified, **HR Pro**, Govt Employee, SMU Alum,
Volunteer (wife & mom too). **Dallas**, TX Joined March 2009.

https://twitter.com › kellysimants   ⋮
Kelly Simants (@kellysimants) / Twitter
Dallas, TX nevadahrteam.com Joined March 2009 ... If you're in the DFW area and an **HR Pro**,
be sure to check out the early bird rates to register for 2019.

https://mobile.twitter.com › johnmsphr   ⋮
John McGregor (@JohnMSPHR) / Twitter
Globetrotting **HR pro** that has been to all 7 continents and over 75 countries, now in dream job
with HRCI. Retweets are not endorsements. Opinions are my own.

https://mobile.twitter.com › texastwitthr   ⋮
Seth McColley (@TexasTwittHR) / Twitter
Husband | Father | #hr pro | #podcast host | #relationshiping enthusiast | #80s connoisseur |
#TexasEx ... **Dallas**, TX sethmccolley.com Joined June 2010.

Figure 7.2 Boolean search results from Twitter

set of rules and real-time performance data. Think CPC, PPC, or SEM but for job ads. In the talent marketplace, programmatic advertising has one significant difference from standard CPC ad buys.

Programmatic advertising allows you to engage job boards and control job targeting strategies to reach new pockets of eligible and qualified candidates.

On-demand talent and programmatic advertising can have exceptional results when it comes to focusing your efforts on diverse candidate groups—such as women in leadership, people with disabilities, or veteran recruiting—by targeting and reaching those candidates where they spend time online and driving them to your specific candidate-targeted career site landing page.

While some traditional job ads work great, others don't, but the cost is the same. Programmatic advertising will move your investment to the jobs that need it. Programmatic advertising is an online data-driven media buying service that uses software (not humans) to improve pay-for-performance media and reduce wasted spending. It has an on-off switch. Programmatic advertising better uses your resources.

Programmatic advertising allows top-of-funnel job distribution that has an on-off switch, which is one of the reasons I love it so much. Recruiters have a level of control and allow teams to set limits and rules to control spending and the number of qualified candidates for each role ahead of time. In short, programmatic job advertising offers companies a lower cost-per-hire and more control over their candidate funnels.

An important added benefit when it comes to programmatic recruiting is the ability to control your ad spending, offering the possibility of lowering your cost-per-hire. For example, using a cost-per-click model, only 6 percent of job ads get over 50 percent of clicks, according to a report published by SourceCon.[6] In contrast, the real-time market bidding of programmatic advertising allows recruiters to automatically direct traffic to jobs in need of applications. By distributing spending so that the budget is concentrated only on the jobs that need more applications or a specific class of applicants, programmatic techniques can lower the cost of a quality applicant by as much as 30 percent.

Once you've harnessed the power of programmatic ad buying, you can focus on optimizing your career site experience in relation to your employer brand. Digital storytelling is social. When your employees are your best brand ambassadors, they're not only bringing you your top source of hire through referrals, they're also champions of your brand. Enable your employees to drive social storytelling through hashtags and videos, or consider a daily employee "channel takeover" (AT&T does this well with its #LifeatATT hashtag). Create a short video featuring employees touting the benefits of your brand. Not only does it give visitors a reason to stick around, you're giving them more memorable information and an inside look at your brand directly from the people who work for your company.

THE BEST SOURCE OF HIRE: EMPLOYEE REFERRALS

What's the best way to recruit—and retain—employees? Company career sites? Networking? Word of mouth? According to studies, it's actually employee referrals. These employees are also shown to stick around for extended periods of time compared with those who are found through different methods. Since referrals are shown to produce better workers, it's important to encourage your current employees and extended network to be involved in the recruitment process.

An employee referral program is a recruiting strategy in which employers encourage current employees or former employees (alumni) through rewards to refer qualified candidates for jobs in their organizations. Employee referrals are a great way to drive qualified candidates from a very active and engaged pool of professionals who are your employees. They know the organization and its culture and can speak to the business brand like no one else. If you're building your employer brand and starting from the ground up expecting your employees to send a flurry of referrals for your open positions, the best place to start is by first creating a brand ambassador program, especially one that is accessible and focused online.

What Brand Ambassador Programs Look Like

At its core, your employee's experience is their story. No amount of policy, NDAs, or "spin" can really change what that means. If your campaign is to be successful, you need to incentivize your workforce and put them in the driver's seat. It needs to be organic, not programmed or forced in any way. Automation and control take this out of the realm of word of mouth and into the realm of advertising, resulting in a loss of effectiveness.

With your employees as the centerpiece, your campaign can tell the story from the right perspective and will address the issues your candidates are most likely to be concerned with. So how do you guarantee that they hit the points you want them to? You don't. Simply stated, this needs to be an organic effort to tell real positive stories about what it really means to be a part of your brand and why others should consider signing on. Let them share the benefits of working for you that have meant the most to them. This is what employment branding really is.

As managers, this idea may bring a flutter of panic, but relax. After all, we are not talking about giving employees your job to do, just allowing them to share their own experiences in their own words. By providing them with structured outlets and maintaining some editorial control, enough safeguards can be put in place while still giving them ownership.

- **Job referral programs:** By rewarding your employees for successful hiring recommendations, you can turn your entire workforce into a recruitment team. This is a baseline, mostly passive, employee referral program. See more on referrals after this section.
- **Open houses and job fairs:** By allowing your employees to represent your organization at events like this, you give the public the opportunity to engage with more than just those who are typically the public face. Encourage them to invite friends and family who might be good candidates for employment.
- **Employee-generated media:** Employee-written blogs on company websites, video testimonials, and other employee-created media assets help tell your story in a way that resonates with candidates.

By opening up your recruiting process and giving employees ownership of driving the content, you can create a narrative that relates directly to job seekers. This in turn can lead to a better understanding of company culture among candidates, leading to successful hires, increased employment longevity, and a better match between employees and company culture.

It's not enough to simply create a program for employee referrals. Sure, you could send an all-company email with instructions on how to refer candidates to open positions at your company and leave it there, but it's likely to fall flat (or get lost in email). Your employees are busy with their life and their jobs. One cannot simply build an employee referral program and expect the employees to come. Tell your employees that you're interested in working with them to build a great place to work and a rewarding culture. Let them know that you will send emails about open positions regularly and would appreciate their recommendations for suitable candidates who fit in with the culture and have the capacity to make important contributions.

How to Promote Your Employee Referral Program

HR and recruiting leaders must be master marketers focused on internal employees as well as company communication. What CEO or HR doesn't want a qualified pipeline of candidates whose cost-per-hire is substantially less? Don't get me started on how employee referral programs also historically have lower turnover rates because those candidates are prepped and given expectations by your best employees.

Roll It Out. As soon as you set up an employee referral program, HR should do more than just send an email. Internal marketing should be a focused, detailed, and long-term process. HR teams should think big picture looking at small opportunities to drive conversation, such as bringing in a lunch or snack, gathering your teams, and talking about the benefits for employee referrals. Position it as a perk ("you're great, you likely know other great possible employees") and don't just leave it there. Combining these more tactical strategies with a larger plan, you are sure to generate positive results.

Celebrate the Small Wins. Send an all-company email when someone's referral is hired—and include what the referring employee will get (X dollars after X days of employment for their referral). Examples like these will incentivize other team members to stop and take a look at their networks to see who they can send your way.

High Performing Employees Refer High Performing Candidates. Ideally, you want to hire referrals from your best employees—and your top performers. Logically, it makes sense that candidates in your employee's network share some of the same traits that you're looking for. Your highest performing teams are likely also the busiest ones. It's key to make employee referrals easy and quick, as well as to include the referring employee in the status of their referral.

Post a Reward. Your staff wants to know that your company cares that they took the time to refer a candidate through your company's referral program. It's a small thing to set up a reward system, whether cash or gift card or a paid day off (once their referral has worked at your company for a specific period of time). Have all-hands meetings. Take the time to thank your team members for their referrals. Recognition is its own reward, but cash is still the most effective employee referral strategy.

Bonus. Offer a 90-day or 120-day retention bonus on top of your first-day start referral bonus. It helps ensure that the employee who's doing the referring is committed to sending the best talent for the long term to your company. This has always been the secret sauce to a robust referral program at any place I was working or consulting.

With a Small Budget, Consider Swag. Referring again to AT&T (because they hire huge numbers of people every year), why not create a killer design for an employee tee with your brand and Instagram hashtag? Or a tagline like "ask me about my amazing job @yourinstagramhandle?" Depending on the number of employees who are willing to wear the shirts around town, at the gym, at grocery stores, putting it on a tee is a fun way to get a conversation about your company started. As a bonus, this contributes to company branding!

SIX KEYS TO MAINTAINING A GREAT ALUMNI NETWORK

Not losing touch with former employees is imperative to creating and maintaining an exceptional alumni network.

- **Go where your alumni are:** Whether it's social media platforms like LinkedIn, Facebook, or a private Google group, let your network dictate the communities and the engagement sources that suit them. If a comprehensive effort to maintain an alumni association is not an option, an employer can consider providing its alumni with an electronic newsletter—either the standard company newsletter or one geared specifically to former employees. The benefits of online publications include instant feedback from readers, interactivity, speed, saving of distribution costs, flexibility, and customization.

- **Provide value in nontraditional ways:** This could be virtual happy hours or in-person alumni events and mixers, as well as career workshops and other learning and development opportunities. It's a small investment to make in a valued former employee who may take advantage of training programs to improve their skills, because when they boomerang, it could be to return in a higher-level position than the one they left. Be willing to show up at alumni events. You might want to even consider hosting them.

- **Practice consistent communication:** Send every team member off well. Thank them for their service and solicit their willingness to stay in touch. A successful boomerang recruiting process begins right before an employee leaves.

- **Spotlight your jobs:** Periodically create content to update alumni on the latest goings on at the company. Include things they may be able to help you with, such as suggesting candidates for a job opening. Rather than directly asking a former employee to return, make sure they have up-to-date information on new job postings (which may include their former position), and let them decide if they want to refer someone or apply themselves.

- **Offer incentives exclusively for your alumni network:** Consider expanding your employee referral bonus policy to your approved alumni. Financial incentives show that you still consider them "part of the family" and trust their referrals as much as you did when they were employed. You might also consider inviting preferred alumni to company events. Engaging with former coworkers could be key to persuading your preferred alumni to return to the fold.

- **Create value in ways that keep them coming back:** As today's employee turnover rates continue to increase, the number of corporate alumni who are available for rehiring also increases dramatically. If you get an inquiry from a potential boomerang employee, acting quickly is imperative. It's important to let them know that they're important to you and your company, even if they haven't actively engaged with your network. Even if they choose not to pursue a second opportunity, this is an excellent way to re-engage them.

Successful Alumni Networks

Bain & Company's alumni network stands at more than thirteen thousand members.[7] The aim of the program is to build enduring relationships with employees so they remain connected to the company even after they have left.

Members can access the contact information of other alumni through the directory, which is a big help for future business partnerships or collaborations. There is also a career development program available for alumni looking to further their own careers or access resources to help find talent for their new teams. Alumni have access to webinars, a private social network, a few perks, and plenty of industry trends and news.

Citi has more than seventeen thousand alumni in 113 countries around the world.[8] The strong alumni network gives back to former employees with benefits such as museum passes, tickets to sporting events, and merchant discounts. It also offers opportunities to stay connected with job vacancies at Citi for those wanting to return or refer someone. Alumni also have the chance to volunteer with nonprofits through the program.

CANDIDATE COMMUNITIES ARE BUILT ON TRUST

Considering that trust in employers is on the upswing, and trust of general media (specifically social media) is trending down rapidly, the opportunity for employers and recruiters to build on communities for talent is limitless. Private groups, networks, and communities are becoming the new norm, and this fundamentally changes recruitment marketing. Trust in the workplace begins with transparency, which means empowering employees with information and opportunities for shared action.

The importance of building your own network and tribe is critical as we begin to experience this shift. This is where alumni networks, private Facebook groups, and targeted messaging can really make a difference, but at the heart of these networks are your employees. They're not only influential, but their faith and reliance on your company's support and transparency make them the brand ambassadors for your company and a top channel for referral source of hire.

If you've been waiting for the right moment to create a company alumni network (employees who left your company in good standing and would be considered for rehire), that moment is now. Your alumni employees have insights into your organization that other candidates and contacts don't. They know the culture and work environment, and are some of the most trusted and reputable sources of qualified employees.

Online alumni associations can be established and maintained through Google, LinkedIn, and Facebook. Once your channel is set up, invite key alumni based on hiring manager recommendations and your own experience. Moving forward, establish what your ideal alumni employee looks like and create an off-boarding process that includes determining which employees are "regrettable turnover," which means that they would be welcomed should they choose to return. The next step lets the departing employee know that their return would be welcomed. And finally, it gets their permission to keep in touch after they leave.

Your community-building efforts don't just pay off in referrals. Tapping into your organization's alumni network can also open doors to new business opportunities. Former employees find new jobs or form their own enterprises, and when they are looking for business partners, they often turn to previous employers. An organization's alumni can serve as a resource for industry trends and keeping up with what the competitors are doing. In addition, well-informed alumni can be powerful ambassadors for the company in the business community.

CHAPTER 8

Making Digital Recruiting Accessible and Inclusive

- **How Recruiting Candidates with Disabilities Can Benefit Your Company**
- **Attracting Diverse Job Candidates in a Digital Landscape**
- **Why Accessibility Matters**
- **What Accessibility Looks Like in Practice**
- **Accessibility and WCAG Guidelines**

So now that we've covered optimizing your mobile recruiting efforts and apply process, boosting email campaigns, and taking a mobile-first approach to recruiting, you're going to be able to take your recruitment marketing to the next level, right? It's not quite that simple. We are operating in an unstable economy with some of the lowest unemployment levels in recorded history, and yet only 29.1 percent of people with disabilities are employed.[1] Companies who are committed to hiring the best talent and improving the candidate experience must also commit to being inclusive and ensure they create a recruitment process that is accessible to all candidates, including those with disabilities.

The Partnership on Employment & Accessible Technology (PEAT) defines accessibility as follows: "Everyone can use the exact same technology as anyone else—regardless of whether they can manipulate a mouse, how much vision they have, how many colors they can see, how much they can hear, or how they process information."[2]

HOW RECRUITING CANDIDATES WITH DISABILITIES CAN BENEFIT YOUR COMPANY

It may seem unusual to some of you that I've focused an entire chapter on accessibility, so let me explain. In the United States, one of the greatest challenges experienced by individuals with disabilities is employment. Research indicates that employer attitudes contribute to this pervasive problem. Specifically, some employers have misperceptions about the abilities of individuals with disabilities and the costs associated with the provision of accommodations. Understandably, employers are concerned with the bottom line.

However, people with disabilities tend to stay on the job longer, are absent less, and have job performance ratings nearly identical to their peers without disabilities. An additional benefit to hiring people with disabilities, according to the study, was the diversification of work settings, which led to an overall positive work environment.

There is also a strong link between diversity and innovation. When companies recruit, hire, and retain individuals with disabilities (including veterans), they benefit from a wider pool of talent, skills, and creative business solutions. New research reported in the *Harvard Business Review* offers compelling evidence that diversity unlocks innovation and drives market growth—a finding that should intensify efforts to ensure that executive ranks both embody and embrace the power of differences.[3]

By correlating diversity in leadership with market outcomes as reported by respondents, the research shows that companies with diversity programs out-innovate and outperform others. Employees at these companies are 45 percent more likely to report that their firm's market share grew over the previous year and 70 percent more likely to report that the firm captured a new market.

ATTRACTING DIVERSE JOB CANDIDATES IN A DIGITAL LANDSCAPE

To reach candidates with different levels of experience, education, backgrounds, and skills, we have to think beyond the personas we developed for our candidate journeys. Diversity as we know it is not a new trend, but reaching diverse candidates and ensuring an accessible and inclusive candidate and employee experience should be a default setting by now. So what exactly should a diverse and inclusive workplace look like? When we think about it holistically, it means that your company's workforce includes people of different races, genders, ages, disabilities, sexual identities, education levels, and religions, and that all your employees are valued, respected, and have access to the tools they need to achieve success.

Expanding your recruiting efforts to reach a more diverse candidate audience through digital recruiting channels means that you can expect a more diverse workforce in general. This is not only important for your company culture, it's also better for creativity, innovation, and keeping up with an extremely fast-paced bull economy that we know won't last forever. We can make the most of it by starting with the people we attract to drive business strategy and execution. Here are just a few data points on how a diverse workforce can benefit your company:

- According to a survey from Glassdoor, 76 percent of employees and job seekers said a diverse workforce was important when evaluating companies and job offers.[4]
- Catalyst research shows that companies with more women on the board statistically outperform their peers over a long period of time.[5]
- Deloitte Australia research shows that inclusive teams outperform their peers by 80 percent in team-based assessments.[6]

So we know that diverse employees perform better, but how do we diversify our digital recruiting efforts to reach them? Consider the following.

Build Diverse Candidate Networks

Step outside the run-of-the-mill e-newsletter communications and build networks that engage a diverse group of candidates. Using your candidate relationship manager (CRM) or a simple Slack, LinkedIn, or Facebook group can create a candidate network that you can use to build a relationship with specific audiences. For example, you can easily set up a Women at Work Facebook group powered by your company name. Tap into your female employees to serve as admins in the group and ask their friends to join. Within the group, you can promote your events and programs and even offer exclusive question and answer sessions virtually (or at offices in person) to talk about your female-friendly perks, benefits, and career programs with the goal of building a community of engaged and interested candidates to fill future roles within the organization.

Focus on Diverse Verticals

Build specific content, conversations, and resources for the communities you wish to reach. For instance, if you're aiming to recruit veterans, home in on the questions and conversations that veterans have. These diversity verticals can exist either inside a social network group like I described previously or within your career site. Be sure to have landing pages that include resources, information, and media to showcase how you engage your targeted protected groups. For example, April is Autism Awareness Month, and if you have an autism hiring program like some companies do, you can create conversations, media materials, and resources for the autism community.[7] You can also use this as an opportunity to speak more broadly about the importance of being inclusive of people with disabilities. By focusing on diversity verticals, you can effectively measure your impact, results, and engagement levels to direct candidates to very specific and targeted positions in which your company is focused on hiring a more diverse workforce.

Get Engaged

No matter whom you're recruiting, there's nothing more valuable than engagement. Find diversity-focused events that give you the opportunity to engage and foster relationships, such as an online diversity recruiting event or a women-who-code conference. In terms of engagement, your audience is twofold. The first is your diverse candidate community and the second is working with nonprofit and diversity groups, conferences, and communities. It's no longer enough to just simply send an email alerting nonprofit diversity groups of your openings. The Office of Federal Contract Compliance Programs (OFCCP) is looking for more candidate engagement and effort by employers in what they call "good faith efforts." A simple outreach letter for your good faith efforts to a nonprofit or community organization that targets a protected class is no longer enough. Employers need to get active and focus on going above and beyond to remain in compliance and avoid fines with the OFCCP.

Ask Questions

Ask your employees and candidates for feedback and recommendations on how to be better. They provide a unique perspective, so listen and make changes. Asking questions and establishing a forum and community for conversation builds trust, drives awareness, and establishes a relationship. All candidates, regardless of their age, race, gender, disability, veteran status, and sex, want the hiring process to be a dialogue and not one-way conversations. You need to ask questions. It helps employers learn just as it does for candidates. Most employers aren't up for the challenge of asking questions or at least putting themselves out there to be engaged because they assume that it results in more work for the recruiting and talent acquisition teams. However, I've found that's not always the case. It might also lead you to communities and conversations that you hadn't considered or been available to connect with previously.

Invest in New Communities Like Reddit and Other Social Networks

The first thing we want to consider when looking for candidates outside of our current marketing personas is having a presence in a variety of online communities to engage candidates with a broader set of skills, different experiences and background, and diverse interests. This means working outside of traditional social channels like LinkedIn, Twitter, and Facebook and turning to platforms where the candidates in your industry with the tenure and experience you're looking for spend their time. Platforms like Reddit, Quora, and Meetup allow you to find candidates who would never turn up in a LinkedIn search or ones who didn't disclose their diversity designation, like military veterans or people with disabilities.

Engage Job Boards and Job-Targeting Strategies to Reach New Pockets of Eligible and Qualified Diverse Candidates.

In the talent marketplace, programmatic advertising has one significant difference from standard CPC (cost-per-click) ad buys. While job ads can be created and scaled, unlike traditional digital advertising, job ads have an end date. Once a position is filled, it should and can be immediately pulled from an ad buy. The biggest benefit to this type of advertising is that you can set specific rules that are directly related to your ad budget to reach a specific audience, for example, or to target a specific conversion rate.

More Focus on Data Outside of Traditional Recruiting Metrics

While time-to-fill and cost-per-hire are baked into your KPIs (key performance indicators), consider drilling down into your source-of-hire and cost-per-applicant to determine the best focus for digital recruiting strategies. Tracking metrics months after hire, you'll also want to take a look at benchmarks for employee engagement, productivity, and success as your company defines it to see where your efforts are paying off on specific teams throughout your organization.

Focus on Building Relationships and Trust

According to the *2021 Edelman Trust Barometer*, employees who trust an employer are far more likely to advocate for the organization (a 39-point trust advantage), are more engaged (33 points), and remain far more loyal (38 points) and committed (31 points) than their skeptical counterparts.[8] It's important to remember that our employees are our best salespeople when it comes to culture, marketing, and storytelling if we're doing our job in building relationships and trust throughout our organization.

I'm asking you to go beyond your corporate requirements and the established federal guidelines and directives. Build plans to exceed expected hiring benchmarks. While yearly reporting and good faith efforts are important, I'm challenging you to approach diversity differently by taking a more holistic approach instead of one that just checks the boxes and allows you to feel better about that quarterly update you sent.

The bottom line is that diversifying your digital recruiting and making your recruiting process more inclusive and accessible has a positive impact on your company's bottom line. Companies that recruit from a diverse set of candidates are more likely to hire the most capable in the labor market. The more competitive the job market is, the more necessary it becomes for HR leaders and teams to increase the diversity of the talent pools we explore.

WHY ACCESSIBILITY MATTERS

For my *Workology Podcast*, I interviewed Sassy Outwater, director of the Massachusetts Association for the Blind and Visually Impaired (MABVI).[9] I was interested in her experience as a person who is visually impaired, as well as in her work with MABVI. She walked me through the application, interview, and hiring process that job candidates face when they have a disability, highlighting the points where candidates with a disability can run into roadblocks caused by a lack of accessibility. I think that every employer should consider the accessibility of each step in the process and work with an accessibility expert who can review their processes, including their career site and connected online application, to ensure they are accessible to people with disabilities.

Accessibility improvements can be as simple as using plain and inclusive language when writing content for your job description or career site, extending length of time for timed assessments, alt-tagging images, captioning videos, labeling elements such as buttons, and other minor adjustments. Many employers don't take accessibility into consideration when building career sites and connecting them to an apply process. It's also important to note that all of the above applies not only to career site accessibility but also to organizations that collect candidate data via an online survey process. The Partnership on Employment & Accessible Technology (PEAT) has an extensive guide on creating inclusive and accessible job descriptions at PEATworks.org.[10]

Many organizations (if you work in the recruiting industry, you know the major players) send surveys to candidates to help human resource professionals and recruiters identify areas where elements of things like the candidate experience can be improved and what benchmarks we should consider in our industry, and offer insight into these processes. This is helpful information, as it allows us to modify our apply process based on data from the candidates themselves. Some organizations even offer awards to companies that are innovating and setting benchmarks for our industry. My concern about these types of awards is that while they bring us together as an industry and highlight the innovators among us, setting examples for benchmarks we should strive for and new processes to implement, the most important pieces of the candidate data puzzle—inclusion and accessibility—are missing.

Because these online candidate surveys are not designed with accessibility in mind, people with disabilities are excluded from the survey response and are therefore unable to contribute feedback (especially where that feedback ties into the candidate experience for disabled individuals). The reports talk about every other aspect of the candidate experience, from communication during the apply process to the time it takes between interview and response, but neglect to benchmark feedback from the 37 percent of candidates who would have been excluded from participating in the process due to inaccessibility of the survey. Of this segment, when surveyed by an organization that focuses on accessibility, 46 percent rated their last experience applying for a job online as "difficult to impossible." Of those, 9 percent were unable to complete the application and 24 percent required assistance.[11] Many candidates with disabilities are not able to participate in these surveys, not to mention your employment process, because the application is difficult or impossible to complete. As a result, they are automatically excluded from being considered for an interview for the job opening.

The employment life cycle must be accessible. Because of inaccessibility in the work experience and the hiring process, a diverse pool of qualified candidates are getting left behind. We are focusing on the overall candidate experience when a growing percentage of job seekers can't even apply for a job, let alone receive a follow-up email or an automated response thanking them for their application.

In addition to missing out on potentially great candidates, inaccessible online job descriptions and applications, websites, social media job posts, mobile apps, and pre-employment testing systems also reflect badly on companies and their brands. They affect the ability of people with disabilities to apply for positions and can also lead to expensive employment discrimination lawsuits.

A June 2019 Twitter thread highlighted how a basic phone number requirement could inadvertently deter qualified candidates from applying for a job.[12] Lisa Kaplan, the founder of Alethea Group, an organization that counters disinformation, said she was helping a homeless woman apply for a custodial job at a public library.[13]

Lisa helped her fill out basic biographical data, putting down the woman's shelter for her home address, but then encountered an email address requirement. To create an email address with the providers Kaplan tried, the woman needed to have a phone number that could receive texts, Kaplan said. The woman only had the landline number for her shelter and did not end up completing the application with Kaplan.

Two-factor authentication is aimed at making your online accounts more secure by requiring an additional verification process, such as a push notification or text message sent to your phone in addition to your password. But in cases of job seekers without smartphones, it can be a deterrent.[14]

Kaplan ended her thread with a plea for action to tech companies: "There has to be a better way. It could be a trusted portal at public libraries or a verification from the librarian, but we need to keep the internet inclusive and accessible—while detecting the manipulation of the internet by nefarious actors."

This story sums up the digital divide that limits who can apply for our job openings. To be a change agent as leaders in the HR space, we must be able to offer an inclusive and accessible application process. And this might involve, as Kaplan suggests, petitioning for resources. If battling giant tech companies doesn't get us anywhere, it could also mean offering alternatives, such as a list of resources for applicants that could include local organizations that provide free or low-cost cell phones

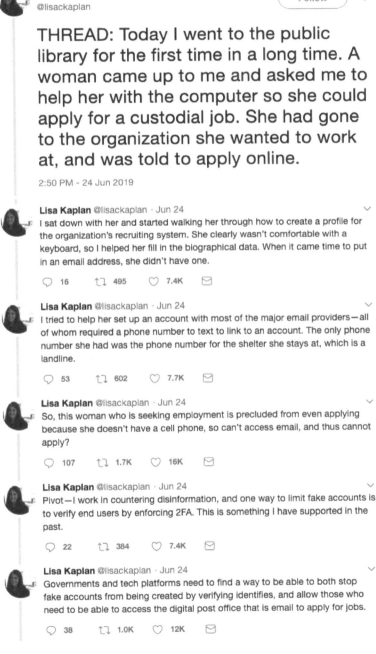

Lisa Kaplan
@lisackaplan

(Follow)

THREAD: Today I went to the public library for the first time in a long time. A woman came up to me and asked me to help her with the computer so she could apply for a custodial job. She had gone to the organization she wanted to work at, and was told to apply online.

2:50 PM - 24 Jun 2019

Lisa Kaplan @lisackaplan · Jun 24
I sat down with her and started walking her through how to create a profile for the organization's recruiting system. She clearly wasn't comfortable with a keyboard, so I helped her fill in the biographical data. When it came time to put in an email address, she didn't have one.

16   495   7.4K

Lisa Kaplan @lisackaplan · Jun 24
I tried to help her set up an account with most of the major email providers—all of whom required a phone number to text to link to an account. The only phone number she had was the phone number for the shelter she stays at, which is a landline.

53   602   7.7K

Lisa Kaplan @lisackaplan · Jun 24
So, this woman who is seeking employment is precluded from even applying because she doesn't have a cell phone, so can't access email, and thus cannot apply?

107   1.7K   16K

Lisa Kaplan @lisackaplan · Jun 24
Pivot—I work in countering disinformation, and one way to limit fake accounts is to verify end users by enforcing 2FA. This is something I have supported in the past.

22   384   7.4K

Lisa Kaplan @lisackaplan · Jun 24
Governments and tech platforms need to find a way to be able to both stop fake accounts from being created by verifying identifies, and allow those who need to be able to access the digital post office that is email to apply for jobs.

38   1.0K   12K

Figure 8.1   2019 Twitter thread by Lisa Kaplan, founder of Alethea Group

and internet access to lower-income and homeless communities. What it really means is that we have to start getting creative when it comes to inclusivity.

It's a fact that lower-income Americans have less access to technology. While the everything-mobile demographic grows, we still have to consider the percentage—no matter how small—of potential job applicants who do not have access to a smartphone or even a desktop computer. According to Pew Research Center, roughly three out of ten adults with household incomes below $30,000 a year (29 percent) don't own a smartphone.[15] More than four out of ten don't have home broadband services (44 percent) or a traditional computer (46 percent). A majority of lower-income Americans do not own tablets either.

WHAT ACCESSIBILITY LOOKS LIKE IN PRACTICE

As a coach and consultant for many companies who request site assessments along with talent brand audits, the first area I encourage clients to consider is accessibility. As an employer brand, especially when so many employers are seeking ways to stand out to candidates in this candidate-driven job market, compliance with standards and guidelines is always a good place to start.

According to a user survey conducted by PEAT, 40 percent of survey respondents reported that they experienced accessibility or usability issues when using social media.[16]

Consider that nearly one out of five Americans has a disability and that one out of eight Americans is over 65. If your website isn't accessible to them, you could be losing out on potential job candidates or new customers and exposing yourself to legal risk.[17]

Under existing regulations for implementing the Americans with Disabilities Act (ADA), discrimination on the basis of disability includes the failure to provide applicants and employees with disabilities with effective and meaningful opportunities of employment.[18] The Department of Justice (DOJ) has entered into settlement agreements with state and local governments that specifically cover accessibility of websites relating to any facet of employment, employment opportunities, and the process of applying for employment. The settlement agreements include a reference to the applicable web accessibility technical standards, like the Web Content Accessibility Guidelines (WCAG).[19]

Here are seven things you can do right now to make your hiring process more inclusive and accessible.

Screen Reader Compatibility

People who are blind or have low vision and people with dyslexia may navigate the web using a screen reader that converts text to speech and provides nonvisual navigation commands. For this assistive technology to work, it's important that you include detailed and consistent navigational elements on your website, including headers, titles, and numbered and bulleted lists. Most operating systems today include a built-in screen reader that you can use to test your website, including Narrator on Windows and Voiceover on Mac OSX.

Video Captions

People who are deaf or hard of hearing often require live captions to participate in meetings and to understand video posts on social media. Hearing loss is common among people of working age and is the most prevalent service-connected disability among American veterans. People with other disabilities may also need captions for focus and concentration. Include captions and transcripts for all media, such as videos and virtual presentations, including those on Facebook Live, YouTube, and other platforms. As a bonus, adding captions has been proven to increase your SEO online and boost user engagement.

Alt Tagging

People who are blind or have low vision may rely on well-written descriptive text (called an alt attribute or alt text, sort for alternative text) visible to screen readers to understand what is being conveyed in the images.[20] There is one basic rule when it comes to alt attributes:

describe the function of the image. This does not always mean that you describe the actual image, and it definitely shouldn't mean one thousand–word alt attributes. Instead, you need to thoughtfully consider how and why you are using each image.

It's important to make online images accessible. This means adding alt-text descriptions to PowerPoint slides that include images, web images, social media, PDFs, and others. The description should include a summary of the purpose of the image and include any relevant supporting research, statistics, or information.

Extended Time to Complete Assessments

People using assistive technology may require extra time to navigate a website and complete tasks. For web page forms, surveys, applications, and others with time limits, the user should have options to turn off, adjust, or extend that time limit.

Color Contrasts

Did you know that red-green color blindness affects up to 8 percent of men? Additionally, low-vision conditions increase with age, and half of people over the age of 50 have some degree of low-vision condition. Ensure that they can use your website by testing your design elements for proper color contrast. There are tools to help you with this, including chromatic vision simulators, which show what your site would look like to people with different types of color blindness and VisionSim, which simulates macular degeneration, diabetic retinopathy, retinitis pigmentosa, and cataracts.

Keyboard Accessibility

One of the easiest initial tests for accessibility is whether you can use a website without a mouse. Can you tab through your website content from start to finish, or are there "keyboard traps?"

Many free automated tools can help you get started with identifying accessibility issues, though please note they are only a starting point. A knowledgeable person will always need to test the site manually. Finally, you can use PEAT's TechCheck tool to assess the current state of your company's technology accessibility practices.[21]

ACCESSIBILITY AND WCAG GUIDELINES

Accessibility is a crucial component of the candidate experience and should be a priority equal to network security, says Accenture's Inclusion and Diversity Senior Manager Dan Ellerman. In a podcast interview, we discussed WCAG and how your company can take its accessibility initiatives to the next level.

WCAG are the global standards that define how to make web content more accessible to people with disabilities, including those with visual, auditory, physical, speech, cognitive, language, learning, and neurological disabilities.[22] WCAG were first established in 1998 and are governed by a global consortium. Other major accessibility laws and regulations also reference and align with WCAG success criteria, including Section 508 for US federal contractors, settlements related to the Americans with Disabilities Act, and the European Standard EN 301 549.[23]

The updated WCAG 2.0 standards were introduced in 2008, and complying with WCAG 2.0 level AA is widely considered a best practice. More recently, a proposed update to WCAG, or WCAG 2.1, extends WCAG 2.0 by adding new success criteria, definitions, and guidelines.

In our podcast interview, Dan reviewed the four major principles of WCAG 2.0 and what each principle means for web accessibility.

Perceivable

"If you don't have one of the senses around vision or hearing or touch, how can you interact with digital information?" This means that company websites must provide text alternatives for any nontext content so that it can be changed into other forms people need, such as large print, braille, speech, symbols, or simpler language.

Additionally, provide alternatives for time-based media. Create content that can be presented in different ways (for example, simpler layouts) without losing information or structure. Make it easier for users to see and hear content, including using adequate color contrast to separate foreground from background.

Operable

"How do we interact with a website if we can't use a mouse?" User interface components and navigation must be operable. Make all functionality available from a keyboard. Provide users enough time to read and use content. Provide ways to help users navigate, find content, and determine where they are.

Do not design content in a way that is known to cause seizures. Make sure your web pages do not contain anything that flashes more than three times in any one-second period and that the flash is below the general flash and red flash thresholds.[24]

Understandable

"Is our website easy to read and presented in a logical fashion?" Information and the operation of the user interface must be understandable. Make web pages appear and operate in predictable ways. Help users avoid and correct mistakes.

Make text content readable and understandable to people with different disabilities. That means individuals with learning disabilities, cognitive disabilities, traumatic brain injuries, and other disabilities, all of which can make using the internet more challenging. What's one of the best ways to meet the needs of these users? The answer is simple, literally. It's simplifying the content you write for the web. Effective writing tactics tend to appeal to all web users, whether they have a disability or not. Use plain language, short sentences, bulleted lists, and lots of white space.[25]

Robust

Sites should be designed to be accessible with current available technology and adaptable with future technology. The site content must be able to render on multiple devices with assistive technology.

In our interview, Dan said that Accenture's benchmarks and standards for procuring technology are the same as the WCAG 2.0 guidelines for building technology. Accenture has updated its supplier code of conduct to reflect the WCAG standards to meet a AA rating.

Says Dan, "It's not as easy as you'd think to meet the criteria, so it's important that your company work with its vendors to help get them where you need them to be." He gave the example of vendors who provide employee engagement surveys for HR that may not be taking assistive technology into consideration. Surveys like these are timed, which may not give people with disabilities enough time to complete them. As your company raises its own bar for accessibility initiatives, it's important to work with both your IT department and third-party vendors to help them adopt the same standards for user experience.[26] To get started with working with WCAG, visit www.w3.org.

Other excellent resources can be found in the staff training resources compiled by the Partnership on Employment & Accessible Technology (PEAT).[27] This page offers resources for training staff across your organization in the accessibility skills relevant to their specific roles. PEAT also offers Buy IT!, which is a purchasing guide for working with vendors to ensure that the technology you purchase conforms to WCAG guidelines.

CHAPTER 9

Compliance, Diversity, Privacy, and Risk

- Office of Federal Contract Compliance Programs Compliance
- When, What, and How Things Changed for Federal Contractors
- Hiring Benchmarks for Diversity, Equity, and Inclusion
- Employment and Hiring Discrimination
- Hiring Discrimination and the Gig Economy
- Age Discrimination, Company Liability, and Age Bias
- Privacy Concerns and How They Factor into Digital Recruiting
- How the EU's General Data Protection Regulations Affect Hiring and Recruiting (Everywhere)
- Are You Hiring Humans?
- Online Privacy and How It Impacts Recruiting
- HIPAA Laws in Human Resources
- Other Risks in the Online Era
- What Can HR Do to Mitigate the Risk of a Data Breach?
- Social Media Policies and Expectations

In a transparent economy, risk abounds. In this chapter, we will discuss employment laws and take a look at bias, discrimination, and compliance requirements specifically for federal contractors.

A digital talent marketplace creates unique challenges for HR leaders and recruiters that go well beyond the standard compliance laws in place before the internet became our primary marketing, outreach, data collection, and communication channel. Compliance has always been a concern for HR teams, but the landscape has changed from paper records to digital, which also means that regulations regarding data privacy, storage, and potential hazards like data breaches have to be top of mind.

The internet, even though it's been in existence since 1983, is still the Wild West. Employment, compliance, and privacy laws haven't caught up with the internet and this changing technology.

OFFICE OF FEDERAL CONTRACT COMPLIANCE PROGRAMS COMPLIANCE

I briefly mentioned the OFCCP in the last chapter. It stands for the Office of Federal Contract Compliance Programs. The OFCCP was created in 1978 with Executive Order 12086 by President Jimmy Carter through a consolidation of all the affirmative action enforcement responsibilities at each federal agency with Executive Order 11246 to the United States Secretary of Labor. The OFCCP's job is to guide, enforce, and administer equal employment opportunity by employers who are federal contractors as directed by three acts:

- Executive Order 11246, as amended.[1]
- Section 503 of the Rehabilitation Act of 1973.[2]
- The Vietnam Era Veterans' Readjustment Assistance Act of 1974 (VEVRAA), as amended.[3]

These authorities prohibit federal contractors and subcontractors from discriminating on the basis of race, color, religion, sex, national origin, disability, and protected veteran status. They also require federal contractors and subcontractors to take affirmative action to ensure equal employment opportunity in their employment processes.

In 2014, the OFCCP announced some changes to its regulations, including VEVRAA and Section 503 of the Rehabilitation Act of 1973. VEVRAA and 503 are just two of the many regulation changes that were enforced as of March 2014 by the OFCCP. The changes are complex, and after a few years we are still left scratching our heads. No matter what your focus, whether compliance or a diverse workforce, it takes action. Building an affirmative action plan (AAP), maintaining compliance with the OFCCP, and reaching diverse candidates calls for engagement and establishing a connection with potential candidates within different diversity groups, both externally and internally. All companies should consider using diversity recruiting programs to move beyond groupthink, expand horizons, and bring forth new ideas between employees, customers, and the company as a whole.

WHEN, WHAT, AND HOW THINGS CHANGED FOR FEDERAL CONTRACTORS

As I mentioned, the changes that began in 2014 have been complex and confusing, especially if, as a federal contractor or subcontractor, you didn't get the memo until after things began to change. To shed some light on the changes, I will break them down in a list by year for your AAP.

Changes as of 2014

Updates to Section 503 of the Rehabilitation Act and VEVRAA regulatory changes that affect AAPs for individuals with disabilities and protected veterans took effect March 24, 2014.

Federal contractors and subcontractors with contracts in excess of $10,000 must take affirmative action to employ and advance employment-qualified individuals with disabilities. Contractors who have fifty or more employees and $50,000 or more in federal contracts or subcontracts must annually prepare a written affirmative action plan for individuals with disabilities.

Employers are required to include the spelling out of "veteran" and "disabled" in equal employment opportunity (EEO) taglines in job advertisements, national utilization goals for Section 503 AAPs, and hiring benchmarks for VEVRAA AAPs. Employers must extend candidate invitations to self-identify veteran and disability status at the applicant stage in order to collect applicant and hiring data for protected veterans and individuals with disabilities.

Changes as of 2015

Federal contractors and subcontractors must treat applicants and employees equally, without regard to their sexual orientation or gender identity. Contractors must list "sexual orientation" and "gender identity" anytime protected classifications are referenced.

Contractors are also required to post the "EEO is the Law" poster supplement, along with the "EEO is the Law" poster, until the OFCCP and the Equal Employment Opportunity Commission (EEOC) update the language.

Changes as of 2016

Federal contractors and subcontractors must comply with EO 13665 (pay transparency final rule), which amended the equal opportunity clause (41 CFR 60-1.4) to add a reference to the new prohibition regarding compensation.

New verbiage must be included in contracts and purchase orders, and the prescribed language must be posted within employee manuals and handbooks and on all company websites and employment applications.

Updates for 2022 and Beyond

All federal contractors and subcontractors subject to OFCCP's jurisdiction should be aware of the following developments: (1) OFCCP received final approval to require federal contractors and subcontractors to provide annual verification of their compliance with affirmative action program requirements, (2) OFCCP announced it will receive and analyze 2018 Component 2 pay data from the EEOC relating to federal contractors and subcontractors as part of its focus on pay equity, and (3) OFCCP is returning to traditional construction compliance reviews instead of the less extensive compliance checks it conducted in 2020.

In August of 2021, the Office of Management and Budget (OMB) approved OFCCP's Affirmative Action Program Verification Initiative (AAVI) in essentially the same form as originally proposed. The OFCCP first launched its AAVI efforts in August 2018 by Directive 2018-07, in response to several criticisms outlined in a 2016 Government Accountability Office (GAO) report.

Federal contractors and subcontractors can expect to log on to the AAVI portal annually to certify that they have developed and maintained AAPs for the year at each establishment or line of business by selecting one of following:

- The entity has developed and maintained AAPs at each establishment, as applicable, or for each functional or business unit.
- The entity has been a party to a qualifying federal contract or subcontract for 120 days or more and has not developed and maintained AAPs at each establishment, as applicable.
- The entity became a covered federal contractor or subcontractor within the past 120 days and therefore has not yet developed applicable AAPs.

Federal contractors can also expect to disclose their entire corporate structure, including any parent companies and all establishments. Collecting this information will likely lead to more parents and affiliates of federal contractors and subcontractors realizing their need to develop AAPs for each establishment, unless they have a separate facility exemption or can assert a defense that they are separate entities for OFCCP purposes.

Going beyond OFCCP Compliance

Particularly considering the broad range of candidate communities we can now reach due to the digitization of recruitment marketing, let's think of OFCCP compliance as the bare minimum, or a low bar that we'd like to rise above. Diversity is a mix of compliance, responsibility, and good business sense. According to a 2018 report by McKinsey, *Delivering through Diversity,* focusing on diversity in recruiting leads to business success.[4] Companies in the top quartile for gender diversity on executive teams were 21 percent more likely to outperform on profitability and 27 percent more likely to have superior value creation. The highest-performing companies on both profitability and diversity had more women in line. But it isn't just gender diversity. Companies in the top quartile for ethnic and cultural diversity on executive teams were 33 percent more likely to have industry-leading profitability. That this relationship continues to be strong suggests that inclusion of highly diverse individuals—and the myriad ways in which diversity exists beyond gender (e.g., LGBTQ, age/generation, international experience) can be a key differentiator among companies. Despite this hard evidence, many companies still struggle with this.

Innovation is hard and bringing in different people who have varying experiences, backgrounds, and are outside of a set expectation or familiarity is uncomfortable. But being uncomfortable is a good thing. That's what I tell myself when I try new things, meet new people, and do something different. It's being comfortable that causes problems, which is why I'm constantly pushing myself to think, do, and be open to different things, including diversity. The truth of the matter is that we've gotten soft. We've relied on compliance with the OFCCP and corporate policy for far too long.

We need to hire diverse candidates to stay competitive just as we need to push our people to learn and think differently. And that starts with surrounding those people with a community of individuals and professionals who aren't carbon copies of the rest of the team. Otherwise, we will never have any new ideas, innovations, or outside-of-the-box ideas, plans, or strategies.

It makes sense that a diverse and inclusive employee base—with a range of approaches and perspectives—would be more competitive in a globalized economy. A small but increasing number of companies have recognized an opportunity to go even further, reframing diversity, equity, and inclusion (DE&I) as an enabler of two of the foremost goals for CEOs: growth and value creation.

HIRING BENCHMARKS FOR DIVERSITY, EQUITY, AND INCLUSION

Federal contractors are expected to hire specific protected categories in numbers that meet or exceed thresholds. The hiring benchmark is a percentage of employees within veterans and persons with disabilities employee groups that meet or exceed the requirements set by the Department of Labor (DOL) with annually published changes and updates. The hiring benchmark is focused on a percentage of hires and should not be confused with a percentage of candidates, which is important. However, the expectation is that an organization must hire and employ a specific minimum percentage of veterans and employees with disabilities.

The hiring benchmark for veterans was updated for 2019 hiring requirements at 5.9 percent.[5] The expectation from the DOL is that nearly 6 percent of all candidate applications for a company that is a federal contractor will be veteran candidates. There is a similar, yet higher, hiring benchmark for individuals with disabilities, and we'll review that later in this chapter.

Companies who are federal contractors must not only comply with federal regulations, but also build trust with the protected job seeker community to strengthen their employer brand. The OFCCP oversees compliance and issues fines, but the DOL is involved in the actual litigation.

I have focused on the diversity side of compliance because these government requirements are often overlooked by many who paint diversity with a broad, sweeping brush. While not every organization is a federal contractor, the expectations set forth provide solid guidance, direction, and reporting for any organization.

All of this is important because it sets the stage when discussing the subject of diversity and, more importantly, diversity disparity. Becoming more aware of diversity disparity within our organizations leads to important conversations that can set forth a movement for change beyond the OFCCP.

Candidate Self Identification

To determine if you meet the hiring benchmarks set forth for hiring veterans and those with disabilities, federal contractors must make sure that candidates self-identify in the hiring process. This normally happens as part of the online application. While the information isn't used in the decision-making process, whether the candidates are offered the job or not, it is important for a company to determine if they are doing enough targeted diversity outreach, engaging the right candidates, and employing them at their company.

Companies like AT&T, which is a federal contractor, provide candidates an opportunity to self-identify early in the hiring process and offer a second chance after a job offer is extended. This helps to ensure they are capturing the correct candidate and soon-to-be employee information, which is then used in their annual affirmative action reporting and available for business leaders and the OFCCP should there be an audit. These hiring benchmarks help provide organizations a minimum level of expectation and a temperature gauge when determining how successful their veteran- or disability-focused diversity program is.

The self-identification process for candidates also allows companies an opportunity to determine how diverse their recruiting efforts are for other diversity programs. It's even more beneficial if the organization captures candidate source information in the form of self-reporting, or data that is tracked with a HTTP cookie (a small piece of data that a server sends to a user's web browser that stores user information), allowing the company to understand the diversity recruiting sources like diversity job boards, affinity communities, and events that lend the highest number of candidates as well as diverse hires by group.

Keep in mind that hiring benchmarks and self-identification are different from good-faith recruiting efforts. They are related, but good-faith efforts aren't always designed to measure the impact, success, volume, or failure of a diverse recruiting source, community, or program.

Hiring Benchmarks for Nonfederal Contractors

It's easy to think that because you are not a federal contractor, you are not required by law to employ diverse candidates. Companies are still required by law to uphold Title VII, the ADA, the Genetic Information Nondiscrimination Act (GINA), and the Age Discrimination in Employment Act (ADEA), as well as many other employment laws. Certain candidate and employment groups are protected from discrimination including age, sex, religion, disability, genetic information, race/color, national origin, and pregnancy. These are federal requirements. Your state or city may have specific requirements that protect other individuals, including LGBTQ communities. This means that employees, as well as candidates, can't be discriminated against as part of the hiring process for these reasons. Sadly, veterans are not included in this list.

The ADA makes it unlawful to discriminate in employment against a qualified individual with a disability. The ADA also outlaws discrimination against individuals with disabilities in state and local government services, public accommodations, transportation, and telecommunications. This part of the law is enforced by the US EEOC and state and local civil rights enforcement agencies that work with the commission. Title I of the ADA requires employers to provide reasonable accommodations to qualified applicants and employees with a disability unless the employer can demonstrate that doing so creates an undue hardship to the employer or poses a direct threat to the safety of the employee or others.[6]

To add another layer to the confusing regulations for protected classes of employees, the EEOC enforces the ADA's employment provisions. Most employers are familiar with reasonable accommodations for persons with disabilities, and federal and state governments support hiring under the ADA with tax credits and financial support for employers. Regulations aside, according to the 2017 *Disability Statistics Annual Report* from the Institute on Disability, nearly one in eight people in the United States has a disability, and that number is rising annually.[7] Companies that succeed in incorporating candidates with disabilities have seen 28 percent higher revenue and two times higher net income, according to a 2018 Accenture white paper on accessibility. Workplace Initiative, a network of companies, nonprofits, and government agencies working to remove barriers for those with disabilities, reports that those companies also experienced reduced turnover, lower recruiting costs, increased productivity, and improved customer outreach.[8]

While companies that aren't federal contractors aren't obligated to meet hiring benchmarks and provide an opportunity for candidates to self-identify, that doesn't mean that organizations are off the hook from diversity efforts, whether it's focused on recruiting, community outreach, or within the organization.

The bottom line is that organizations perform better when they have a diverse employee community. Employees deserve to be treated fairly and consistently regardless of their protected class, which is why organizations should be focused on creating an inclusive workplace while providing organization leaders with training to handle a variety of employment situations.

EMPLOYMENT AND HIRING DISCRIMINATION

For more background, in the United States, diversity generally falls into what the EEOC defines as a protected class. These protected classes include individual workers who are protected in the employment and hiring process under a number of federal US employment laws and include the following groups:

- Age (over 40)
- Disability

- Genetic information
- National origin
- Pregnancy
- Race/color
- Religion
- Sex

There is also a ninth protected class for organizations that are federal contractors that include veterans and military.

Federal contracting companies are required to engage candidates and encourage them to apply for positions, including those where diversity disparity exists within the organization. Filing an annual EEO-1 report is mandatory for companies that employ at least fifty employees and have a contract with the government resulting in at least $50,000 worth of business each year. They are also expected to not only engage protected classes on the basis of sex as mentioned above but also must complete outreach to members of the LGBTQ community.

Additionally, these same contractors are expected to meet certain candidate percentage thresholds. The percentage threshold is referred to as a hiring benchmark and changes annually. The benchmarks provide thresholds for two of the nine classes: veterans and people with disabilities.

Companies must request all job candidates self-identify their protected class early in the hiring and application process. This information isn't used in the hiring process but is part of federal contractor requirements, as mentioned previously. In 2019, federal contracts were required to ensure that at least 5.9 percent of employees hired were veterans and 7 percent of hires were people with disabilities.

On August 27, 2013, the US DOL announced a final rule that changed the regulations of Section 503 of the Rehabilitation Act of 1973. This prohibits federal contractors and subcontractors from discriminating against employees with disabilities. Although this rule has been in place for over four decades, the change required federal contractors to actively ensure that 7 percent of their workforce is made up of people with disabilities. This change became effective on March 24, 2014.

Social Media Discrimination and Social Media Recruiting

Another new territory that developed along with the digital landscape is social media. Most companies have a social media presence online, but companies are also using social media sites as part of their recruiting and candidate selection process. With more than 5.6 billion Google searches per day, chances are that your HR team, recruiters, or managers are searching the internet for candidates.[9] Maybe it's part of your regular candidate sourcing process. You search LinkedIn, Facebook, and Twitter, build lists, make friends, and fill positions. Or maybe you use tools to search across social media networks by keyword. Depending on how a candidate restricts and controls their privacy on social media sites, a recruiter or manager can learn a great deal of information that shouldn't be included in their decision to interview or even hire a potential employee.

So back to those protected classes that, according to the law, are considered information that should not be factored into the decision-making process when a candidate is evaluated as part of the hiring process.

Imagine if a hiring manager Googles a candidate and visits their Facebook profile only to learn that their top prospect was 20 weeks pregnant. This position is very important and is responsible for a project that goes live just about the time that the candidate would be on maternity leave. The manager considers this information when making their final hiring decision and decides to offer the position to a candidate who is not expecting.

Or maybe a company representative learns about a current employee's family medical condition from their personal blog. According to their blog, the employee needs a heart transplant. Your company is a small organization, and a costly surgery like this will result in thousands of dollars of expense for your company, especially since they currently cover 100 percent. The CEO is very specific that he doesn't want health care costs to increase, and your leadership team's bonus is heavily influenced by your corporate P&L. A decision is made to lay off the employee before he is added to the transplant list and a surgery is scheduled.

Unfortunately, situations like these are not far-fetched and have yet to be tested in the court system, as social media is a relatively new business tool. As social media becomes the communication method of choice, companies should be concerned about the potential liabilities from online unconscious bias. In 2007, the EEOC began focusing their efforts on unconscious bias. Unconscious bias is the concept that individuals can have a bias at an unconscious level that influences decision-making in ways that the individual is unaware. Essentially, employers and hiring managers demonstrate, and are unaware of, behaviors that are biased against a protected class.

Since Facebook's launch in 2004, university experts have been studying the correlation between Facebook users' offline and online behaviors. Their work over the last decade supports the fact that the key to social media platforms like Facebook is that pre-existing offline community factors and behaviors complement the use of the social media site. And because of studies like this, it makes sense to assume that employers would exhibit the same biases online as they already do offline. The only difference is the ease at which employers can have access to this protected information, thereby allowing their unconscious biases to become more prevalent.

A new field study in the *Journal of Economics & Management Strategy* sheds some light on how social media could lead to discriminatory hiring practices.[10] Researchers found that some employers use job applicants' country or city of origin—information that was only available on their Facebook profiles—as an indicator of whether to call them back or offer them positions. Though the study was based in France, the results speak volumes for any job market. The researchers sent out over eight hundred job applications from two fake applicants—one of whom had local origins, while the other had foreign roots. While both applicants sent in résumés and cover letters that didn't include their hometowns, their Facebook pages revealed their countries of origin to employers.

At the start of the experiment, the researchers found a nearly 42 percent difference in the applicants who received callbacks. The foreign applicant proved to be at a significant disadvantage when it came to being contacted back compared with the domestic applicant.

However, in the midst of the experiment, the researchers noted a massive change in the layout of Facebook. Once Facebook implemented profile tabs, users' personal information like country of origin and languages spoken were no longer available on the homepage. Instead, the changes required users to click more in-depth into others' profiles to find that information.

Following the change, when job recruiters could no longer tell with one click what country the applicant hailed from, the researchers noticed similar callback rates between their two fake applicants. This finding was perhaps the most important in the study, as it shows the layout of social media was a major factor behind the discriminatory actions.

The researchers are calling on social media companies to be aware of these findings and keep them in mind when designing future updates or page layouts, as they could have life-changing implications.

"This study illustrates that design choices made by online platforms can dramatically affect a decision like calling back, or not, an applicant for a job interview," said coauthor Dr. Matthieu Manant. "Internet companies should integrate this fact into their design thinking."

Until social media sites and search engines can mask these factors, companies need to be prepared for a new era of discrimination claims from using social media.

HIRING DISCRIMINATION AND THE GIG ECONOMY

As more and more companies transition from hiring full-time employees to using independent contractors (a.k.a. gig workers), the gap in employment discrimination protections for these workers is coming into focus.

The US Department of Justice provides the following helpful summary of Title VII of the 1964 Civil Rights Act, the federal law that prohibits employment discrimination:

> Title VII makes it unlawful to discriminate against someone on the basis of race, color, national origin, sex (including

pregnancy and gender identity) or religion. The Act also makes it unlawful to retaliate against a person because the person complained about discrimination, filed a charge of discrimination, or participated in an employment discrimination investigation or lawsuit.

What most people don't know is that Title VII covers only "employees," not "independent contractors" and gig workers, and this could have a significant impact on hiring discrimination. According to the Brookings Institution's reporting, at least 15 million people in this country are primarily employed as a gig worker.[11] This figure represents a 20 percent increase from 1995, and I expect the number of gig workers to only increase. The definition of "employee" and "independent contractor" is a topic of litigation, especially since it affects whether the person must be paid minimum wage and overtime, as well as other issues like worker's compensation.

CASE STUDY: UBER

In May of 2017, Uber released its first state of diversity report, adding fuel to the fire of controversy surrounding Uber leadership and the future of the company.[12] Their diversity numbers were less than ideal, especially when you look at the employee population in technology roles. According to the report, the company had nearly 85 percent men in technology roles within the organization, and overall the US-based Uber team consisted of the following race and ethnicity breakdown: 30.9 percent Asian, 49.8 percent Caucasian, 4.3 percent multiracial, 5.6 percent Hispanic, and 8.8 percent African American.

If Uber aspires to become a federal contractor, they will need to have all employees and candidates self-identify for affirmative action plan (AAP) reporting purposes. In 2017, Uber had already been the target of numerous lawsuits related to its recruiting, hiring, and employment practices. The company, aware that its success depended on its employer brand and not paying billions of dollars annually to settle lawsuits, made some changes in leadership as well as in its diversity and inclusion programs. The rideshare company has since released 2018 and 2019 state of diversity reports. Its 2019 report was released along with this statement:

> At Uber, our mission is to ignite opportunity by setting the world in motion. We see direct parallels between how we ignite opportunity through our company and how we ignite it within our company. But we also know that a solely data-driven approach will never be sufficient, because D&I is more than a box to check or a target to hit. The numbers matter, but they're only a starting point; a commitment to diversity and inclusion has to run much deeper. That's why we've set an audacious goal: to make Uber the most diverse, equitable, and inclusive workplace on the planet. And we're not just setting high expectations for our own good. We're aiming sky-high because we know from experience that reducing and eliminating inequity is hard to do if all you shoot for is incremental change.

From Uber's 2019 Diversity & Inclusion report, here are a few noteworthy year-over-year total population changes at Uber from 2018 to 2019:[13]

- The population of women overall grew 42.3 percent. This growth was most notable in tech (where the headcount of women grew by 47.9 percent) and tech leadership (35.3 percent growth).
- The region with the highest increase in headcount of women was Latin America, where the population of women grew by 88.3 percent.
- In the United States, the populations of Black/African American and Hispanic/Latinx employees grew by 44.5 percent and 73.5 percent, respectively, from 2018. This growth was most notable in tech (up 65.0 percent and 74.3 percent, respectively).

Uber's closing statement from the 2019 report read,

> This year, we began looking more deeply at our workforce data by exploring intersectional views. When we consider the intersection of race/ethnicity and gender (in the US), we're able to make more meaningful and insightful observations of key trends, and thus pursue more impactful and inclusive strategies to continue closing gaps and improving our culture. Overall, white men still make up the majority of Uber's employee population (30.1%) in the US. This pattern is especially pronounced in leadership roles, tech roles, and, most acutely, tech leadership roles. These observations stress the importance of improving diversity and inclusion at Uber across the employee journey (recruiting, hiring, development, and retention). In 2020, and in each subsequent year, we'll be able to look at the intersectional representation data to assess how well our people processes are working and how inclusive our culture is for different groups at Uber—particularly women of color, whose intersectional identities often result in invisibility, especially in tech.

While the company is still dealing with many issues around DE&I, it has come a long way since 2017. From an employer brand perspective, transparency and acknowledgment of mistakes was key for this company. The legal problems had created a negative outlook for the company brand and the company was too large to simply brush past them, hire a head of diversity, and try to improve the numbers.

AGE DISCRIMINATION, COMPANY LIABILITY, AND AGE BIAS

The Age Discrimination in Employment Act (ADEA) forbids age discrimination against people who are age 40 or older. It does not protect workers under the age of 40, although some states have laws that protect younger workers from age discrimination. It is not illegal for an employer or other covered entity to favor an older worker over a younger one, even if both workers are age 40 or older. Discrimination can occur when the victim and the person who inflicted the discrimination are both over 40.

According to the US Bureau of Labor Statistics (BLS), about 40 percent of people ages 55 and older were working or actively looking for work in 2014. Through 2024, that number, known as a labor force participation rate, is expected to increase the fastest for the oldest segments of the population—most notably, people ages 65–74 and 75 and older. In contrast, participation rates for most other age groups in the labor force aren't projected to change much over the 2014–2024 decade.

Our aging workforce is growing, and our economy is strong, but so many people over 40 are struggling to find a job.

If You're Over 40, This May Sound Familiar
If there's one thing I've learned in my years as a writer and speaker in HR, it's that there is power in a personal story—which is what you're about to hear. Age discrimination is topic that is hidden away behind closed doors, but the simple fact is that we are all growing older.

In August of 2018, I had the pleasure of interviewing Jo Weech for my *Workology Podcast*.[14] Jo is the founder of Exemplary Consultants and she had recently published an article on LinkedIn that had garnered more than ten thousand comments and likes, shining a spotlight on the topic of age discrimination in the hiring process. Jo courageously shared her personal story and has helped others find the courage to share their own experience with age discrimination.

If you're over 40, Jo's story might ring way too true. If you're an HR leader or recruiter, you can take personal responsibility and work for change in our industry. We're not helpless. We're actually not as scared to take on a company for age discrimination as someone else might be for other types of discriminatory behavior. Jo has some great suggestions for recruiters in her piece and you can read it in its entirety at www.linkedin.com/pulse/over-40-interviewing-have-things-happened-you-jo-weech.[15]

The topic of age bias in hiring is getting more scrutiny after growing concerns on age discrimination hiring practices when it comes to using ads and targeted campaigns on social networks like Facebook and LinkedIn. Workers over 50 total about 54 million Americans, and they are now facing much more precarious financial circumstances: a legacy of the recession. More than half of workers over 50 lose longtime jobs before they are ready to retire, according to a recent analysis by the Urban Institute and ProPublica.[16]

Facebook allows for ad targeting based on age, gender, and zip code. This was originally intended for use in consumer ad targeting but has found its way into recruiting and hiring. Until recently, you could target which Facebook users saw your sponsored post or update based on the language they spoke or read.

This won't be the last time you hear about age discrimination. We are all not getting younger, myself included. In a federal court in California, a class-action lawsuit against the global accounting firm PwC that claims "substantial evidence of age disparities in hiring" was certified in April of 2016.[17] The company noted on its careers website and in reports that the average age of its 220,000-member workforce was 27, and that 80 percent of the staff members were millennials (born after 1981).

PwC responded that the company's "hiring practices are merit-based and have nothing to do with age." It added, "The plaintiffs' accusations are false, and we will prove that in court." I'm sure we will be seeing more lawsuits like the one against PwC in the future.

PRIVACY CONCERNS AND HOW THEY FACTOR INTO DIGITAL RECRUITING

With the speed and convenience of all things digital comes some pretty serious privacy concerns. Recruiters, in particular, live and die by candidate data, which has become a legal minefield in the past decade. From social media to public trust and ethical use of data to HIPAA regulations, untangling data compliance in a digital world is probably the most complicated issue we as HR leaders have to deal with.

HOW THE EU'S GENERAL DATA PROTECTION REGULATIONS AFFECT HIRING AND RECRUITING (EVERYWHERE)

Now that the European Union's (EU) General Data Protection Regulations (GDPR) is in effect (as of May 25, 2018), companies must focus on compliance with the regulation, particularly in HR and recruiting, which rely heavily on candidate data.

The GDPR was designed as a replacement for the Data Protection Directive 95/46/EC with the purpose of reconciling country-specific and sometimes conflicting European data privacy laws.[18] Most importantly, it aims at changing the way organizations operating in the EU, or those collecting personal data from EU citizens, approach data privacy. It also provides a harmonization of the data protection regulations throughout the EU, thereby making it easier for American companies to comply. In simpler terms, it means that it will now be unlawful to use an EU citizen's data without their explicit consent.

It's important to note that the GDPR isn't just about companies who hire in the EU. It's also about employers who are employing EU citizens wherever they may live. The GDPR applies worldwide to any company that offers goods or services (even if they are free) within the EU, or collects, processes, or maintains personal data about European residents (again, not just citizens). Recruiters are going to need to restructure candidate engagement, sourcing and recruiting programs that focus on candidate data, and HR technology, and refocus on building candidate and employee relationships.

From the application process to background screening, companies recruiting or employing EU citizens must adhere to strict regulations with regards to data. Under GDPR, you are required to ask for explicit consent, clarify how you will use individual candidate's data, and make sure that the data remains secure. This involves more than simply adding a clarification and a checkbox to data collection forms. Your vendors—such as your ATS, payroll, and recruiting software—must be GDPR compliant.

The GDPR introduces direct obligations for data processors for the first time. Processors will also now be subject to penalties and civil claims by data subjects for the first time. This means that, if you haven't already, it's imperative that HR and recruiting leaders speak with and understand if their vendors and partners are taking steps to be compliant with GDPR.

Next is a short list of questions that you should ask your vendors and partners in relation to GDPR compliance. It's imperative that your HR technology vendor is compliant with the new regulations, as well as liability for violations and noncompliance.

- Have their contract terms changed with GDPR?
- What level of consent do you seek when applicants submit their data?
- What is the process for storing, collecting, and deleting data?
- What is the timeline for auto deletion—circumstances and data type?
- What is a documented timeline for keeping data?
- What processes exist to keep data up to date?
- Have they appointed a data protection officer?

Do You Need a Data Protection Officer?

In relation to the last question above, Section 4 of the GDPR outlines the requirement for applicable firms to appoint a data protection officer (DPO). According to Article 37(1), data controllers and processors shall designate a DPO where:

A. The processing is carried out by a public authority or body, except for courts acting in their judicial capacity;
B. The core activities of the controller or the processor consist of processing operations which, by virtue of their nature, their scope and/or their purposes, require regular and systematic monitoring of data subjects on a large scale; or

C. The core activities of the controller or the processor consist of processing on a large scale of special categories of data pursuant to Article 9 and personal data relating to criminal convictions and offenses referred to in Article 10.

Most firms required to appoint a DPO would fall under subparagraphs (B) and (C). Article 39 outlines five minimum tasks that the DPO must perform:

- Inform and advise firms and employees who carry out data processing on applicable data protection provisions.
- Monitor compliance with the GDPR, other data protection provisions, and additional internal data protection policies; this includes training and auditing.
- Advise on data protection impact assessment (DPIA).
- Cooperate with the supervisory authority.
- Serve as main contact for the supervisory authority.

A word of caution: in many cases, the business can be both data controller and data processor. However, because the GDPR makes the distinction, we'd like to consider the shared responsibility of both parties.

Companies that determine the means of processing personal data are controllers, regardless of whether they collect the data directly from data subjects. For example, a recruiter (controller) collects the data of its clients when they apply for a job, but your recruiting technology (processor) stores, digitizes, and catalogs all the information. These companies can be ATSs or full-suite recruiting software companies. Both organizations (controller and processor) are responsible for handling the personal data of these customers.

Recruiting Strategy Changes Post-GDPR

Because short-term recruiting programs, or what we refer to as "reactive recruiting," will come at a price in part due to the GDPR, HR teams must focus on building candidate relationships and providing value for the long term. The value of building relationships, sharing information, and providing resources will be more important than ever to engage and recruit candidates.

If you've already begun adapting your recruiting model to GDPR compliance, you're probably ahead of other companies when it comes to compliance and hiring. The consulting firm Gartner estimates that more than half of the companies that are subject to the GDPR will not be in compliance throughout this year. They will be at risk.[19]

If you're in the half that is not yet compliant with the GDPR, consider it an opportunity to revamp your current practices and candidate outreach.

When it comes to GDPR in recruiting and hiring, your tech should comply with new regulations while still supporting the broader mission of the recruiting and hiring side of your organization. This gives you the peace of mind on the compliance side, allowing you to focus on improving your hiring processes and candidate quality.

GDPR Impacts Every Employer (Especially Those Who Hire Humans)

Europe has always had stricter standards when it comes to online privacy. In 2012, European courts upheld the "Right to Be Forgotten" which allows individuals to erase their online history in certain circumstances. In 2014, an EU court decided that Google must comply with requests to remove some search results in a decision that became known as the right to be forgotten. As part of that decision, European users can submit a request to Google asking the company to delist results that are "no longer relevant" or otherwise outdated. The GDPR just builds upon that.

Under the GDPR, candidates will have the "right to be forgotten" or "right to erasure," meaning that candidates can request for their data to be erased when it is no longer necessary for the original purpose. This is the future into which we are heading—a place where GDPR is a global program designed to protect consumers, candidates, and our data from the prying eyes of anyone and everyone who is selling it for a buck instead of thinking about people and humanity.

HR departments will play a crucial role in ensuring that employee data is processed lawfully and appropriate information is given to employees about the use of their data. The GDPR will require a significant shift in how companies deal with this aspect of data protection compliance.

It's important to note that the GDPR isn't just about companies who hire in the EU. In the short term, it's about employers who are employing EU citizens wherever they may live. Recruiters are going to need to build candidate engagement, sourcing, and recruiting programs that focus on building relationships.

HR is saddled with a lot of compliance responsibilities, many of which are not of its own making. It can be process-driven, and this might be a great time to consider splitting the department into two areas, compliance (the processes) and HR (the human side), or clearly defining when to use technology and when to put people back into the mix. With the right balance, HR teams can be more productive, more engaged, and use the human element to attract and retain top talent.

ARE YOU HIRING HUMANS?

It's timely to note that at the heart of the fear of being replaced by robots is the feeling of being less than human, when you're a number or a line item for your employer, or "human capital," rather than being treated like a human being. Humans don't want to be data; at the least, they want more control over how their data is used. A phone call or personalized email can mean the difference between considering a role at your company or moving on for a candidate.

The solution isn't more technology, it's better technology. Your tech should support not only compliance with new regulations but also the human side of recruiting. Tools like machine learning, natural language processing, personalized recommendations, and other AI-enabled technology that bring hyperpersonalization and a human-to-computer interaction model should enhance the candidate and employee experience.

Unless your recruiting strategy is focused on hiring and employing robots, engagement is here to stay. However, the robot revolution is inching closer . . . especially since a robot in Saudi Arabia was the first to be granted citizenship in 2017.[20]

ONLINE PRIVACY AND HOW IT IMPACTS RECRUITING

Let's start with Facebook. It has had a bad run, between Cambridge Analytica, Congressional testimony around election advertising (among other things), and recently topped off with a $5 billion dollar fine in July 2019 and a testimony before Congress in October 2021.

The Federal Trade Commission (FTC) began probing Facebook in March 2018 following reports that political consulting firm Cambridge Analytica had improperly accessed the data of 87 million Facebook users. The FTC approved a record $5 billion settlement with Facebook over the company's privacy policies—the largest fine ever imposed by the FTC against a tech company. Ouch.

In July of 2019, Facebook said it will make advertisements for jobs, loans, and credit card offers searchable for all US users following a legal settlement designed to eliminate discrimination on its platform.[21] The plan disclosed in an internal report voluntarily expands on a commitment the social media giant made in March of 2019 when it agreed to make its US housing ads searchable by location and advertiser.

Ads were only delivered selectively to Facebook users based on such data as what they earn, their education level, and where they shop. The audit's leader, former American Civil Liberties Union executive Laura Murphy, was hired by Facebook in May 2018 to assess its performance on vital social issues.

Targeted ads tailored to individuals are Facebook's bread and butter—accounting for all but a sliver of its more than $50 billion in annual revenues last year. It's unlikely that making the ads searchable would have a significant effect on Facebook's business. Analysts have cautioned, however, that any restrictions on Facebook's ability to target ads could scare off advertisers.

How do we feel about Ads Manager now? My advice is to stay on top of what Facebook is up to and react accordingly with your ad budget.

Another thing we can thank Facebook for is that privacy is a bigger concern than ever before, leading to users abandoning social media platforms (yes, even LinkedIn). Amid public concerns over Cambridge Analytica's use of Facebook data and a subsequent movement to encourage users to abandon Facebook, there is a renewed focus on how social media companies collect personal information and make it available to marketers.[22]

Pew Research Center has studied the spread and impact of social media since 2005 when just 5 percent of American adults used the platforms.[23] The trends tracked by data tell a complex story that is full of conflicting pressures. On one hand, the rapid growth of the platforms is testimony to their appeal to online Americans. On the other, this widespread use has been accompanied by rising user concerns about privacy and social media firms' capacity to protect their data. While there is evidence that social media works in some important ways for people, Pew Research Center studies have shown that people are anxious about all the personal information that is collected and shared and the security of their data.

Overall, a 2014 survey found that 91 percent of Americans "agree" or "strongly agree" that people have lost control over how personal information is collected and used by all kinds of entities. Some 80 percent of social media users said they were concerned about advertisers and businesses accessing the data they share on social media platforms, and 64 percent said the government should do more to regulate advertisers.[24]

HIPAA LAWS IN HUMAN RESOURCES

When it comes to topics of privacy, especially concerning employee health care benefits, HIPAA is one of the most misunderstood and miscommunicated policies for employers and employees. HIPAA is nebulous, and in combination with any employer health care plan it creates a great deal of confusion and frustration for managers, HR, and employees, especially in our digital lives.

The HIPAA Privacy Rule as outlined by the US Department of Health and Human Services establishes national standards to protect individuals' medical records and other personal health information. The HIPAA Privacy Rules apply to health plans, health care clearinghouses, and health care providers that conduct certain health care transactions electronically.

The rule requires appropriate safeguards to protect the privacy of personal health information and sets limits and conditions on the uses and disclosures that may be made of such information without patient authorization. The rule also gives patients' rights over their health information, including the right to examine and obtain a copy of their health records, and to request corrections.

An employer is considered a health plan if they pay for a portion of the cost of the medical care. If, as an employer, you pay for a portion of an employee's health plan, you fall under HIPAA privacy guidelines. HIPAA controls how a health plan or covered health care providers disclose protected health information to an employer, including a manager or supervisor of a company.

As an employee, if you pay for a portion of the total cost of an employee health care plan, you are required to follow HIPAA. Employers have access to health care information including benefit enrollment, any benefit changes, Family Medical Leave Act (FMLA), and wellness program information that falls under HIPAA privacy.

Employees must authorize health care providers first before they are able to disclose any health care–related information to their employer, unless other laws require them to disclose it. This is one reason why employees must complete FMLA paperwork authorizing a medical professional to share an employee's health care information before typically granting them FMLA leave. It asks for information including date of birth, diagnosis, and social security number.

Under the HIPAA law, employers must protect your health information in the following ways:

- Protection of sensitive health care information and changes. For example, benefit paperwork falls under the privacy law and any plan changes associated with them if this information includes any data that comes from the electronic health record.
- Provide HIPAA training for employees who have access to sensitive employee health information.
- Protection of FSA or Wellness Program Information. These fall under HIPAA's privacy guidelines, meaning program administrators and employees affiliated with these programs are provided with specific HIPAA training and must ensure the employee health care information is protected.
- Protection of Occupational Health Records. Also known as OHR or Employee Health Records, these are a result of a post-offer employee physical, workers compensation, or other workplace injury under OSHA. HIPAA requires the health facilities and agencies to keep this information secure. Employers are obligated the same way.

Additionally, employers must have HIPAA privacy laws displayed, as well as state-specific ones, and must notify employees of their specific privacy policies for the company. Employers must also have a defined policy and process related to the notification and investigation that takes place if an employee notifies the organization of a potential privacy violation. HIPAA's privacy protection is key.

What HIPAA Doesn't Protect

HIPAA doesn't protect the following information:

- Your employment records. Employee medical and health care benefit information should always be filed separately for the individual employee file. Employee new hire paperwork, performance review, and documentation are generally not protected under HIPAA.

- Employment decisions based on health information including absences and time off work unless they include all the information disclosed by a medical professional bulleted above.
- Managers or HR from sharing health care information with coworkers or the boss. For example, if an employee was sick because they were pregnant and emailed that to the team, this is not a violation of HIPAA privacy.
- Workplace or office gossip. While the workplace grapevine is never fun, the sharing of personal information like a cancer diagnosis isn't typically HIPAA protected.

Recommended HIPAA Resources

HIPAA privacy laws are extremely complex, and this article in no way fully articulates the complexity of the law. HIPAA was put in place to protect a patient's health care record while also providing patients and a patient-authorized person or organization access to those records. I recommend checking out the following resources to learn more about HIPAA privacy laws, starting with the Department of Health Services' Health Privacy Information Page. The site has a variety of resources, but for health care consumers, I recommend visiting their Consumer HIPAA Resources for more in-depth information on HIPAA privacy guidelines and other frequently asked questions. I also suggest you contact your employment attorney to answer specific questions and help you establish an employee investigation and communication process at your company.[25]

OTHER RISKS IN THE ONLINE ERA

With all of the information we need to do our jobs living in the cloud or in our databases, email, and other accounts, it's nearly impossible to prevent security breaches. Data breaches can lead to enormous liability for any company. Some losses are easy to calculate, such as time spent on help desk activities, investigations, and legal defense. Other losses are harder to quantify, such as reputational damage to the business. But it's clear that the costs can be staggering. According to the Ponemon Institute's 2020 *Cost of Data Breach Study*, the global average for a data breach is $3.83 million, but the average cost of a data breach in the United States has hit an all-time high of $8.64 million.[26]

Is Your HR Tech and Information at Risk From Hackers and Phishing?

Phishing attacks are one of the most common security challenges that both individuals and companies face in keeping their information secure. Whether it's getting access to passwords, credit cards, or other sensitive information, hackers are using email, social media, phone calls, and any form of communication they can to steal valuable data. Businesses, of course, are a particularly worthwhile target.

Phishing is a type of social engineering attack often used to steal user data, including login credentials and credit card numbers. It occurs when an attacker, masquerading as a trusted entity, dupes a victim into opening an email, instant message, or text message. Phishers aim to lure or lead people to fake websites where they trick their victims into providing their personal information such as their Social Security numbers, credit card numbers, PINs, and account numbers.

In contrast, spear phishing is a phishing attack targeted to a specific individual or company. These attacks usually rely on tailored methods and resources, such as attempting to clone the login interface for corporate intranets, as well as using personal information gathered in advance (perhaps from a prior breach) about targets to increase the likelihood of success. Spear phishing attacks conducted against senior executives are referred to as whaling.

The most frequently used—and most reliable strategy for attackers—is to disguise a malicious link as pointing to a legitimate or trusted source. These types of phishing attacks can take any number of forms, such as exploiting misspelled URLs, creating a subdomain for a malicious website, or using confusingly similar domains.

And the hackers are getting smarter about finding their way into our data. One in seven organizations have experienced "lateral phishing"—a situation in which an account inside an organization is compromised and the credibility of that same-domain account is leveraged to send phishing emails to other people within the same domain, along with frequent contacts external to the company. This was documented in a report published in July 2019 by Barracuda Networks in cooperation with researchers at UC Berkeley and UC San Diego.[27]

For organizations that have fallen victim to lateral phishing attacks, over 60 percent have had multiple account compromises, with researchers analyzing 154 compromised accounts and over one hundred thousand unique recipients. This type of attack relies strongly on implicit trust that comes with custom, organization-provided email accounts as opposed to free email services provided by Google, Microsoft, or Yahoo.

WHAT CAN HR DO TO MITIGATE THE RISK OF A DATA BREACH?

In large part, data security is an issue for the technology department, but HR professionals can help ensure that effective programs are in place, according to information from the 2018 SHRM Employment Law & Legislative Conference.[28] Specifically, HR can lead the way by: taking the following steps:

- Knowing who is hired. Protecting personally identifiable information (PII) starts with properly vetting job candidates who will have access to sensitive information: those being considered for HR, payroll, and finance positions, to name a few.
- Accounting for equipment. During the onboarding process, employers should complete a checklist so that they have a record of all the equipment each employee receives. Then, at the time of separation, the checklist should be consulted to ensure

that all equipment is returned and workers don't walk out of the building with sensitive information.

- Training employees to spot issues. Workers may not always know how to identify an issue—such as a phishing scam through which a cybercriminal sends an email that looks like it came from someone in the company. An employee may quickly respond to the message and divulge personal information that can be used to access payroll and other information. Employees should be trained on how to identify scams and also should know what to look for in a legitimate company email, such as a standard signature line, a photo of the sender, and a company email address.
- Encouraging workers to speak up. When a breach or attempted breach occurs, employees who handle PII must feel comfortable stepping up and notifying the appropriate staff. This is essential not only for resolving the situation but also because employers must provide certain notices when information is compromised.
- Carefully crafting Bring Your Own Device (BYOD) policies. BYOD policies may turn into "bring-your-own-breach" policies in practice. The more mobile the device, the easier it is for an unauthorized person to walk away with the device and any sensitive information that is stored on it. If employers are going to have a BYOD policy, they should have written policies about what will happen if the device is lost or stolen and what will happen upon termination of employment. Among other things, they should also have a procedure for remotely wiping data from the device.
- Building a culture of compliance. Representatives from different business functions—IT, HR, security, and finance—should work together to ensure that data security measures are ingrained in the organization's practices. Moreover, compliance and cooperation must start in the C-suite. HR can play a role in influencing senior management about the importance of having everyone in the organization follow security procedures.

SOCIAL MEDIA POLICIES AND EXPECTATIONS

Often it's your company's marketing department, public relations, or information technology departments that are monitoring or using social media in external brand development or promotional efforts. These departments can share situations and scenarios they may have already encountered when branding on social media networks.

As more people are being drawn to online communities, chances are someone in your company has already used social media for branding in some form. The issue of control concerning employees and what and when they post on social networking sites is a common question. Let me make it clear that social media is not a fad. As technology has evolved over the last 30 years, we have become more dependent on it as a part of our daily lives and especially in a business context. Consider how technology changes impacted your business, like fax machines, the internet, cellular phones, and even email. As someone who grew up with a rotary phone and party line, I am still a child of the internet. It's hard for me to imagine life without technology like Google Maps, my laptop computer, and wireless internet. Without them, I wouldn't be in the industry I am today and you certainly wouldn't be able to download and read this book.

Companies and senior leaders of organizations are under the belief that before the popularity of social networking, they had control of what their employees said and didn't say about their managers, company, and working conditions. This is not the case. While social media has gained popularity since the MySpace era, the internet over the last 20 years and creation of chat rooms, forums, and even blogs has provided individuals an opportunity to publicly air their personal opinions online. These online forums and platforms are not unlike the editorial section of the newspaper, and I have yet to work for a client or company that monitored and scrutinized these for their brand like they do the internet.

HR and Your Company's Social Media Policy

The responsibility to develop reasonable social media policies and ensure employees understand what type of content is appropriate to share falls solidly on the shoulders of HR departments. Legal considerations should also be taken into account regarding this policy.

First, banning your employees from using social media demonstrates a lack of trust, but it also represents a lost opportunity in engagement for your company's social channels. A responsible and dedicated employee knows what needs to be accomplished and will estimate the time required to meet objectives.

Typical examples of companies and employees using branding through social media include the following:

- An employee or former employee connecting with the company's branded Facebook fan page.
- Employees posting corporate event photos on Flickr or sharing company videos on YouTube through intercompany email or via corporate servers.
- A manager receiving a LinkedIn recommendation request from a former or current employee.
- LinkedIn or Facebook alumni or customer groups created without corporate's brand consent or knowledge.
- Live streaming or video recording from smartphones on the company premises.

By opening discussion with your workforce about these potential situations, you will learn more about what your policy should or should not include.

Your corporate social media policy, just like the rest of your employee handbook and policy and procedure manual, should be custom-created with your company and organization in mind. Education, research, and collaboration among other employees and other departments outside of your human resource team are key in ensuring that your social media policy properly reflects your company's culture, values, and business goals.

When evaluating your social media policy and determining how to incorporate it into your company's employee handbook, standard operating procedures, or policy manuals, constant communication is key. Many organizations fail to properly communicate a policy change using an employee acknowledgment as a failsafe crux. Because your social media policy is so critical to your organization, it makes sense that the corporate social media policy that can affect your organization so swiftly should require more than a single employee signature. I call this "one and done."

I suggest communicating your company's social media policy in a variety of ways including the following:

- **Memo from the CEO:** A policy change like this should come from the top and not just your HR or IT departments.
- **Front-line manager meetings:** As the new social media policy is being rolled out, this change should be communicated first to your management teams providing them an explanation that clearly states what the specific corporate policy is. Managers are now using Google and social networks as a form of employee background check.[29] To avoid this scenario, it's important to explain to managers the expectations as well as the boundaries for themselves as well as their employees and provide social media training if needed.
- **Signed acknowledgment form and annual training:** Chances are your legal teams will advise you to include an acknowledgment form of some kind, and I agree. I personally recommend that all employees receive annual social media training or classes to remind them of the guidelines, pitfalls, and suggested practices. The landscape of social media is changing rapidly (e.g., Instagram, TikTok) and each platform should be considered for company brand value as well as guidelines for employees on the use of each.
- **New hire social media training:** In addition to annual social media training for all employees, I advise all companies

to include social media guidelines in their new hire training. As these social networking sites become more popular, it's important to talk about what the expectations are. If you are a company like SHRM, they have a process in place for all corporate Twitter accounts. Social media classes and clear communication like this should be discussed to avoid any potential misunderstanding.

What to Include in Your Social Media Training

- Include a review of common social media platforms, including tips for setting up an account, the difference between social platforms for personal use and business use, and what to include in your social media personal bio to protect your right to your own opinions.
- Outline some examples of social media mistakes that could impact individuals or the company.
- Cover case studies of successful social media strategies that are relevant to your business, for example, recruiting or marketing. Coca-Cola has a social media certification program that any employee who wants to represent the company online must pass. Zappos includes social media training (for personal use and for company customer service) during its new hire orientation.
- Provide an overview of your company's social media policy, including legal risks, actionable offenses, and definitions of and how to report online bullying or workplace harassment (see next).

A Note on Social Media and Workplace Harassment

In the age of digital and social media, harassment can happen on social media platforms. The United States EEOC recommends that workplace anti-harassment policies incorporate dealing with social media. Even if employees post harassing or derogatory information about coworkers away from the workplace, for example, an employer may be liable for a hostile work environment if it was aware of the postings or if the harassing employee was using employer-owned devices or accounts. As a result, the EEOC found that "harassment should be in employers' minds as they draft social media policies and, conversely, social media issues should be in employers' minds as they draft anti-harassment policies."[30]

CHAPTER 10

Business Outcomes and Success

- **The Path of Least Resistance**
- **Metrics Can Turn Recruitment from Cost Center to Revenue Center**
- **Making a Recruiting Business Case for Leadership**
- **How Google Analytics Focuses Your Recruitment and Hiring Efforts Online**
- **Using NPS Data for Recruiting and Candidate Experience**
- **Important HR Metrics: Source-of-Hire**

In this chapter, we'll cover acceptable business outcomes and how to measure success in recruiting in the digital space. We'll look at data, metrics that matter, measurement of engagement and sentiment, and the importance of tools like Google Analytics, Net Promoter Score (NPS) surveys, email metrics, and how to establish the return on investment (ROI) of recruiting and human resources within your organization.

Being able to measure business outcomes is critical in any business initiative, but especially in the digital space for recruiting where the majority of decision makers are not digital natives (although that trend is changing considering that the millennial generation is turning 40). To establish the ROI and benefits that recruiting has on the larger organization, we must be able to measure activities that focus on performance and revenue generation (and savings). Otherwise, we can't justify our roles in HR and the value we bring to the company, nor can we get credibility, trust, and sponsorship from the leaders and stakeholders at our company.

THE PATH OF LEAST RESISTANCE

In order to implement new processes and procedures and make proposed changes, you need the following: reports on results with analytics compared to industry benchmarks to make your case, a solid idea or plan for change, and executive or senior leadership support in the form of an executive sponsor.

Data is imperative in testing and scaling (or scaling back) successful changes in an organization. Perpetual data collection and analysis is the only way to improve your departmental processes. If you're not aware of the success and problems within your organization, it's nearly impossible to make educated adjustments to your programs. The review of metrics is key to understanding the value of implemented changes.

By focusing on analysis and forecasting, HR can predict potential difficulties in processes or possible resistance from employees. You can then develop a plan to communicate effectively with the appropriate people within the company and develop a solution.

Data is the key to improving metrics in the areas of time, cost, and quality. To hit all three components effectively, metrics and analytics will allow you and your recruiting team to make the best informed decisions about what to automate, where to spend time on high-touch tasks, how to reach candidates more quickly and in a targeted way, and how to manage costs.

Using analytics beginning at the sourcing stage can help you quickly identify top prospects for your hiring funnel. This is one function you can streamline via automation. Using assessment programs and hiring algorithms allows you not only to quantify the skills you've identified in top talent but also to identify candidates who are not a good cultural fit or may pose a turnover risk.

METRICS CAN TURN RECRUITMENT FROM COST CENTER TO REVENUE CENTER

When considering the most important metrics for your recruiting team, most of us will want to place a priority on the KPIs that show the revenue saved by the company to demonstrate value. As recruiting leaders, we need to find ways to establish our value that equate in not just expenses but cost savings, as well as missed revenue or revenue generated opportunities.

When working with leadership, there are three challenges that are top of mind for most recruiting leaders. The first is educating leadership on common recruiting practices, metrics, and terminology. This establishes a knowledge baseline for leaders. The second is using recruiting metrics that truly demonstrate value and help leadership understand the recruiting landscape along with tools and processes that are producing results. The third is doing all this in a way that speaks the language of business by aligning metrics with numbers such as revenue or lost productivity when a position is left vacant for a day versus an extended period of time.

Here are the recruiting metrics you should measure when you're the person responsible for reporting to leadership:

- **Time-to-fill:** The average number of days the position is posted to the time a candidate accepts a job offer.
- **Time-to-start:** The average time between when a candidate accepts an offer to their first day as an employee.
- **Candidate-to-hire ratio:** These ratios can vary from the number of applications to hires, to the applicant-to-interview ratios for initial interviews as well as final interviews.
- **Source-of-hire:** What applicant sources are performing the best across the board by position and among recruiters?
- **Quality-of-hire:** Recruiting metrics that measure which source of hire produces the best-performing candidates or those with the longest tenure.
- **Lost productivity per open requisition, per day:** Determining a lost productivity metric for all positions, as well as specific ones per day, can help establish how recruiting impacts the bottom line.

While metrics are a great way to facilitate conversations about recruiting, it's important to be transparent in the performance of your talent acquisition function. Don't oversell your performance, and if you don't meet leadership expectations you've set for you and your team, own up to it. Transparency is key to communicating value to leadership.

Metrics, including those in recruiting, need to tie into the broader workplace trend showing success or failure. They are a solid foundation for more detailed conversations about common business goals for the entire organization and how small changes can make big waves when it comes to recruiting and hiring.

Each metric has specific benefits when it comes to setting goals and analyzing results, and each can be leveraged in reporting to company leadership to demonstrate recruiting ROI. One of the most import-ant is source-of-hire, or what applicant sources are performing the best across the board by position and among recruiters.

It's important to lead with organizational goals when considering what data you need for your reporting purposes.

MAKING A RECRUITING BUSINESS CASE FOR LEADERSHIP

As a recruiting leader, you have done the work of auditing your team's recruiting and hiring processes, made recommendations based on your audit, and have a rough plan of action. The real challenge isn't neces-sarily recruiting the best talent—it's communicating what your team is doing and not doing, as well as making a business case to add tools or increase recruiting spend to drive the best recruiting performance to support your company. The goal when it comes to recruiting metrics is educating your executive leaders on the challenges you face as a support team within a company and the impact that small changes can make on your recruitment and hiring.

Presenting a solid business case for a budget to improve your recruiting processes, whether through new technology, staffing, or other support, means that you have to be fully up-to-date on your company's strategy to understand what may or may not be possible within the current forecasted budget and business strategy. Part of this is understanding how the leadership in your company measures success. If success is measured more on whether a particular goal is reached rather than monetary measures, you may have to adjust your selling strategy to better appeal to that goal. Keep in mind that ROI is difficult to prove in HR efforts without key performance indicators (KPIs), so you'll want to focus heavily on your team's results based on past progress.

If you can clearly define a return on investment in relation to the organization's business strategy, you're already a step ahead. When presenting your business case, you'll want to highlight the following areas to speak the same language as the leadership at your company:

- **The payback period:** This is the length of time it takes for an investment to make back the money initially allocated for the project. Your proposal should include the total investment and how it ties into your goals, with a focus on the timeline in which your team expects to see results. In short, how long will it take to see an impact of the investment?
- **Internal rate of return:** This is the interest rate at which the net present value of all cash flows from a project or investment equals zero. This includes both positive and negative flow. You'll want to include net gains and net losses (prospective and past) in relation to the budget you're asking for.
- **The profitability index:** This is the ratio of payoff to investment of a proposed project. Slightly different from your expected length of return, this should demonstrate expected success metrics and how an investment can improve areas that directly impact cash flow, such as reducing time-to-hire, reducing staff overhead (if you're working to streamline processes), or improving lost productivity per open requisition.

To measure the potential of a program's effectiveness, outline the following:

- Increased revenue attributed to new hires as a result of your proposal.
- Decrease in the time-to-hire attributed to your proposal.
- Increased quality of hire (performance of new hires versus current employees).
- Your company's brand (percent of positive recognition as a great place to work) as measured by industry surveys.
- The project's overall ROI.

If you can clearly define each of these elements, your proposal will answer the important questions regarding the profitability of the project. It helps your case to speak the language of a CFO, using terms like ROI, human capital investment, stakeholders, and fiduciary responsibility.

Presenting a Business Case to Drive Results

Let's use employee productivity as an example. In a *Workology Podcast* episode, I spoke with Jason Hopkins, director of talent acquisition and internal marketing at Emerus Holdings. Jason's work that focuses on lost productivity is the one metric that stands out to help position recruiting and HR as a revenue center instead of a cost center.[1] This means that you can pin a number on the value of an inefficient process. If your recruiting team cuts time-to-fill by one day for each position when a company does 2,500 hires per year with a lost productivity metric of $150 a day, this equals $375,000 in revenue that recruiting has provided the company.

By tying a dollar amount to lost productivity when a position is left unfilled—even for a day—you can demonstrate to leadership the broader impact of recruiting while making a great business case for how a new technology or process change can decrease lost productivity by shortening time-to-fill.

Besides speaking the language of your C-level leadership, your results-based presentation that's tied into your company's bottom line metrics, and a strong case for a new initiative, you'll also want to consider the following when you're presenting to your company:

- Be prepared to back up your numbers. You can be sure that a CFO will want to know the logic behind your calculations. If you're using your presentation to "show your work," you'll want to be very comfortable talking about the logic behind your numbers.
- Show market benchmarks. In human resources, when proposing an initiative that your team hasn't previously executed, using industry benchmarks can help give your CFO an idea of how your

organization ranks comparatively. Your competitor analysis should include regional and national benchmarks based on solid evidence. SHRM is a great resource for industry benchmarks in recruiting.

- Include case studies of other organizations that have been successful at implementing a similar initiative. These don't have to be competitors, but case studies can help you demonstrate how your proposed initiative can potentially impact your company's success. If it works elsewhere, it's likely to work for you.

- Have a realistic implementation plan. This has to include both the financial aspects of the implementation as well as the staff resources, such as the time to completion and the resources needed to execute your proposal. Remember to include third-party vendors if, for example, you're proposing using new technology to streamline recruiting processes. Your vendor can even help you create use case scenarios to develop this part of your proposal.

- Keep it simple. Include an executive summary and an offer to follow up with more complex data. You don't want to present to a room full of busy executives by reading from a lengthy PowerPoint presentation. Topline items are key, with slides to back them up that your leadership team can focus on after your presentation.

To successfully drive results and get your leadership team's buy-in, you will need a strong understanding of your organization's goals, extensive research into your hiring initiative's requirements for success, and a well-presented business case.

Recruiting Dashboards and Data

Recruiting dashboards can be a great way to see the performance across the board not only by region or geography but for individual performers as well. Dashboards can provide a quick snapshot of the time spent focused on specific recruiting processes by segment and activities. This includes time spent on the following:

- Sourcing
- Reviewing candidates
- Conducting initial candidate screenings
- Scheduling interviews
- Gathering interview or hiring manager feedback
- Onboarding

When analyzing this data, the focus is on scaling and streamlining the process by measuring the service and value that the recruiting function brings to the table.

While dashboards and reporting are a great way to display data and view trends, it's important to remember that this data should help improve processes and drive efficiency. Recruiting is challenging to scale. The best way of doing so happens to be by using recruiting tools and technologies, or additional headcount to target candidates and create volume, that quickly drives them into your recruiting and hiring funnels. By simultaneously monitoring recruiting metrics like time-to-fill, you can uncover trends that show how an investment in recruiting can produce results that can make a large impact on the revenue of the company.

This small change in presentation and positioning changes recruiting from a cost center to a revenue center, allowing your department to seek investment for different enhancements and new technologies by using forecasts that demonstrate how the adoption of a process change or technology can impact the larger bottom line, and by offering up different forecasting models from conservative to aggressive.

I know it's extremely challenging to measure and communicate the value that recruiting brings. As HR grew in complexity, it became more involved in business forecasting and establishing ROI that could be directly tied to future and current business success. HR and talent acquisition pros are now strategic business partners involved in the success of organizations by evaluating—not just hiring, firing, and filling traditional advisory roles. We are now challenged with "proving" the value of what often is not measurable, pivoting recruiting from a cost center to a revenue center. Recruiting dashboards and metrics are a great first step to moving the conversation forward in the broader organization around the value that recruiting brings.

Company leaders value transparency, and more and more are understanding that talent acquisition is key not only to company productivity, but also to employer brand and culture. McKinsey and Company's study on CEOs indicated that talent was a top priority for CEOs in 2020.[2] The report, which polled newly promoted CEOs about what they wished they had done when they first assumed the role, found that the majority wished they had focused more on talent within the organization. Recruiting dashboards and metrics are a great way to partner with your CEO on this initiative.

Your executive stakeholders who have an eye on the bottom line want to see results based on data. While previously many human resource operations have been focused on employer brand, candidate experience, and other areas of HR that are difficult to tie to revenue, assigning value to things like days of lost productivity due to a poor hire or a decrease in time-to-fill impacting that same metric is the key to being able to show these results. Having analytics for recruiting initiatives that drive your primary goals and using that data to demonstrate preventing lost revenue can be part of what drives cultural, strategic, and process decisions for your organization, moving HR from cost center to revenue center.

If you are looking for a sample recruiting dashboard to help you organize your metrics, visit www.digitizingtalent.com to download a sample recruiting dashboard template.

Planning for Change: How to Use Data to Take Action

Once you have your data, you can see where the potential opportunities lie. Looking at the analysis, you can start to determine what your first and most important plan of action should be.

Personally, I think the career site is the center of your recruiting universe and is the first priority on which to focus. This can take time and is also dependent on your IT team and your HR technology vendor. In

Chapter 4, I went into a lot of detail about how to optimize your career site and how to measure success with analytics for user behavior. Career sites are the lowest hanging fruit for digital recruiting, and a few small changes in content, SEO, speed, and even the placement of your apply buttons can improve traction. HR technology is a must-have in today's marketplace, but you're going to need to create reporting and data that show how the effort you put into your career site pays off in application rate, site traffic, employer brand visibility, and so on.

Plans that support your company initiatives are going to speak to your company leadership. This includes initiatives like employee self-service or succession-planning programs that support business growth and executive focus. SHRM.org., ERE.net., Recruiting Brainfood's newsletter, Matt Adler's *Recruiting Future* podcast and my *Workology* blog and podcast are all great resources for identifying new initiatives in our industry and how to plan for them. In order to create a balanced hiring plan and strategy, it's vital that you know what initiatives your organization will be focusing on. Your department's role is critical to company success, so it's important to be in the loop for your entire company's organizational planning.

Schedule meetings with department heads and executive team members to assess what they'd like to focus on in the coming months, along with their goals and expectations. Ask how your department can assist and in what capacity, include this information in your forecasting, and you'll have the executive buy-in you need for planning ahead of your formal report.

Here are a few top-level initiatives to consider if you're not already working them into your strategy for the coming year.

Artificial Intelligence (AI). Chatbots are already in place, primarily for customer service and support roles. Many companies have already adopted this technology for human resources. Employees need assistance, and employers need to free up the time of their HR team from tactical work. So chatbots are the right answer to manage both these things in a balanced way. Your applicant tracking system (ATS) might already have this technology enabled or have it in the works. Now is the time to connect with your vendor and find out.

Online Learning and Centralizing your Onboarding and Training. Just as reskilling becomes a trend, online training has emerged as a great way to help employees learn. There is tremendous potential to use this learning approach, especially with a younger workforce. More organizations are using technologies that not only support online learning but also allow them to set benchmarks, centralize company educational resources, and standardize onboarding training.

Talent Pipeline and Automation of HR Processes. In a near-zero unemployment economy, focusing on building an active talent pipeline to fill requisitions and shorten your time-to-hire is no longer optional. If you've started initiatives to improve and streamline these initiatives, now is the time to go all-in. In departments like HR, we must be able to show improved KPIs to support investment in technology and human resources that can address the tight talent market.

HOW GOOGLE ANALYTICS FOCUSES YOUR RECRUITMENT AND HIRING EFFORTS ONLINE

As our work in recruitment and hiring becomes more digital, we need tools, reporting, and metrics that help us understand the needs, interests, and activities of our candidates for the positions we are recruiting for—not to mention our specific company brand. There are ways to accomplish this that require some planning but provide talent acquisition leaders with a more holistic look at the digital recruiting landscape.

Google Analytics is a free tool for websites to monitor online activity and visitor reporting. The reporting tool allows recruiting teams to monitor activity on their website, allowing them to better understand online job seeker behaviors and habits. This tool allows recruiters to gather more data and information around online sources of job seeker traffic, including social media, job boards, and employee reviews sites, which then allows recruiting teams to better assess the ROI of these digital recruiting tools.

Setting Up Google Analytics: The Basics

Setting up Google Analytics is easy and free. The hardest part is working with your IT department to add the required code to the career site itself. You or IT will need a Gmail account to set up. From there, you and your IT team can decide whether to allow for shared access between IT and recruitment or if you want to share reporting access to other Gmail accounts. IT teams tend to like the shared reporting access option because they can control security and revoke reporting access should someone exit the organization who had access to the reporting and data information.

You can use Google Analytics to set up cross-domain tracking between your ATS, career site, and candidate relationship manager (CRM). It can track all of them at the same time to give you a full line of sight from initial candidate entry to a completed application so you can deeply understand candidate behaviors and optimize your recruitment marketing funnel. It may seem complicated when you first get started, but Google Analytics can help you achieve your primary goal of understanding your candidates and learning the best tactics to find them.

Google Analytics provides you and your talent acquisition team web-specific activity data, including the following seven reports that should help you get started:

Type of Device and Browser Used to Access Your Webpages. The tool provides you with data on browser usage like Chrome versus Safari and device type. This includes desktop, mobile, and tablets, providing insights into how many candidates are accessing your site with a mobile device. For example, if you can see that a high percentage of site visits are from a mobile device, you'll want to focus development of your career site on improving user experience on mobile, beginning with a responsive website that works just as well on mobile as on desktop.

Time on Site. How many minutes or seconds are candidates spending on your website? What pages are they lingering longer on and how deep within your website are they digging? The pages on your career site should be "sticky" and lead the user through an informational experience or engagement. Including links to "learn more" and "about us" can help keep a user on your site longer, as it makes it easy for them to navigate to other information they might want to find out about your company.

Video content is another way to increase time-on-site, as users tend to engage with relevant visual content that has an engaging narrative. This could be employee testimonials, video job descriptions, an "about us" video that focuses on your company culture, or video from company events that showcase the perks you offer your employees (outings, happy hours, and so on).

Bounce Rate. If you notice that a specific page on your career site has a high bounce rate, consider re-evaluating the page content, metadata, SEO title, and so on. You can surmise that a high bounce rate means (1) users aren't finding the content useful or easy to navigate, so they leave; (2) organic search results (meta description) are not matching the page content; or (3) the page with a high bounce rate should be redesigned, rewritten, or changed in your site map. Take a step back and review your site map. Is the page with the highest bounce rate necessary? Is it relevant? If not, consider eliminating or housing the content elsewhere and redirecting the URL.

Traffic Sources. One primary function of web analytics is to tell you where your site traffic comes from. No matter how much traffic you attract to your careers page, if you don't know where your traffic came from, you won't understand which of your campaigns and channels are effective. Common traffic sources include the following:

- Organic traffic (from search engines like Google and Bing)
- Paid advertising

- Social media (LinkedIn, Facebook, and others)
- Job boards
- Direct traffic (visitors going right to your website)
- Email

Analyzing traffic sources also allows you to set measurable goals and adjust campaigns based on the results. This is important when considering paid versus unpaid traffic, not to mention your sources of hire that are netting the highest quality candidates. If you aren't using Google Analytics, you are probably unaware that both Indeed and Glassdoor can provide free job seeker referral traffic. So can Google for Jobs (see later section). This data is important to have because it helps you plan on the type of digital recruiting investments your talent acquisition team wants to make.

Web Traffic. Sources are important, but so is understanding which days have the highest traffic on your site. This helps with job post planning and other digital as well as in-person recruiting campaigns. For example, you might find that a landing page for a career expo produces better results before the event versus after the fact, leading you to do more premarketing and planning with job seekers using social media or with the local college, university, and chamber of commerce.

Conversion Rates. It's important to remember that the channel that brings the most traffic to your site might not be your most effective platform. Your end goal is not to boost traffic but to boost applicants. So a channel that brings a lot of people to your site might seem effective, but if none of those site visitors submit applications, how valuable is it actually?

Google Analytics allows you to set specific goals—or the action you want people to take when they visit your site. For recruiters, the end goal is a submitted application. Track this by placing a tracking pixel on your thank you page or by setting your thank you page URL as a goal in Google Analytics. Then you can see which platforms convert visitors to applicants at the highest rate.

You'll use UTM codes (Urchin Tracking Module codes, which are snippets of code attached to the end of a URL) in Google Analytics to track campaign results and sources. A UTM code is a simple code that you can attach to a custom URL to track a source, medium, and campaign name. This enables Google Analytics to tell you where searchers came from as well as what campaign directed them to you.

Keyword Search. Available in Google Search Console (part of Google Analytics), you can view an organic search traffic report that tells you what users search for to find your career site. This can help you identify the top keywords you'll want to use for content (SEO) as well as keywords that you'd like to rank higher for. If you want to capture user traffic for a specific phrase, this is where you'll want to look to see what users search for, in what format, and what page on your site they land on from an organic search source.

Access to all this data and information from Google Analytics can provide you so many insights and nuggets of wisdom in your recruitment planning. For example, one of my clients made a simple change to their job postings by adding a second "apply now" button to the top of every job posting and changing the button color to draw more attention to the call to action. The company wanted higher candidate conversion rates after spending so much time and money driving them to the postings. With the small change of color and adding an additional button, we saw a 200 percent conversion increase over a period of 90 days.

USING NPS DATA FOR RECRUITING AND CANDIDATE EXPERIENCE

The Talent Board reports that 73 percent of candidates were never asked for feedback on their experiences in the application process. It found vast differences in candidate satisfaction in the area of perceived fairness.[2] There was a 128 percent difference between those who felt they were being treated the most fairly—with ratings averaging 4.4 stars—and those who rated application fairness the lowest, or around 1 star. And according to Career Arc, nearly 60 percent of candidates have had a poor experience, and 72 percent of them shared the experience either online or with someone directly.[3]

So how do we collect this data? Many HR departments are using surveys to collect information from candidates. Taking a page out of the marketing handbook, the Net Promoter Score (NPS) is a tool that is used to gauge the loyalty of customer relationships. It serves as an alternative to traditional customer satisfaction research and claims to be correlated with revenue growth. This method can be used with candidates and, in fact, is being used by many companies today. In recruiting, the NPS metric is based on how employees or candidates answer one question: "On a scale of 0 to 10, how likely is it that you would recommend this company as a place to work?"

I had the pleasure of interviewing Will Staney for a 2019 *Workology Podcast* episode on how to use NPS in recruiting.[4] Will is the founder of Proactive Talent, a recruiting and employer branding consulting and staffing company, as well as the cofounder of Talent Brand Alliance, a professional community for employer branding and recruitment marketing professionals. In marketing, using net promoter scores to measure consumer or customer experiences is common. In Will's time at Twilio, he used some awesome coding skills to build a small integration where the candidate received a text message asking the candidate to rate their experience. This text was sent using Twilio's own platform a short time after the candidate's interview was complete, allowing the candidate to provide quick feedback on what the interview and selection process has been like. Will said that candidates were quick to answer because of the timing of the messaging and the use of text.

Not all NPS surveys have to be done this way. Will said that using a simple survey through a technology platform like SurveyMonkey could quickly ask employees and job candidates how their experience was. Recruiters and HR leaders could use the information and data to alert them to possible bad experiences. This quick scoring system helps HR and recruiting pros decide whether to dive deeper into the process and experience. You are looking for scores to better understand what your candidates want and to open a dialogue on how to fix or improve.

What's an Average NPS Score for Recruiting and the Candidate Experience?

NPS scores are 0–10. Will shared what a good NPS score is (9 and above) and what an average score would be (7–8), with concerns for NPS scores of 7 and below. This is important because, in my experience, there isn't a lot of benchmarking and data available around NPS for recruitment and hiring. Your NPS score is less about what your peers and recruiting competition are doing and more about how those you are asking are rating you and what their expectations are from you.

Using NPS surveys to help improve hiring and retention, turn employees into brand ambassadors, and measure the impact of changes in your workplace can be a game hanger for HR teams, especially when it comes to employer branding.

IMPORTANT HR METRICS: SOURCE-OF-HIRE

By consistently capturing a small amount of information during your interviewing process, you can assess data points that will help you optimize your hiring efforts when recruiting at high volume. With the acquisition of talent being one of the most expensive and critical functions in the company, improving upon it is not just a good idea, it's essential. Improving how well your hiring process performs can save thousands of dollars on each employee that you hire. At the minimum you need to know how many people you need to forecast, when the hires will be offered, and when they will be onboarded and fully trained to help fill holes in your organization. There are also standard metrics like turnover by location or position, employee engagement, and general turnover rate.

Calculating Source-of-Hire

At the fundamental level, tracking source-of-hire will help you distribute your hiring resources to the most effective recruiting channels. Calculate this metric by dividing your recruiting source yield by number of applicants from the recruiting source. Use this metric to determine which sources, job boards, or websites are most effective for hiring for your business.

Depending on the type of ATS you use, it should record the application source a candidate entered your pipeline from through automated tracking. Create and review a report to view the distribution of candidates and hires among different sources. You can also collect this data via candidate surveys or using a drop-down self-selection menu as part of the application, although these two are not as reliable because the candidate is providing the data and information. Source-of-hire shows what percentage of your overall hires entered your pipeline from each recruiting channel or source (e.g., job boards, referrals, direct sourcing). This information can help you allocate your recruiting budget more effectively and direct more resources to the most valuable channels.

According to an iCIMS survey, more than 65 percent of employers agree that employee referrals fit better with their company culture.[5] If you discover through data that referrals represent a significant percentage of hires, it might be worthwhile to increase (or add) a bonus for employee referrals. If you discover that a recruiting channel isn't working as well as you predicted, you can drop or adjust these sources.

One of the methods to measure source-of-hire is self-selection at the beginning of your application process. Candidate self-selection is the moment during the application process that the candidate is asked "How did you hear about this job opportunity?" The candidate then selects from a drop-down list that includes your career site, employee referral, specific job boards, and other sources. This response is then collected by the ATS for reporting.

While this is valuable information, there are some problems with the reliability of data collected. The limited accuracy might lead you to make decisions about your source-of-hire that are less informed.

In the early part of your application process, the candidate is more focused on submitting their résumé and references, and a high number of candidates may report the wrong source when asked. Additionally, candidates may have discovered your job posting through multiple sources and may in turn be confused about what to select from your drop-down menu. A more flexible solution should be implemented to capture tracking from multiple sources; for example, if a candidate decided to seek out your career site based on seeing a listing on LinkedIn and on a job board (and perhaps also an employee referral).

With the technology available to us today, there are better ways to track source-of-hire than a self-selection drop-down menu. We can use cookies on our career site and technology that tracks a candidate from interest to application. Tracking traffic to your career site based on sources is likely to be more accurate than a self-selection report if the data you want to collect is purely analytical. You can have reports on both self-selection and traffic source and analyze both for their results and standard deviations from each other.

Most modern ATS solutions provide the ability to do source-code tracking. This ensures that the correct source automatically gets passed into the system for candidates that apply without candidate involvement.

Important HR Metrics: Time-to-Fill

First, to avoid any confusion, it's important to understand that the difference between time-to-fill and time-to-hire is the point you start counting. You may start counting time-to-fill before a job is published, but your time-to-hire timeline starts when your best candidate applies or gets sourced. So time-to-fill tells you how fast your hiring process moves. Time-to-start differs from time-to-hire because it measures the time between when your candidate accepts the offer and their first day as an employee:

- Time-to-fill is the average number of days the position is posted to the time a candidate accepts a job offer.
- Time-to-start is the average time between when a candidate accepts an offer to their first day as an employee.

Recruiting Metrics: Time-to-Fill Key Points

Measuring time-to-fill is an important way for recruiters to demonstrate their efficiency. The longer a position goes unfilled, the more productivity will be disrupted, and the more the responsibilities of that job will be distributed to other staff members. By accurately measuring time-to-fill, you can evaluate the speed of your team's recruitment processes and provide hiring managers with realistic time frames for filling their vacant positions.

The time-to-fill metric also provides you with insight into your recruiting strategies, as well as guidance for resource allocation and budget planning. Longer time-to-fill periods may lead to higher cost-per-hire figures, as more expensive recruiting practices might have to be employed after a position has been vacant for too long. Analyzing metrics like cost-per-hire and time-to-fill, along with the individual recruitment stages that make up time-to-fill, can help identify the most time-consuming and costly aspects of your talent acquisition strategy. It can also help direct your budget and resources to the most efficient and effective strategies.

To accurately analyze and reassess your time-to-fill KPIs, it helps to break this metric down into segments, such as the following:

- Time to advertise an open position on all channels.
- Time to select acceptable candidates.
- Time to complete all interviews.
- Time to complete background checks (if needed).
- Time to create and extend offers.
- Time for candidates to accept offers.

By separately analyzing these segments, you can identify the weaknesses in your talent acquisition strategy and focus on the areas in need of improvement. For example, if your time to identify an acceptable candidate is increasing for certain positions, you might consider re-evaluating the job description's required qualifications or your screening process. It could mean that your hiring manager has unrealistic expectations for quality of hire based on the current marketplace or that there might be a flaw in your employment strategy when it comes to the quality of candidates you're reaching with your job postings.

Recruiting Metrics: Time-to-Start Key Points

If it takes weeks or months before a new hire starts, your company is losing productivity. So what can you do to decrease the length of time between a candidate's acceptance and their first day? When it comes to reporting, time-to-start may be a more significant metric if you see excessive "position vacancy days" based on industry benchmarks or if it begins trending higher. This is because delayed start dates negatively impact revenue generation and productivity.

Time-to-start is typically impacted by things that are outside of recruiting control, including orientation dates, background checks, and other postoffer processes. Time-to-start is a great metric to measure because it helps shine a spotlight on process challenges and bottlenecks that nonrecruiting leaders might not be aware of.

Reducing the time involved from a candidate's offer acceptance and their start date takes a bit of creativity and flexibility. There are few internal factors you can streamline, so you'll want to focus on (1) expecting candidates to put in two weeks' notice at their current job (and potentially wanting some down time before starting at your company) and (2) what you can legally ask of the candidate during the period of time before they officially onboard.

If your company can be flexible with assigning a "prestart" date based on setting up a candidate on payroll immediately or offering a bonus to the candidate for an "overlap period," you can work with your new hire to begin their onboarding and training while they are still technically in their notice period with their current company. You can arrange to meet with your new hire outside of their current company's hours or on a weekend to get this started, or ask the candidate to begin your online training courses on their own schedule.

Consider setting up a "meet the team happy hour" for your new hire with their coworkers-to-be. Offer food and refreshments or hold the event off site. This will give the team a chance to interact with their new team member and gives the new hire a chance to get to know who they'll be working with.

As long as your new hire is able to be flexible and your company leadership understands that these activities may kick off pay for active employment, these can be very effective methods to speed up time-to-start.

Finally, don't attempt to entice a candidate to avoid working out a notice period for their current employer. After all, when an employee leaves your company, you'd expect them to give notice. Would you want to hire someone who was willing not to give their current company notice?

Time-to-fill and time-to-start are two of the most difficult gaps to close in your recruiting metrics, but it can be done and done ethically. When you can demonstrate success to your company leadership by moving these numbers in a positive direction, they'll be even more invested in your recruiting team's efforts and the impact on company productivity and the bottom line.

Recruiting Metrics: Qualified Candidates Per Hire

This metric measures the number of candidates who make it past the first stage of your hiring process. It helps to show how effective your sourcing, advertising techniques, and qualifications provided by the hiring manager have been in attracting the right candidates to your job posting and opening.

If the number of candidates seen before a candidate is hired varies widely or is too high, it indicates your entire hiring process is not targeted or focused enough. For high-volume positions, a hiring manager should only need to see two to three people before hiring a person. Shoot for four if it's a unique, critical, or senior-level spot.

A bonus metric to consider is the number of candidate ratios in total to help forecast and plan for high-volume hiring. This is key for forecasting applicant numbers needed for new location openings or when hiring for seasonal or temporary positions.

Recruiting Metrics: Candidate Acceptance Rate

A company's offer acceptance rate is a fairly simple metric—it essentially provides an indication of how likely a candidate is to accept an employment offer. In a sense, it measures the overall success of your recruitment process.

This is an important metric because it is directly tied to your candidate experience. According to research from IBM on *The Far-Reaching Impact of Candidate Experience*, better candidate experiences are linked to higher acceptance rates.[6] The study reveals that candidates who are satisfied with their experience are 38 percent more likely to accept a job offer. Most candidates (over 60 percent) talk about their experiences with friends and family. With mobile and social media, feedback (good and bad) spreads faster than ever. This affects not only the reputation of the hiring organization but also their ability to attract other candidates in the future.

The calculation for an offer acceptance rate is straightforward. Just take the number of accepted job offers divided by the total number of job offers given within a period of time. Taken as a percentage, this rate represents the percent chance that someone will accept a job offer from your company.

Recruiting Metrics: Interview-to-Hire Ratio

An interview-to-hire ratio measures the number of conversations your hiring staff has with prospective employees, from phone conversations, to assessments, to various rounds of interviews. Interview-to-hire ratio shows the effectiveness of a company's recruiting efforts and whether they could be improved. To find your ratio, divide the number of interviews completed over a period of time by the number of hires over that period of time.

When companies have a high interview-to-hire ratio, it usually means they are spending valuable time interviewing, which could result in interviewing too many candidates for each job. While it is important to interview several viable candidates to find the best person for each open position, it is equally important to be able to identify the top few candidates before interviews begin. When recruiting in high volume, it's crucial to implement a screening process that ensures you effectively screen out candidates who are not likely to be a good fit. This can be done via online surveys or assessments, a tool that prescreens résumés for specific keywords relevant to the position, or quick phone screens. Companies can also re-evaluate their minimum job posting qualifications or by creating opportunities for candidates to learn more about the company and position prior to formally applying for the job. Taking some time at the beginning of the process will save time for your hiring managers, bypassing candidates that aren't qualified or would not be a good fit.

Improving the Interview-to-Hire Ratio

Break down your average interview-to-hire ratio report into individual roles and see if one specific job opening is responsible for skewing your results. Do the same by hiring manager and department to see who is struggling. You can also break it down by hiring stage to see if your numbers are lower or higher at the screening or initial interview stage versus the final hiring manager interview. If they are higher at the end stage, you can work with your hiring managers to offer support so that they better understand the qualifications and expectations from the posted roles.

This metric is key in being able to speed up your time-to-hire and streamline your recruiting processes from start to finish. Being able to break it down by stage is an easy way to identify the slowest areas of your hiring funnel. If more people are being interviewed without offers being extended, it could also ultimately impact the candidate experience and your employer brand.

Using these metrics to streamline your recruiting processes is imperative to the function of your human resources team. They are also key in recruitment planning, forecasting, and budgeting. Without them, it's difficult to justify budget increase requests for new programs and technology that could further improve the productivity of your team.

The acquisition of talent is one of the most expensive and critical functions in your company. Using metrics for these particular ratios can help you work with your team on specific areas and improve on how well you're screening and interviewing, which can save your company thousands of dollars on each employee you hire.

CHAPTER 11

Artificial Intelligence and Other New Recruiting Technology

- **Trends in Intelligent Recruiting Technology**
- **Recruiting Technology, Venture Capital, and Technology Adoption**
- **What We Expect from a Modern ATS**
- **How HR Buys HR Technology**
- **Artificial Intelligence Basics in HR**
- **Artificial Intelligence, Chatbots, and HR**
- **Recruitment Marketing Platforms**
- **Artificial Intelligence and Programmatic Advertising**
- **Finally, Fool Me Once . . .**

Today's recruiting technology is collaborative and comprehensive focused on the candidate experience as well as hiring manager and recruiter engagement, to make the hiring process agile and flexible. It also allows companies to hire quickly and effectively in these changing markets, which makes the technology indispensable for successful recruiting. The pain points along the way are the same with any other technological evolution: How do we keep up? How do we implement new technology? Where are our IT partners? Do we need to learn how to code? Do we outsource to a third-party vendor or maintain new technologies in-house? How do we even understand what this new technology does?

To understand the changing landscape of technology that supports recruiting and the digital revolution in human resources, we must first understand a basic history of HR technology and how it has impacted our industry.

I mentioned previously the modern applicant tracking system (ATS) was first developed in the 1990s as a way to house online applications for the purposes of online storage and compliance. Personnel professionals were overjoyed with the functionality as it made much of the hiring process paperless. We said goodbye to the file cabinets filled with handwritten job applications and replaced them with file cabinets filled with interview notes from those same candidates.

Fast forward 20-plus years and today's recruiter expects much more from an ATS. Companies that develop these systems have also helped turn the ATS from a simple compliance-friendly database into a highly engaged tool designed to enhance the entire hiring lifecycle.

In this chapter we will focus on a variety of technologies that are emerging and increasingly important in how a digital talent acquisition team sources, hires, and engages talent. I'll discuss a variety of technologies, some you may be familiar with and some not.

Before we go any further, I want to point out that human resources is highly dependent on candidate data, and the technology they use must be more than compliant. This technology must be easy to use, be collaborative for multiple users in the hiring process, and enhance the candidate experience. Rather than simply storing data, intelligent recruiting technologies are a partner for recruiters, streamlining day-to-day processes and freeing up time for recruiters to spend on human-to-human interaction.

TRENDS IN INTELLIGENT RECRUITING TECHNOLOGY

An Increase in Mobile Applications

According to a study by Pew Research Center, 28 percent of all Americans have used a smartphone for part of their job search.[1] For 18- to 29-year-olds, that number jumps to 53 percent. And they're not just reading job descriptions—more and more want to apply for a position right then and there on their phone. Your recruiting software should be responsive for mobile and allow integration with social accounts such as LinkedIn to make it as easy as possible for candidates to apply on your careers page.

The Gig Economy

Your ATS should allow customized workflows and contractor skills categorization. A study by Intuit predicted that gig workers will make up 43 percent of the US workforce by 2020, and recruiting technology must keep up with this trend by making it expedient to quickly hire and onboard contractors; otherwise they'll move on to their next gig.[2] It's a zero-unemployment, candidate-driven market. Intelligent recruiting software should shorten your time-to-hire significantly to engage and retain contract candidates.

Employee Referrals

According to a LinkedIn survey, 48 percent of recruiters say referrals will be their top source of quality hires this year.[3] Referrals are hired faster, perform better, and stay longer at a company than your standard applicant.[4] An employee referral portal allows current employees to connect their social media accounts and broadcast job openings to friends, family, and acquaintances quickly and easily. Your ATS should be able to track employee referrals in the hiring funnel and notify the referring employee as changes occur, as well as calculate referral bonuses and rewards.

Your Employer Brand

A strong brand impacts whether qualified candidates will decide to join your team—or accept a competitor's offer instead. According to a LinkedIn survey, 72 percent of recruiting leaders worldwide agree that employer brand has a significant impact on hiring.[5] There's plenty of evidence that a great employer brand makes it easier to recruit, and it also impacts the business's bottom line in more than one way. For most companies, those numbers can equate to millions of dollars in savings and reduced time to recruit. Your ATS should allow for career site branding customization and consistency across channels, as well as multimedia integration. A Glassdoor US site survey reports that 75 percent of candidates are likely to apply to a job if the employer actively manages its employer brand (e.g., responds to reviews, updates their profile shares updates on the culture and work environment).[6]

Today's recruiters expect software to handle everything from job postings to application to onboarding and employee training, and these expectations are reasonable. The ATS has moved far from a compliance database into a highly engaged and developed tool designed to enhance the hiring process. The modern ATS must be able to integrate with existing HR solutions, such as human resources information systems (HRISs), background check screening, sourcing, interview technology and candidate relationship managers (CRMs).

RECRUITING TECHNOLOGY, VENTURE CAPITAL, AND TECHNOLOGY ADOPTION

The new talent landscape involves many different moving parts—from career sites, job boards, and recruitment marketing technology to ad buying, interview technology, referral tools, and to social media searching. It is complicated, with the focus on talent tech combined with the infusion of venture investment that exceeded $2 billion in venture investment in 2019, according to George LaRocque, founder and principal HCM market analyst for LaRocque LLC. In fact, the company tracked $1.448 billion of venture capitalist investment in the second quarter of 2019, which is more than any quarter in 2018. This means that, at the midpoint in the year, we're less than $1 billion away from all of the venture capital tracked in 2018.[7]

"Across industries, everyone has a talent problem," LaRocque said. "They are competing with each other for a limited talent pool, and they have to get creative in the way they source." That is spurring them to adopt applicant tracking systems and recruiting apps, as well as in-house tools to engage workers and manage succession planning faster than they might have in the past. "HR is being pushed to find more innovative ways to address the talent issue," LaRocque said. "It is driving the adoption of more HR applications in small businesses."

While the growing pains that come with new technology adoption are consistent for small and large companies, not making time for technology will create a much larger pain point in the future. The time savings we can achieve in recruiting and HR from new tech make these tools immediately worth the investment—and what company isn't suffering from understaffed HR teams! The future solution is to be able to automate and streamline the most time-consuming tasks we take on so that our HR and recruiting teams can focus on high-touch and personal relationship and talent funnel building.

WHAT WE EXPECT FROM A MODERN ATS

The ATS has moved from a compliance database into a highly engaged and developed tool designed to enhance the hiring process. Today's ATS must be able to integrate with existing HR solutions, such as HRIS, background check screening, sourcing, interview technology, and CRM. At a very basic level, this is what we should expect from our ATS:

A System That Is Customized to Suit Our Needs

An ATS should be specific, yet its interface should not be too complex, making it user friendly for all parties who are involved in the hiring process, from the recruiting coordinator, to the candidate, and especially the hiring manager. If recruiting is going to change, the technology needs to suit all their needs.

A Simple Yet Robust Reporting Dashboard

Data, metrics, and information are the key to great hiring, and yet only a small percentage of ATS technology users actually interact with the reporting dashboards of our software in favor of Excel spreadsheets.

Easy Search

Whether it's searching for a specific candidate or a group of candidates to determine our organization's speed to scalability, I want a technology that can provide me with information and resources so I can be a part of business leader conversations. I want to be able to discuss not just things like our time-to-hire but also the anticipated speed at which we will be expected to hire for a new location, facility, or a division of employees based on our current candidate database.

Designed for Productivity and Efficiency

I want an ATS that doesn't require pushing candidates through seventeen steps before I make a hire in the system. I want an ATS that allows me to see the complete hiring process so I don't waste time fumbling through piles of interview notes and spreadsheets. I want an ATS that automatically adds iCal invites to my busy work schedule. I want a technology that knows intuitively how to make the most of my time for maximum productivity.

Designed For a Team

Best-in-class hiring for an organization takes a team, a village, and your entire company. An ATS needs to incorporate all team members who are involved in the hiring process, providing them with customized access, unique information, and reporting. I want a technology that allows my entire organization to claim ownership for the hiring and talent attraction process.

A System Focused on Cultivating Candidate and Prospect Relationships

A modern ATS is a system that allows for ease of information, communication, and the candidate experience. It's a hybrid ATS/CRM that helps to build a talent pipeline of prospects to fill those new and yet to be forecasted roles within my organization. It's a technology that makes the hiring process more fluid and flexible to our organization's growth needs.

Because of the complexity of these systems and the integration with other recruiting and HR technology, it's important to have a list of expectations when considering upgrading and implementing a new ATS, as well as to use for a check-in with your current ATS technology vendor.

HOW HR BUYS HR TECHNOLOGY

If you've been following *Workology* for any length of time, you already know that one of the things I get fired up about is the selling, marketing, and engagement process between human resources and recruiting professionals with industry service providers and vendors. In my personal opinion, there is a great deal of misinformation about the buying, demo-ing, and selection process leading to plenty of missteps by a handful of eager sales professionals and organizations that hurt the rest of the industry.

I believe it is our responsibility as HR leaders and buyers to educate the market, not the other way around. That's exactly why I am seeking to educate HR technology vendors and service providers on buying practices and expectations. In 2018, I created an HR and Recruiting Buyer Survey to ask readers how they purchase and discover their HR and recruiting technologies, as well as how they use them.[8] The survey had an amazing response, some expected and some not so predictable. I'm excited to share the results with you here, as well as in some ongoing work to help recruiting tech vendors and providers, with data that show what we in the recruiting industry (I'm including talent acquisition as well) expect and want from our technology evaluation and buying experience.

With regard to company size, the majority of respondents work for companies with fewer than 50 employees (23 percent), with the remainder pretty evenly distributed from 10,000 or more employees (13 percent) to 1,000–5,000 employees (13 percent) and 101–250 employees (15 percent). This is a nice snapshot of the variety of company size in our industry.

The majority of responses to "How many technologies do you consider and demo as part of the buying process?" fell into one to three products (66 percent), with 31 percent considering four to eight products. As far as the number of people involved in the evaluation process, most survey respondents said fewer than three (56 percent), with 31 percent responding that between four and eight people are involved in the process. When you consider that these evaluators are looking at three products on average, with more than three stakeholders involved in the process, vendors should understand that this decision-making process will lengthen the time from demo to decision.

I also asked about the final decision. More than 65 percent of respondents said they were responsible for evaluation and recommendation, and just 20 percent responded that they were the final decision-makers, meaning that the majority of recruiters and HR pros have to get buy-in from someone else at their company, likely a CEO or other C-level executives. Another key point for vendors to consider is that it's just as important to help your contact "sell" their decision as it is to sell your software.

The industry of respondents varied wildly, but the technology and telecommunications industry led with just over 21 percent of responses. What I find interesting about this trend is the adoption factor.

Technology companies tend to be early adopters, frequent purchasers, and typically involve their IT departments in the decision-making process. I always recommend that any company involve their information technology department when buying and considering new recruiting or HR software, as it's imperative to the adoption of the software as well as predictive buying (i.e., how will this work for us with our future technology adoption). The next largest industry segment to respond was consulting at 11 percent, which makes sense considering that one of the roles a consultant plays in the recruiting industry is technology consideration and adoption.

The majority of responders role was within human resources (52 percent), followed by "Other" at 18 percent. "Operations" and "Corporate Recruiter or Talent Acquisition" were equal at 9 percent each. One of the interesting factors, however, is in the first question I asked. In response to level of experience, 28 percent had three to seven years of experience, 22 percent were senior level (sixteen or more years) in the industry, and just 10 percent were C-suite level. Just 9 percent were entry level (zero to three years of experience). This means that vendors targeting C-level execs for recruiting technology purchases are missing the mark. Their real demographic is midrange in experience and likely has a great deal of influence on the final decision, even if that decision is made by a C-suite exec.

ARTIFICIAL INTELLIGENCE BASICS IN HR

In September of 2018, I attended an HR technology conference where the phrases "machine learning" and "artificial intelligence" were at peak hype levels. While everyone at the conference was talking about AI, I felt like we needed to step back a bit and get some foundational information on what AI is and how it works in human resources tech. Naghi Prasad is an HR technology cofounder and CEO with an AI technology called Astound. He has a master's degree in machine learning from MIT and a PhD in AI.

Naghi says that, at a basic level, AI is about developing computer systems and algorithms that are able to perform tasks normally associated with human intelligence like visual perception. Surprisingly, AI has been around for over 50 years. Naghi says that there was a wave of innovation in natural language processing in the 1970s and 1980s. AI again experienced innovation in the area of expert systems in the 1980s and early 1990s, followed by machine learning through the 1990s. In the 2000s, computer technology and resources became more affordable and could house larger amounts of data, resulting in AI further evolving with a focus on deep learning.

AI is focused on building human-like intelligence focused on automation. Naghi sees a lot of use cases for AI in HR technology in the areas of talent sourcing, candidate evaluation, employee engagement, and what he calls "employee service." Imagine a technology that can quickly answer employee questions using AI. Naghi talks about how AI technology can help us understand, respond to, and customize responses to employee questions (like, for example, an employee who is looking for information on how to find their W-2).

I believe everyone who has worked in an HR generalist-type role understands the need for a type of AI technology like Naghi describes. While questions about FMLA paperwork, time-off requests, and how to set up or change direct deposit are important, they are extremely time consuming and repetitive. AI technology in HR can help change that.

ARTIFICIAL INTELLIGENCE, CHATBOTS, AND HR

AI is becoming more and more common, and people know they're not talking to a real person, but it allows you to find out what your candidates are asking about the job or your company. You can implement dynamic content personalization based on a conversation with a chatbot. You can gather information about a candidate's level of experience that might not be in their résumé or LinkedIn profile, which allows you to deliver more qualified candidates to your hiring managers. This responsive technology can be on your website, your social platforms like Facebook Messenger, and even email automation.

Automation technology allows us to develop scripted responses and nurturing messages that drive results in an industry where relationships are everything and recruiters are focused on candidates to hire and conversion goals.

One of the focus areas when it comes to automation and building candidate relationships is marketing to passive candidates. In this talent market, the right candidate is out there, but they may not be ready for an interview. To help warm them up, you can lean on CRM technologies to automate emails and other communication touch points to help candidates learn about a company and why they would want to work there. This is crucial for building and nurturing your candidate funnel.

How Chatbots Can Help Improve Productivity in HR

First, let's define what a chatbot is. According to SHRM, it's a computer program that can simulate conversation—either via text or voice.[9] Chatbots, powered by AI and armed with machine learning, can interact with humans and become increasingly agile with each interaction. Chances are you're familiar with robo-assistants like Amazon's Alexa, Apple's Siri, and Microsoft's Cortana. If you've ever interacted with one of these tools, you were interacting with a chatbot.

As a small business owner and entrepreneur, I'm all about productivity and prioritizing my time to ensure that I can do my best work while juggling clients and growing my business. The feeling of never having enough time and too much to do is constant. However, it is really not that much different than when I worked in HR. In fact, it's exactly the same.

In the world of entrepreneurship, productivity is critical to your success. However, in my experience, employees are not always celebrated for being productive or highly proficient with their time or effort. I think much of this stems from fear: the fear that if we are too good at our job or if we find an easier way to do something, we will be rewarded for our creativity and productivity by automating ourselves out of a job. I want to believe this isn't true. I think that those who are productive should be rewarded through additional projects, new training, and different opportunities within the business. Unfortunately, this doesn't always happen, and I think that those who are highly efficient are seen as the enemy and become a target for roadblocks and office politics.

It's easy to get bogged down in the small stuff, like those emails that seem to never end. It's those administrative requests like paperwork filing, employee questions, and business leaders. It's that small stuff we keep sweating, and chatbots can help drive productivity, allowing us to focus on the more strategic efforts by still providing a level of service that our employees and business partners expect.

In 2018, I quietly launched a chatbot on *Workology*. We've tried and experimented with a number of different ones. At present, I am using Facebook Chat. It's not AI, but you do have access to a live person over Facebook Messenger to ask questions and interact with. It's been a great way for customers to quickly get access to resources and answer questions without the heaviness of email messaging.

Using chatbots has become easier through open source development, and most require little or no coding. If you have a business page on Facebook for your company, you can even use an intuitive chatbot, like Chatfuel, for messaging via Facebook 24/7. Voilà, you have a 100 percent response rate for your business page.

Chatbots are unlikely to replace the human factor in recruitment. Ideally, they can take on the more labor intensive, transactional elements of the application process, freeing up your time to focus on high-touch tasks in your recruiting funnel.

How Chatbots and AI Can Support HR
Recruiters are overwhelmed by too many open positions. Candidates are frustrated with hiring processes that they view as too slow. So how can chatbots help your HR team?

Allegis Global Solutions conducted a survey in 2016 of two hundred job candidates to determine how comfortable they were interacting with "online robots" during the interview process. The results included the following:

- About 57 percent of respondents were either "fairly" or "extremely" comfortable interacting with AI applications when answering initial questions during the application and interview process.
- Candidates were most comfortable interacting with bots during the scheduling and interview preparation process; 66 percent were either "fairly" or "extremely" comfortable.

These tools can support recruiting professionals with the human interactions common to the hiring process—receiving a résumé or application, setting up times for interviews, conducting interviews, making an offer, receiving an accepted offer, and beginning the onboarding process. In short, chatbots can save time, expedite the hiring process, and reach more candidates. Here are seven ways chatbots can help HR and recruiting and free up your time to focus on high-touch tasks.

Appointment Scheduling. Chatbots can allow candidates to schedule phone or in-person meetings (similar to how Calendly works). A lengthy interview scheduling process can damage your employer brand. It could also mean that you miss out on the best candidates because they get tired of waiting and accept a job with your competition instead.

Using a chatbot that's calendar-synced, candidates can book their interview through the chatbot. With calendar sync, it can access the calendars of the interview panel members. This means that the interviews will be booked based on their real-time availability. This can prevent double-bookings or having to reschedule because not everyone was free at the agreed time.

Customer Service. This is important to both candidates and employees. Candidates have frequently asked questions. Employees spend hours each month searching for basic company-related information. Chatbots can quickly get the answers they are looking for, improve your candidate experience, and make employees more productive and satisfied.

Chatbots are especially relevant for millennials, as this group relies heavily on mobile messaging platforms and new technology to stay connected. Chatbots are also extremely useful for the 3.7 million employees that work remotely and don't have face-to-face access to HR. As a result, more talent will be retained due to better, faster, and easier forms of communication.

Candidate Screening. A chatbot can help in the screening process by not only getting prospective employees' information but also performing quick background checks. Immediate answers hold onto potential applicants longer because they provide instant responses that keep potential applicants interested. As a result, there will be an increased number that actually complete applications.

Answers provided to potential applicants by chatbots are generally quite accurate and complete. This high rate of accuracy may reduce the need for follow-up questions. And without any additional questions, this will speed up an applicant's decision-making about whether they want to apply. A high accuracy rate is possible because recruiting questions generally cover a very narrow range and most questions are easily predictable. As a result, you don't need advanced AI technology to produce satisfactory answers about your jobs and the company.

Onboarding. When a new employee is hired, the onboarding process tends to be repetitive, and many questions from new staff members are predictable. The same applies to many parts of the training process for new employees.

A startup called Talla, based in Boston, develops chatbots designed to help new workers get up to speed and be more productive. The company is using advanced machine learning and natural language processing techniques in an effort to create software that is smarter than the average bot. Talla launched a prototype bot for managing to-do lists on the workplace communications platform Slack. So far, about six hundred companies have added the chatbot to their Slack channel and are using it.

Benefits Enrollment. Some large HR software providers are already experimenting with chatbots as a new employee interface, allowing them to select benefits, choose 401(k) options, and enroll in various company programs (such as gym membership or lunch options).

Rather than trying to remember everything at once, a chatbot for HR will answer questions in real time, resulting in faster decision-making for employees. A chatbot for HR teams creates an effective approach to answering crucial questions such as "When do we get paid?" or "How can I switch dental providers?"

Employee Communication. Companies like Overstock.com are using AI chatbots for its customer service employees. Overstock's chatbot is called Mila. In addition to "chatting in sick," employees can use Mila to schedule time off, check their schedules, and do a variety of other tasks that used to require making a phone call or sending an email. Now the company can fill schedules and replace workers faster, which ultimately saves money.

Microsoft has a chatbot for employees called Adbot that mines the corporate directory for information. The company is also working on building a bot on top of its intranet so employees can ask a digital assistant simple questions, such as "What's for lunch at the café?"

Companies like MeBeBot have changed the game for companies that don't necessarily have the dedicated staff to create chatbots for internal use, as it can be added as an integrated AI assistant that allows organizations to achieve the same results as a larger organization.

Training and Development. Using chatbots for training is effective because it offers more interactive participation by employees rather than sitting through a standard training video or watching a PowerPoint presentation.

The evolution from using a chatbot as a productivity tool to using a chatbot to facilitate employee learning and development is natural because a good chatbot can communicate with learners in the same way friends and colleagues do. Learners won't ignore a message from a dear friend, and they likely won't ignore one from a chatbot if the chatbot is smart, friendly, and adds value to their day.

Having a chatbot that provides hundreds of answers a day means that recruiters don't have to write up answers or take as many phone calls from potential applicants. As a result, chatbots free up valuable recruiter time to do more important tasks.

Getting started using chatbots is a simple process if you already have data to train the bot, like company knowledge bases, employee training documentation, internal service ticket records, and FAQs, to name a few. Take these essential documents and pair them with one of the many chatbot solutions out there, and you can get started in no time.

If you take a look at every aspect of the HR value chain, ask how you can alleviate the repetitive tasks to spend more time with candidates. One of the major future skills needed will be critical thinking. Your company's AI can handle the basics, but we will need to upskill our human workforce to handle complex tasks. There aren't enough people currently being educated for AI, and we see that as a skills shortage, so if you want to be adaptive for the future workforce, this is something you should consider now.

The bottom line is that your company needs to have a clear AI strategy. We have historically seen "mobile first," and that is rapidly shifting to "AI first." Be prepared to tackle the obstacles your company will face with AI. At the end of the day, we're still dealing with people and people have feelings that must be considered when you're adapting to a new technology.

Questions to Ask HR Tech Vendors about Their AI Technology

While I know that many of us are looking hard at adding AI into our HR technology stacks, there are a number of companies that, while they claim to have AI, do not have actual AI in their HR tech. And because all demos are slide decks and demo environments, it is extremely hard to vet that technology. This is why Naghi shared a list of questions to ask the HR technology provider you are considering:

- How does the software get more accurate and learn from questions and interactions?
- How does the technology understand employee responses or questions and their variations? Does it respond differently or provide a canned response like a FAQ?
- What is the AI technology plan for changing and evolving (with the larger business but also with the clients)?
- How does the technology recognize and respond to workplace policy changes that necessitate a new or updated response?
- When your AI cannot answer a question or provide a satisfactory response, what happens? Who is notified of the request for information, and how do you work with your client to make sure that the information is updated or changes are made?

The Role of Artificial Intelligence in the Recruitment and Hiring Process

Automation is going to take our jobs, according to a lot of articles about the talent marketplace and the future of work. A lot of people are making the claim that AI is the end of jobs. It sounds scary, but the good news is, they're wrong. While AI will eliminate some work, it will primarily free people up to do different things, fine-tune their skills, and allow businesses to lower prices on products and services because automation saves time and money.

One example I discussed in 2018 with Talroo's CEO Thad Price was that the automated checkout introduced in the 2000s in retail was supposed to be the end of front-of-store cashier positions. Except it wasn't. Instead, business and payroll shifted, but the cashier role ended up transitioning into a higher level customer service position. Yes, it was still a checkout, but it also helped the customer. Thad mentioned a visit to Lowe's, which has had automated checkouts for quite some time. Years ago, industry experts predicted that automation would lead to self-service frontline employees would be absent, and companies would use technology so they didn't have to hire retail staff. But at Lowe's, while there were customers using the self-service checkout, there were people in the signature blue smocks all around the front of the store, helping customers choose paint colors, walking them to where the lightbulbs are giving advice on indoor and outdoor plants . . . you get the picture Automation didn't cut the number of frontline staff that Lowe's retains it simply allowed its frontline staff to focus on customer-oriented tasks No more wandering around a big-box store talking to yourself and wondering where the employees are.

This is a great example of what AI can do for recruitment and hiring There will always be a human element to human resources, and if we need more of anything, it's free time for high-touch personal contact So if you're in recruiting and think you might be replaced with a chatbot at some point, think again. The robots aren't taking over, and companies are adopting AI at a record pace, particularly in the tech sector but also in retail, restaurant, manufacturing, shipping, and just about any industry with repetitive tasks that can be automated. Machines used to perform mechanical tasks, but with today's technology, machines can also "think" (meaning that they do what we program them to do) Consider autonomous vehicles, smart algorithms that Amazon uses to predict what you might buy next, and data mining and collection.

The Role of AI in Recruitment and Selection

In the recruiting lifecycle, automation has advanced to the point where it can help streamline just about every facet of recruiting, screening and selection. Programmatic job advertising is a great example of being able to "set and forget" targeted job postings. In recruiting, here are five stages of the recruiting life cycle that AI can impact:

1. **Automation:** Automation includes chatbots and interview scheduling automation tools. Many companies have already adopted this technology for human resources. Employees need

assistance, and employers need to free up the time of their HR team from tactical work. So chatbots are the right answer to manage both these things in a balanced way. Your ATS might already have this technology enabled or have it in the works. Now is the time to connect with your vendor and find out.

2. **Matching:** Matching as an automated process means that you no longer have to spend hours slogging through hundreds of résumés for a single position. Automation technology allows companies like Talroo to program job-matching algorithms that scan résumés for keywords in your job description or based on parameters you have identified for the role. This technology can narrow your hundreds of résumés down to dozens of qualified candidates. The promise of AI for improving the quality of hires lies in its ability to use data to standardize the matching between candidates' experience, knowledge, and skills and the requirements of the job.

3. **Qualifying:** Once the initial match screening has been completed automatically, AI allows us to adapt the job qualification process from someone on the team sending out a list of questions to potential candidates to setting a list of qualifying questions that are autogenerated based on an online application. Does it affect the candidate experience? Not negatively. Your recipients don't know (or care) if the questions are autogenerated or sent by a human being. And that human being can now focus on personalization of messages for candidates that are farther down in your hiring funnel.

4. **Reach:** This is where we really get excited about the potential of AI. By using data and targeting, intelligent algorithms can allow advertisers to exponentially improve the effectiveness of their campaigns, particularly in the area of targeted reach. Intelligent algorithms are constantly learning, which means that the more you use them, the better they work for you. Programmatic is built on this concept, and it's what Talroo does really well. For example, once your posting is ready, your

targeted reach is projected based on audience size and geo-graphic data. In real time, automation can assess the efficacy of your campaign reach, make recommendations on what to adjust to improve reach, and optimize the performance of your cam-paign so that you're getting more mileage out of every dollar in your advertising budget.

5. **Analytics:** So we're still going to need data analysts, and those data analysts are thrilled that they no longer have to run seven different reports using five different systems to create ten spreadsheets to analyze benchmarks for your organiza-tion's hiring key performance indicators (KPIs). Automation means that once a report is set up, the data can be aggregated from multiple sources and parsed in multiple ways, generating a single report or series of reports that allow our data analysts to spend their valuable time assessing data and making adjustments based on data (as opposed to collecting it).

List of HR and Recruiting Artificial Intelligence Resources

If you are looking to brush up on the topic of artificial intelligence in recruitment and human capital, I've put together a list of recommended resources, including an assortment of books, podcasts, articles, and other resources to help you become well-versed in the subject quickly and thoroughly. Over the last several months, I've written a number of arti-cles and white papers for clients on how HR leaders can prepare for how AI is changing our workplace landscape.

These resources below have been my favorite go-to sources for myself and my friends:

- *Artificial Intelligence for HR: Use AI to Support and Develop a Successful Workforce*

  Ben Eubanks has a new book out that provides a nice frame-work for use of AI. Ben's background as an HR practitioner provides the reader with robust insights.

- *Circa 2118: What Humans Will Do When Machines Take Over*

  Peter Weddle, job board and talent acquisition expert, wrote a book that provides book provides an interesting look at the future employment landscape and what HR and recruiting leaders can expect.

- "Podcast Ep 154—Artificial Intelligence Basics for HR and Recruiting"

  This is a *Workology Podcast* interview that dives into the basics of AI with Dr. Naghid Prasad, who has a PhD in AI.

- "Podcast Ep 121—How Artificial Intelligence Creates Discrimination in HR & Recruiting"

  This is a *Workology Podcast* interview with Dr. Jutta Treviranus on the subject of AI and how it could create discrimination in hiring and recruiting.

- "A Look at How AI *is* Powering HR and the Future Workplace"

  This post discusses several sessions and impressions from the HR Technology Conference on the subject of how AI is changing and driving innovation in human resources.

RECRUITMENT MARKETING PLATFORMS

I am a firm believer that the new world of recruiting is marketing focused. Recruiters must be comfortable on multiple social media channels including Twitter, Facebook, and other position-specific communities by job title, vertical, or niche. With the prevalence of recruitment marketing comes recruitment-marketing software. Recruitment marketing has followed the trajectory of traditional marketing platforms like Marketo and Hubspot. Recruitment marketing platforms have evolved from HR leaders using heavily modified traditional marketing software programs to vendors that are developing recruitment-focused marketing platforms that allow you to use automation, integrate with your ATS, and offer improved analytics and integrated data in a single source. These platforms support your marketing, employer branding, outreach, and career site.

There are a lot of platforms out there, but the real standouts have an eye on future technology and integration that goes beyond your ATS to serve as a candidate management system (CMS), recruiting software, automated marketing technology, and single source for email marketing (nurture, drip, and job-posting email campaigns) and take personalization to the next level with scoring for personas based on cookies on your career site and what your candidates are sharing on social media.

Software review site G2 defines and qualifies recruitment marketing platforms as follows:[10]

> Recruitment marketing platforms offer a variety of features to facilitate recruiting marketing efforts including social recruiting tools, job distribution features, and candidate relationship management (CRM) capabilities. Many of these features are similar to those that support inbound marketing efforts within marketing departments. Organizations use recruitment marketing platforms to market job openings, engage with candidates, nurture their interest, and encourage the submission of applications. Many of these platforms also offer tools for identifying candidates at events such as campus recruiting events. Recruitment marketing platforms are traditionally implemented in HR departments and used by internal recruiters to build talent pipelines. These platforms enable users to treat candidates as "leads," qualifying them in a similar manner as leads in sales operations. Organizations can use recruitment marketing platforms to increase the volume and quality of applicants. Recruitment marketing platforms can be implemented either as a standalone solution or as part of

an integrated HR management suite. These platforms can also be integrated with applicant tracking systems (ATS) and onboarding software to form a talent acquisition suite. Many features present in recruitment marketing platforms are similar to those found in email marketing, customer relationship management (CRM), and organic search marketing products.

To qualify for inclusion in the Recruitment Marketing category, a product must:

- Provide tools that help optimize employer branding on career sites, job portals, and employee testimonial pages.
- Streamline the distribution and marketing of job openings.
- Offer a candidate relationship management (CRM) system to track and organize candidates.
- Facilitate employee referrals and social recruiting efforts.
- Offer a built-in applicant tracking system or integrate with third-party ATSs.

As the need for more outbound recruiting increases, the demands on recruiters to work faster, smarter, and better to win over top talent have increased. The biggest challenge is that we don't have enough time to execute outbound recruiting at scale. Automation technology has been helping other departments scale for decades. The same AI, machine learning, and predictive analytics that are helping marketing teams target new leads and sales teams manage customers can now be applied to candidate recruiting as well.

The five overarching stages of recruiting are planning, strategy development, search, screening, and evaluation and control. The first four can be developed in a vacuum, but as you reach the evaluation and control stage, data is an imperative. And without technology, we don't have data.

Looking at the big picture, you can identify areas for improvement in recruitment planning and strategy development with an eye on productivity and implied success (as opposed to applied success data) For search and screening, you can make some modifications to streamline both with recruiting technology. In fact, many HR teams are not taking full advantage of existing technology that is already available in an ATS or CMS. The new recruitment marketing platforms require minimal effort to set up basic automation technology for candidate response, application status, welcome emails, and personalization via email or text.

The fifth step, evaluation and control, typically feeds the first four. It's the difference between "guessing" and "knowing." Most HR leaders have an idea of what needs improvement in steps one to four, but without data, we cannot isolate exactly where or by how much. Given that recruiting teams run on data, making decisions about candidate outreach, engagement, screening, and other high-touch tasks requires reporting and metrics, even if you only focus on the bare minimum.

Even if you're using basic dashboard and reporting, Google Analytics to understand traffic on your career site, source-of-hire reports from your ATS or CRM, and other performance reporting from technology partners, you're spending a lot of time gathering and parsing data from multiple sources. While most modern ATS platforms have dashboards and reporting functionality, we must take the time to set those dashboards up to see the high-level metrics that help us do our jobs. A single-source data reporting dashboard within an integrated recruitment marketing platform is literally the future of our industry.

Sourcing Technologies and Tools

When we look at the talent acquisition (TA) process, one of the most important pieces is proactive recruitment or sourcing. Instead of relying on candidates to find us, we use the internet and find them. I had the opportunity to interview Mike Cohen for a 2019 *Workology Podcast* episode on sourcing technology.[11] You might know him as Batman in talent acquisition and sourcing circles. He is a sourcer, TA leader, frequent speaker at conferences such as ERE, and writer at SourceCon.

Mike walked us through a list of his favorite sourcing and recruiting tools. As a sourcing geek and recruiting practitioner, he is passionate about finding not just the coolest tool but the one that helps improve those recruiting pain points that seem to suck the most out of our day. The podcast interview has a laundry list of recruiting tech "who's who."

His favorites include (1) Hiring solved; (2) HireEZ, formerly Hireutal; (3) EngageTalent; (4) SeekOut; and (5) HumanPredictions. Mike loves sourcing in a place that we often overlook, and that is Facebook. He offers up a number of free and paid tools to use to leverage the data your potential candidates share on the social media platform we love to hate. That includes Intelligence Search, peoplefindthor.dk, and Osint Tools.

Prior to our interview, I asked Mike if he could walk listeners through the basics of Boolean and Google X-Ray sourcing. His response surprised me in that he recommended we DON'T talk about Boolean logic. He says there are so many tools that can do the dirty work of Boolean for you without knowing the operators and logistics. In fact, he recommends Prophet II, which is a new and free tool by Hiring Solved that is a Boolean builder and searcher.

Sourcing is more than just cool tools—it's also engaging and qualifying candidates while building that trust. But how many times should you touch the talent through phone and email? The magic number is 7–11 times before a candidate responds to your messages, emails, or requests. As recruitment marketing follows traditional marketing, we must follow our sourcing efforts to evaluate the number of engagements to conversions. This means we have to understand touchpoints along the candidate journey. Each touchpoint is a message that literally "touches" a customer (candidate). Collectively, touchpoints create the candidate experience. Touchpoint marketing analyzes the assets and processes that make up the touchpoints and maps them according to where they lie in the candidate journey. Digital touchpoints refer to engagements with your brand online, which include your career site, job ads, search engine results, and social media.

I love technology and all the cool tools and tech. It seems to be endless when it comes to recruitment and sourcing. What I find interesting is that so many of the tools that Mike mentioned are originally sales and marketing tools that have found their way to recruitment and hiring. There isn't a platform, program, chatbot, AI feature, or anything else out there that is going to solve all of your problems, make this job easy, or get you all your placements automatically. There are only tools and users of tools. Some tools are a better fit for some people and organizations based on a variety of reasons and factors.

Sourcing with Matching Technology

This is where sourcing technology and AI meet. Matching technology tech companies focus on parsing and matching résumé and job description data. It has evolved from Boolean keyword searches to natural language processing, semantic search, and other matching technology that involves other observable and procured data or machine learning.

Not only are we accustomed to using matching technology, but candidates now expect job matching services to match them to relevant jobs that suit their experience levels, skill set, and geographic preferences. These jobs are increasingly being accessed via their mobile device first, with candidates following up later via desktop to apply or express interest if the platform or the career site is not mobile-enabled.

An exciting trend in job-matching technology comes in the form of candidate matching, where smart-search technologies are being developed to crawl the web and match candidates that meet hiring and job description criteria. Companies like Pocket Recruiter, Series C-funded Entelo with its Sonar product, and ThisWayGlobal are turning traditional jobs and matching on its head and using their technology to notify employers of job candidates who have new profiles or job experiences that match a specific job opening. Quite often, companies like those mentioned here are offering services and solutions beyond the scope of simple job matching, further muddying the waters of the recruiting technology landscape.

As a segment within the matching technology vertical, matching systems include companies that provide matching services based on a variety of inputs, including semantic-based matching, assessment outputs, and preference "signals" (e.g., observable data about what types of talent companies are interested in and which jobs candidates are interested in). Matching systems companies may engage in some or all of these functions to deliver services to their consumer, enterprise, or HR tech, publisher, or job board clients:

- Use algorithms, advanced natural-language processing, and AI to identify skills, requirements, and experience in both the job-posting requirements and the candidate résumé profile in the right context to identify a match.
- Create pairings of jobs and applicants anonymously so past and current employers do not know prospective candidates are searching for new jobs.
- Focus on certain industries (e.g., restaurant and hospitality) with high turnover rates to match relevant candidates when companies need them most.
- Focus on high-demand job families (e.g., tech talent for start-ups) to match candidates and companies based on skills and experience, as well as identified preferences to help maximize technical and cultural fit.
- Leverage location as a key matching point.
- Use "smart" algorithms to refine matches based on what talent companies prefer and what jobs candidates prefer.
- Allow candidates to apply through the matching system.
- Direct messaging or brokered connections through a matching platform.
- Provide recruiters with a list of job candidates who are often highly specialized and match with specific job posting or hiring criteria.

Matching systems companies generally charge for platform access and provide matching services free to candidates in an attempt to build the most robust talent pools.

One of the cutting-edge tech topics in recruiting is how intelligent algorithms are now able to provide us with invaluable predictive knowledge for a set of attributes that represent the interests and needs o our target audience, or candidate base. This is also called "programmatic."

In the simplest terms, programmatic and automation are the same. I job advertising, programmatic is the automated buying and placemen of job ads using technology and not human beings. Automation ca improve your current traditional bidding and advertising process becaus programmatic advertising tasks include making real-time, split-secon decisions about increasing or decreasing bids for specific jobs and plac ing the most relevant job ads in front of your target candidates.

Programmatic advertising has grown into a major marketing tech nique over the past few years to the point where now some two third of all ads delivered on the web are using the technology, according t eMarketer.[12]

ARTIFICIAL INTELLIGENCE AND PROGRAMMATIC ADVERTISIN(

AI has a wide use case that employers and supporting HR technologie can tap into, and ad placement to reach job candidates is just the begin ning. Each area of the recruiting lifecycles mentioned in the previou section fits into areas of programmatic for hiring, onboarding, engage ment, and benchmarking. Where programmatic really shines in this life cycle is in automating the process of requisition and job advertising.

There are three areas in the advertising process where programma tic rules:

- Programmatic advertising tools can reduce your cost-per-hire significantly through proactive job ad bidding based on predic tive analytics. This means that the jobs that have enough appli cants have a lower budget or bid, and your budget and resource are diverted to the positions that still need applicants.
- Programmatic tools are efficiency times 100. One example is th "weekend effect," or the increase in applications on the week ends as compared to weekdays. Being able to automate your

job ad spend and display for the weekends to make up for lost traffic on weekdays is a game changer in the recruiting marketplace. If your competitors are manually managing their ad buys, someone is going to have to be on top of the ad buy outside of the traditional work week (and they're not). This means that by using programmatic tools, your company has the advantage of early adoption of automation and can capture an audience that your competitor typically cannot.

- Programmatic can take your quality-of-hire to the next level using matching taxonomy. Programmatic tools rank applicants in real time based on how well they match your specified criteria for an open position. This results in better-matched applicants for all of your job postings.

How Programmatic Intelligence Helps You Compete for Talent

On the most simple level, programmatic advertising is similar to buying clicks through Google Adwords. You define the bids, monitor those bids, and make changes as needed. In recruiting, the goal is to drive qualified applications through clicks, which lead to conversions. The campaigns required monitoring. However, with AI there is one significant difference—programmatic is now automated.

In a market where Google for Jobs is pushing search traffic away from traditional job boards and to its own algorithm and job postings, programmatic is your ringer. And because we're still in the early adoption stage, it also might be your little secret. Even the most advanced SEO experts are still trying to figure out how to drive traffic to job postings. Advice like including a salary range in your job posting is great, but when it comes to your budget for job advertising, algorithms are less significant.

Job boards have been using programmatic ad buying to drive qualified candidates to specific job postings for years now. The difference is, with automation, those same programmatic tools are now available to you and your recruiting team. You can throw your budget at a CPC ad buy, but you're literally throwing your money at a "post and pray" methodology. Programmatic technology lets you move past traditiona advertising and automate your bidding, audience, reach, and spend. Once you've identified your target audience and qualifying keywords programmatic does the work of an advertising business manager.

On a meta level, programmatic works like pixel tracking or cookies on a website. Using hundreds if not thousands of points of data—the websites we visit, the keywords we search, the products we buy forms we've filled out, newsletters we receive, and so on—ad servers used by programmatic software can figure out if you or I are a qualified target when we load a webpage, and deliver (or not deliver) targeted ads accordingly.

Make the best use of your vendor partners to develop creative strategies like programmatic advertising. By using data and targeting intelligent algorithms allow advertisers to exponentially improve the effectiveness of their campaigns, particularly in the area of targeted reach. Intelligent algorithms are constantly learning, which means that the more you use them, the better they work for you. Programmatic i built on this concept, and it's what Talroo does really well. For example once your posting is ready, your targeted reach is projected based or audience size and geographic data. Automation can assess the efficacy of your campaign reach in real time, make recommendations on what to adjust to improve reach, and optimize the performance of your campaign so that you're getting more mileage out of every dollar in your advertising budget.

FINALLY, FOOL ME ONCE . . .

One important side effect of having the power of programmatic at your fingertips is eliminating the possibility of ad fraud. At the inception of this technology, it was available to large companies and ad agencies who created a long, opaque supply chain of programmatic environments, including various types of video ad fraud where less desirable display units were repackaged and arbitraged as high-CPM video ac units (for example, a 300 × 250 in-banner video ad being paraded as a full-screen, pre-roll ad). Having tools and technology for real-time bidding (RTB) protocols, blockchain-based solutions, and programmatic trading means that the ad buying process is transparent, from posting to display to reporting and analytics.

Programmatic tools and transparency in the process give you confidence that your analytics are solid, that you can base future targeting on past campaigns, and that your postings and keywords are hitting the right notes. In short, if robots ARE taking jobs from humans, it's an entry-level scammer job. We're okay with that.

Conclusion: Workplace 2040

- **Building Workforce 2040**
- **Investing in STEM (Science, Technology, Engineering, and Mathematics)**

What's next? Looking back on what we've reviewed, the natural next step is to turn to the future. Where is recruiting heading in terms of digital? How can we prepare for advancements, changes, and increased candidate competition in the short term as well as the long term?

Digital recruiting technology is more automated, customized, and scalable than ever before. And that's a good thing, because in the coming years, we're facing a significant talent shortage and an exodus of boomer employees that will lead to a considerable skills gap. The "Great Resignation" that has followed the pandemic only contributes further to that shortage. Artificial intelligence (AI) is advancing faster than we can adopt the new technology. After two years spent in the chaos of a global pandemic, our economy hangs in the balance and another recession isn't out of the question.

What we do know is that we don't have enough candidates for our open positions. Digital recruitment and employer branding is a relationship that takes time to evolve. Your efforts now may not pay off until we're recruiting the post-Z generation, but we do know that they will pay off.

We also know that our core team, the human beings that keep the "human" in human resources, is always going to be at the heart of recruiting and maintaining a successful and thriving workforce. If we learned anything from the COVID-19 pandemic, we came away with a strong sense that a workplace without empathy will also be a workplace without a positive employer brand or engaged employees, and the actions that companies did or did not take during the earliest days of the pandemic will not soon be forgotten.

BUILDING WORKFORCE 2040

I've been thinking a lot about my 13-year-old daughter and how her future job and career has likely not been developed yet. I encourage her to participate in technology development (she can create a website and produce videos like a pro, says the proud mom), but I can't say for certain how the skills she's learning today will be relevant for her future.

How do we set up strategies for our future workforce for jobs that haven't been invented yet while also planning our HR and business forecasting for the next decade? The fact is, if we look at how much the talent landscape has changed in just the past ten years or even the last two since the beginning of the pandemic, we shouldn't be surprised at how much it will change in the next decade, and we're already seeing the signs. We're operating in a near-zero unemployment economy, we've been introduced to the gig economy, boomers are retiring in droves, and the skills gap is widening. As HR leaders, there are some areas we can focus on now that can help us with a predictive model for what our future workplace will look like.

INVESTING IN STEM (SCIENCE, TECHNOLOGY, ENGINEERING, AND MATHEMATICS)

Just a few years ago, the Bureau of Labor Statistics said we'll need 9 million STEM workers by 2022 to fill the growing demand in the tech economy. And here we are in 2022, looking at a skills gap and a dearth of candidates for these skilled positions. Consider how much this demand will increase in 10 or 20 years. By investing in STEM education, we can introduce today's students—our current and future workers—to opportunities in the new economy.

Despite the efforts we've made in the United States over the past several years, girls and young women remain less likely to pursue education and careers in STEM, according to a 2018 report from Microsoft. The report *Closing The STEM Gap* has data on the gap between the perceptions and realities of girls and young women contemplating their roles in STEM careers and the educational experiences required to build STEM competencies.[1]

According to Microsoft's research, over 75 percent of girls who participate in hands-on STEM activities outside the classroom feel a sense of empowerment. That finding drops to under 50 percent for those who only experience STEM activities in the classroom. Many students are finding external opportunities to collaborate through real-world challenges. This means that a focus on getting a traditional four-year college degree may not always be the best option for every student. Offering opportunities like apprenticeships, internships, and training programs that give hands-on, real-world experience, combined with a two-year degree or no college degree at all (given the student loan debt crisis we're currently experiencing) seem to be a logical step.

Apprenticeships and other types of job training programs in which companies can "grow their own" have been gradually increasing. Companies are rethinking the criteria for certain jobs, and instead of looking for specific types of degrees or certifications, they're looking for candidates who want to grow their careers and setting up internal formal training programs to close the skills gap. These programs also level the playing field for candidates when it comes to diversity and accessibility. Google isn't just hiring Stanford grads anymore (in fact, they were one of the first to develop internal training programs and look for smart candidates to participate). Remote work can be a game changer for accessibility, as candidates have established necessary accommodations and do not have to wait for their employers to adopt technology like screen readers and voice assistants.

Automation and the Changing Nature of Jobs

In 2019, I had the opportunity to interview Peter Weddle for the *Workology Podcast*. Peter is an innovator in the HR and job search space. He's published multiple books including his most recent, *Circa 2118 What Humans Will Do When Machines Take Over*.[2] He's also the CEO of TA Tech. In podcast episode 168, "How Robots Will Change Our Workplace," we discussed how the world will be changing as a result of robots, AI, and other types of technology.

Peter talked about his book and also cited some intriguing research to support how quickly tech is being adopted.[3] A report from Boston Consulting Group reports that up to 23 percent of all industrial tasks will be automated by robots by the year 2025, and PwC says that 38 percent of all jobs will be automated just five years after that (by 2030). These adoption rates of technology in our workplaces combined with the likelihood that employees will be shifting to different jobs and areas of the business puts HR in a unique position to really be the champion of change. And the opportunity for HR to become a leader in the workplace when it comes to the AI conversation means educating ourselves on these topics so that we can prepare our workplace and leaders for the future workplace and business landscape.

I talked a lot about AI in Chapter 11, but it's important to note that this technology swiftly became mainstream while many worried about robots taking jobs. Instead, AI technology is enabling companies to do things they have never been able to do before. Major companies across industries including Hilton, Humana, Procter & Gamble, and CapitalOne use AI and machine learning to navigate through thousands of applications, organize interviews, conduct initial screenings, and more.[4] Companies like AT&T have created custom content on a scale that is generated for candidates throughout the hiring process, including AI-generated video that is customized to language, job title, and just about any other field on an application.

The Growth of the Gig Economy

How we work is changing, and we really can't talk about the rise of the gig economy without talking about the global pandemic that accelerated it. Freelance writers, designers, and web developers have been using platforms like Fiverr and Upwork for years, but the pandemic created a surge in workers signing up on ODT (on-demand talent) platforms. Furloughed employees wanted to work while they waited for companies to reopen. Unemployment numbers were high throughout the pandemic, and many essential workers left frontline industries so they could work safely from home. These platforms offer greater flexibility and agency for workers, and for employers, they make it easy to find and directly engage with gig workers who are willing to do temporary jobs, most of them remote.

Upwork's *Freelance Forward 2020* report found that 59 million Americans freelanced this year amid the COVID-19 public health crisis.[5] That's 36 percent of the total workforce in the United States. For those who freelanced, the following statistics applied:

- 75 percent of those who left an employer to freelance say they make the same or more income than they did in their traditional job.
- 58 percent of traditional workers who began working remotely during the pandemic are now considering working independently moving forward.
- Freelancers surveyed reported lower rates of negative impact of COVID-19 on their overall well-being and financial health than those in the traditional workforce.

The report found that even throughout a global recession, the independent workforce has remained a pillar of the US economy, with independent workers contributing $1.2 trillion dollars to the US economy in annual earnings—a 22 percent increase since 2019.

Additionally, research from PRO Unlimited found that 40 percent of all white-collar workers already fall into the temp or gig category and it was expected that over half of skilled workers would be independent gig workers by late 2021.[6] A FlexJobs survey also reported that 36 percent of workers in the United States have been freelancing during the pandemic, an increase of 2 million since 2019.[7]

While we tend to think of gig workers narrowly—temporary entry-level office roles via staffing agencies, gig workers driving for Uber or Lyft or delivering DoorDash and Postmates, or freelance contractors (1099 workers) operating either on their own or via a platform for freelancers like Fiverr—the industries that are most popular for gig workers have expanded in unexpected ways.

According to research from The Gig Economy Data Hub, the top three industries for gig economy workers are business services (20.6 percent), a diverse category that includes accountants, architects, janitors and administrative support workers; construction (17.2 percent); and education and health services (14.2 percent).[8] Online platform technology has made new forms of work possible, and as this and related technologies develop, they are likely to continue to shape the workforce and contribute to changes in the gig economy.

It is important to note that these workers have different expectations:

- One of the benefits of using ODT platforms is that workers can sign up and start earning almost immediately. Reducing your time-to-hire to get as close to immediate hiring as possible is key.
- Asynchronous, remote, and flexible work arrangements have become commonplace and are central to candidate engagement. For roles that can be done remotely, keep them remote. This also expands your talent pool, as geographic barriers are no longer necessary.
- Employers need to be more flexible to accommodate an independent contract-minded workforce. This doesn't just mean shift work; it also means committing to employee autonomy and allowing workers to schedule work time around what has become their new normal.

All of this suggests that, in simplest terms, the traditional employer-employee relationship is being replaced by the emergence of a diverse workforce ecosystem—a varied portfolio of workers, talent networks, gig workers, and service providers that offers employers flexibility, capabilities, and the potential for exploring different economic models in sourcing talent. And what this means long term is more than simply working within a candidate's market—it's making the shift from hiring employees to engaging consultant candidates for a specified period of time.

Design Thinking and Employee Experience

The difference design thinking can make is similar to how agile project management methodologies help HR and recruiting teams organize, anticipate, and adapt to changes, but carries the thought process a step further into intentional design and how it impacts the user (employee) interaction and experience. This applies to all areas of employee engagement, from candidate experience to onboarding to leadership.

Design thinking is a human-centered approach to creating new, often innovative, solutions to complex challenges impacting human experiences around products, services, environments, and interactions. It is a method traditionally used by designers across various design disciplines, elevated by the technology industry and successfully introduced to the corporate world by companies such as Apple, Phillips, and Google.

Given the changing nature of a global workforce and rapidly growing percentage of next-generation employees, concerns regarding skills shortages and the gradual shift of "power" to the employee, as well as changes in consumer behaviors related to new technologies, the employee experience should be a primary focus area for any HR transformation program, digital redesign projects for a company portal, and employee interaction tools.

Design thinking can help your team understand and redesign each aspect of employee experience, leveraging new technologies and responding to the changing aspirations and needs of tomorrow's workforce—starting from recruitment and new employee integration through learning and development, work environment, collaboration and reporting.

Josh Bersin at Deloitte predicts HR teams will stop designing "programs" and instead design integrated, high-value "experiences" that excite, engage, and inspire employees. HR can leverage design thinking via the following:

- Organizational design, which can incorporate design thinking when restructuring roles or the organization itself.
- Engagement, which research shows can be driven by using design thinking to make work easier, more efficient, more fulfilling, and more rewarding.

- Learning, in which new, self-directed learning experiences can be shaped by design thinking's central principle of putting the user experience ahead of the process.
- Analytics, in which data analysis and design thinking can be linked to recommend better solutions directly to the employee.
- HR skills, which must be upgraded to incorporate an understanding of digital design, mobile application design, behavioral economics, machine learning, and user experience design.
- Digital HR, where design thinking is critical in developing new digital tools that can make work easier and better.

Finally, while the concepts surrounding design thinking are not new and have been used by the design, engineering, and marketing industry for years, they have not always been applied to the kinds of challenges that HR leaders face. But design thinking concepts and approaches are becoming more common and are having a positive impact on the design, delivery, and success of HR programs and HR technology solutions. As HR has more of a spotlight shining on it because of the war for talent, whether it's retention, development, or recruiting, HR can use design thinking as a way to become more strategic and create better solutions and experiences for employees.

While it's difficult to predict exactly what the workforce will look like in twenty years, we can see indicators in all of the areas discussed thus far. It's not enough to have a culture that appeals to next-generation candidates; companies must also invest in change management, training and development, and technology that allows us to be adaptive to what the future model *could* look like.

What's exciting is that in this time and place that we are living in, we have the ability to shape not only the now as we step out of the pandemic but the workplace for the next ten, twenty, or thirty or more years. I don't know about you, but my future workplace and how I work will be on my terms, and it will likely be by a beach with a piña colada in my hand all while working, learning, and collaborating with my clients, team, and peers. In fact, that's my dream destination to work on my next book, consult with clients, and lead my team and company

I think that's the future we all want: the future of choice, the future of personalization, and the ability to find the workplace that's perfect for us in that specific moment, time, and point in our life wherever and whenever we need to be. Because what I need right now in a workplace is very different from what I needed even two years ago. My daughter is on the cusp of high school where she will likely be attending in person on a traditional high school campus, but maybe she won't And that's okay too. Maybe she will succumb to my dreams and decide to finish out her high school at a virtual school taking online classes in a foreign country on a beach. Our future workplace is wherever work gets done that works for us, and how we reach, engage, and collaborate with candidates, colleagues, and our HR teams will also be highly personalized, flexible, and unique. That's digitizing talent. It's leveraging technology and online tools to elevate our work, business, and life.

Notes

CHAPTER 1. THE POWER OF DIGITAL

1. Joseph Johnson, "Global Digital Population as of April 2022," Statista, May 4, 2019, https://www.statista.com/statistics/617136/digital-population-worldwide/.
2. Simon Kemp, "Digital Trends 2019: Every Single Stat You Need to Know about the Internet," *The Next Web*, January 30, 2019, https://thenextweb.com/contributors/2019/01/30/digital-trends-2019-every-single-stat-you-need-to-know-about-the-internet/.
3. *2020 North American Candidate Experience Report*, Talent Board, 2020, https://3cmsd11vskgf1d8ir311irgt-wpengine.netdna-ssl.com/wp-content/uploads/2021/02/TB_NA-Report_Final-02-02-2021.pdf.

CHAPTER 2. RECRUITING REVOLUTION OR EVOLUTION

1. *ISO 30414:2018(en): Human Resource Management—Guidelines for Internal and External Human Capital Reporting*, International Organization for Standardization, 2018, https://www.iso.org/obp/ui/#iso:std:iso:30414:ed-1:v1:en.
2. Jeff Dickey-Chasins, "A Brief History of Job Boards (Infographic)," *Job Board Doctor* (blog), December 4, 2012, http://www.jobboarddoctor.com/2012/12/04/a-brief-history-of-job-boards-infographic/.
3. *24th Annual Global CEO Survey: A Leadership Agenda to Take on Tomorrow*, PwC, 2021, https://www.pwc.com/cl/es/publicaciones/pwc-24th-global-ceo-survey.pdf.
4. Jessica Miller-Merrell, "Episode 266: Making Sense of Human Capital ISO Standards," February 4, 2021, in *Workology Podcast*, https://workology.com/episode-266-making-sense-of-human-capital-iso-standards/.

5. "Intellectual Capital Index," Talent Growth Advisors, 2016, https://talentgrowthadvisors.com/our-big-idea/ici.

CHAPTER 3. THE TRUST ECONOMY

1. *The 2021 Edelman Trust Barometer*, Edelman, 2021, https://www.edelman.com/trust/2021-trust-barometer.
2. "Why We Study Trust," Edelman, accessed May 9, 2022, https://www.edelman.com/trust.
3. *2020 Recruiting Metrics: Candidate Experience Report*, CareerPlug, 2020, https://12gno23uo3pg18e2lq1vatuv-wpengine.netdna-ssl.com/wp-content/uploads/2020/08/Candidate-Experience-Report.pdf.
4. Kevin W. Grossman, "CandE Recruiting Focus 2021," Talent Board, December 10, 2020, https://www.thetalentboard.org/article/cande-recruiting-focus-2021/.
5. Tallulah David, "23 Surprising Stats on Candidate Experience—Infographic," CareerArc, June 14, 2016, https://www.careerarc.com/blog/candidate-experience-study-infographic/.
6. Frederick F. Reichheld, "The One Number You Need to Grow," *Harvard Business Review*, December 2003, https://hbr.org/2003/12/the-one-number-you-need-to-grow.
7. "Understanding Millennials and the Opportunities They Bring to the Workplace," Impraise, accessed May 9, 2022, https://www.impraise.com/blog/understanding-millennials-and-the-opportunities-they-bring-to-the-workplace.
8. Rebecca Gowler, "More Millennials Embracing Freelancing," *HR Magazine*, February 11, 2015, https://www.hrmagazine.co.uk/content/news/more-millennials-embracing-freelancing.
9. Patrick Murray, "Four Ways to Improve Employee Survey Follow-Up," American Management Association, January 24, 2019, https://www.amanet.org/articles/four-ways-to-improve-employee-survey-follow-up/.
10. Steve Cooper, "Make More Money by Making Your Employees Happy," *Forbes*, July 30, 2012, https://www.forbes.com/sites/stevecooper/2012/07/30/make-more-money-by-making-your-employees-happy/?sh=599790115266.
11. Chris Groscurth, "Why Your Company Must Be Mission-Driven," *Gallup*, March 6 2014, https://www.gallup.com/workplace/236537/why-company-mission-driven.aspx.
12. Talent Board, https://www.thetalentboard.org/.
13. *2020 North American Candidate Experience Report*, Talent Board, 2020, https://3cmsd11vskgf1d8ir311irgt-wpengine.netdna-ssl.com/wp-content/uploads/2021/02/TB_NA-Report_Final-02-02-2021.pdf.
14. Kate Reilly, "Five Insights from LinkedIn's Latest Research on What Candidates Want," *LinkedIn Talent Blog*, July 24, 2017, https://www.linkedin.com/business/talent/blog/talent-strategy/linkedin-new-research-inside-mind-of-todays-candidate

15. *Candidate Engagement Archives*, Talent Tech Labs, accessed May 9, 2022, https:// talenttechlabs.com/blog/vertical/candidate-engagement/.

16. "Reporting Inappropriate Content (Flagging a Review)," Glassdoor, updated March 15, 2022, https://help.glassdoor.com/s/article/Reporting-inappropriate-content?language=en_US.

CHAPTER 4. DEMYSTIFYING DIGITAL

1. Andrew Perrin and Monica Anderson, "Share of U.S. Adults Using Social Media, Including Facebook, Is Mostly Unchanged since 2018," Pew Research Center, April 10, 2019, https://www.pewresearch.org/fact-tank/2019/04/10/share-of-u-s-adults-using-social-media-including-facebook-is-mostly-unchanged-since-2018/.

2. Brooke Auxier and Monica Anderson, "Social Media Use in 2021," Pew Research Center, April 7, 2021, https://www.pewresearch.org/internet/2021/04/07/social-media-use-in-2021/.

3. Mansoor Iqbal, "LinkedIn Usage and Revenue Statistics (2022)," Business of Apps, updated May 4, 2022, https://www.businessofapps.com/data/linkedin-statistics/.

4. *LinkedIn's Economic Graph: A Digital Representation of the Global Economy*, LinkedIn, accessed May 9, 2022, https://economicgraph.linkedin.com/.

5. Brooke Auxier and Monica Anderson, "Social Media Use in 2021," Pew Research Center, April 7, 2021, https://www.pewresearch.org/internet/2021/04/07/social-media-use-in-2021/.

6. AT&T (@att), Instagram, https://www.instagram.com/att.

7. "How to Post a Job on Facebook: A Step-by-Step Guide," BetterTeam, accessed May 9, 2022, https://www.betterteam.com/how-to-post-a-job-on-facebook.

8. "Frequently Asked Questions," Reddit, accessed May 9, 2022, https://www.reddit.com/wiki/faq.

9. Theory of Reddit, "The Glossary," Reddit, accessed May 9, 2022, https://www.reddit.com/r/TheoryOfReddit/wiki/glossary.

10. "Recruitment Marketing Benchmark Report," Appcast, accessed June 30, 2022, https://www.prweb.com/releases/covid_19_impact_on_recruitment_mobile_apply_rates_overtake_desktop_for_the_first_time_ever/prweb17748001.htm.

11. Jessica Miller-Merrell, "Episode 299: The Role of the CHRO in the Restaurant Industry," July 22, 2021, in *Workology Podcast*, https://workology.com/episode-299-the-role-of-the-chro-in-the-restaurant-industry/.

12. "eRecruiting & Accessibility: Is HR Technology Hurting Your Bottom Line?" PEAT, November 30, 2015, https://www.peatworks.org/erecruiting-accessibility-is-hr-technology-hurting-your-bottom-line/.

13. "Live and Work from Anywhere," Airbnb, accessed May 9, 2022, https://careers.airbnb.com/.

14. "14 Examples of the Best Company Career Sites (2018)," *Ongig* (blog), 2018, https://blog.ongig.com/company-career-site/examples-of-the-best-company-career-sites-2018/.

15. "Designing Engaging Mobile Experiences: Which Approach Is Right for You?" Aberdeen Strategy & Research, June 16, 2015, https://www.aberdeen.com/ techpro-essentials/designing-engaging-mobile-experiences-which-approach-is-right-for-you/.
16. Keywords Everywhere, https://keywordseverywhere.com/.
17. Mike Madden, "5 Email Marketing Strategies to Try in 2018," *Marketo* (blog), July 2018, https://blog.marketo.com/2018/07/5-email-marketing-strategies-try-2018.html.

CHAPTER 5. EMPLOYER BRAND BASICS

1. Jessica Miller-Merrell, "Employer Review Sites for Employers & Candidates," *Workology* (blog), December 27, 2017, https://workology.com/best-employer-review-sites/.
2. "Strengthen Your Employee Value Proposition," Gartner, accessed May 9, 2022, https://www.gartner.com/en/human-resources/insights/employee-engagement-performance/employee-value-proposition.
3. Brooke Auxier and Monica Anderson, "Social Media Use in 2021," Pew Research Center, April 7, 2021, https://www.pewresearch.org/internet/2021/04/07/social-media-use-in-2021/; Brooke Torres, "Job Seekers: Social Media Is Even More Important Than You Thought," The Muse, accessed May 17, 2022, https://www.themuse.com/advice/job-seekers-social-media-is-even-more-important-than-you-thought.

CHAPTER 6. MOBILE, MOBILE EVERYWHERE

1. "Mobile Fact Sheet," Pew Research Center, April 7, 2021, https://www.pewresearch.org/internet/fact-sheet/mobile/.
2. "Average Email Performance Metrics Worldwide, by Message Type, Q2 2021," Insider Intelligence, August 1, 2021, https://www.emarketer.com/chart/249420/average-email-performance-metrics-worldwide-by-message-type-q2-2021.
3. J. Clement, "Share of Global Mobile Website Traffic 2015–2021," Statista, February 18, 2022, https://www.statista.com/statistics/277125/share-of-website-traffic-coming-from-mobile-devices/.
4. *Cisco Annual Internet Report (2018–2023) White Paper*, Cisco, March 9, 2020, https:// www.cisco.com/c/en/us/solutions/collateral/executive-perspectives/annual-internet-report/white-paper-c11-741490.html.
5. Brooke Auxier and Monica Anderson, "Social Media Use in 2021," Pew Research Center, April 7, 2021, https://www.pewresearch.org/internet/2021/04/07/social-media-use-in-2021/.

5. Katrina Kirsch, "The Ultimate List of Email Marketing Stats for 2022," *Hubspot* (blog), updated May 6, 2022, https://blog.hubspot.com/marketing/email-marketing-stats.

7. Joseph Johnson, "Number of Emails per Day Worldwide 2017–2025," Statista, October 19, 2021, https://www.statista.com/statistics/456500/daily-number-of-e-mails-worldwide/.

8. Joseph Johnson, "Global Email Platform Market Share 2021," Statista, October 21, 2021, https://www.statista.com/statistics/709596/most-used-e-mail-platform-by-market-share/.

9. Joseph Johnson, "Global Email Client Market Share 2021," Statista, October 21, 2021, https://www.statista.com/statistics/265816/most-used-e-mail-service-by-market-share/.

10. "COVID-19 Impact on Recruitment: Mobile Apply Rates Overtake Desktop for the First Time Ever," *Cision*, February 23, 2021, https://www.prweb.com/releases/covid_19_impact_on_recruitment_mobile_apply_rates_overtake_desktop_for_the_first_time_ever/prweb17748001.htm.

11. Barry Schwartz, "Google Begins Mobile-First Indexing, Using Mobile Content for All Search Rankings," *Search Engine Land*, November 4, 2016, https://searchengineland.com/google-begins-experimenting-mobile-first-index-hopes-expand-upcoming-months-262527.

12. "It's Official: Google Says More Searches Now on Mobile than on Desktop," *Search Engine Land*, May 5, 2015, https://searchengineland.com/its-official-google-says-more-searches-now-on-mobile-than-on-desktop-220369.

13. *Mobile-Friendly Test*, Google Search Console, accessed May 9, 2022, https://search.google.com/test/mobile-friendly.

14. "Responsive Web Design," Google Search Central, accessed May 9, 2022, https://developers.google.com/search/mobile-sites/mobile-seo/responsive-design.

15. *2021 Connectivity and Mobile Trends Survey*, Deloitte, 2021, https://www2.deloitte.com/us/en/insights/industry/telecommunications/connectivity-mobile-trends-survey.html.

16. Paul Lee, Mark Casey, Craig Wigginton, and Cornelia Calugar-Pop, *Deloitte's 2019 Global Mobile Consumer Survey*, Deloitte, November 19, 2019, https://www2.deloitte.com/us/en/insights/industry/telecommunications/global-mobile-consumer-survey-2019.html.

17. *2021 Recruitment Marketing Benchmark Report*, Appcast, 2021, https://info.appcast.io/whitepaper/2021-recruitment-marketing-benchmark-report-website.

18. Daniel Zhao, *The Rise of Mobile Devices in Job Search: Challenges and Opportunities for Employers,* Glassdoor, 2019, https://www.glassdoor.com/research/app/uploads/sites/2/2019/06/Mobile-Job-Search-1.pdf.

19. "#SHRM19 Las Vegas Unofficial Party & Event Guide," *Workology* (blog), June 15, 2019, https://workology.com/shrm19-unofficial-party-guide/.

20. EZTexting.com, *2019 Mobile Usage: Report: How Consumers Are Really Texting*, 2019, https://cdn.brandfolder.io/YAYWC2JN/at/5j668ngq5jk54hg425jm769f/2019_Mobile_Usage_Report.pdf.

21. *2017 US Cross-Platform Future in Focus*, Comscore, March 22, 2017, https://www. comscore.com/Insights/Presentations-and-Whitepapers/2017/2017-US-Cross-Platform-Future-in-Focus.

22. *Peak Posting Performance*, CareerBuilder, https://hiring.careerbuilder.co.uk/hubfs/ Resources/Downloads/Whitepaper_-_Peak_posting_performance.pdf.

23. *Cisco Visual Networking Index: Forecast and Trends, 2017–2022*, Cisco, 2019, https:// twiki.cern.ch/twiki/pub/HEPIX/TechwatchNetwork/HtwNetworkDocuments/ white-paper-c11-741490.pdf.

24. R. J. Johnson, "Study: About 67% of Americans Play Video Games (Mostly on Smartphones," iHeart, September 11, 2018, https://www.iheart.com/content/ 2018-09-11-study-about-67-of-americans-play-video-games-mostly-on-smartphones/.

25. Jessica Miller-Merrell, "Gamification in Talent Acquisition," *Talroo* (blog), March 14 2019, https://blog.talroo.com/gamification-in-the-talent-acquisition-space/.

26. "The Interview," Heineken, accessed May 9, 2022, https://goplaces. theheinekencompany.com/en.

27. Tim Lee-Thorp, *Viceroy Energy Leadership Identification*, Vimeo, February 4, 2018, https://vimeo.com/254413808.

CHAPTER 7. JOB SEEKER AND CANDIDATE TARGETING

1. Jessica Miller-Merrell, "Episode 91: Understanding Sourcing's Role in Recruitment and Hiring," April 3, 2016, in *Workology Podcast*, https://workology.com/ep-91-sourcing-recruitment-hiring/.

2. Cotton Delo, "Facebook Admits Organic Reach Is Falling Short, Urges Marketers to Buy Ads," *Ad Age*, December 5, 2013, https://adage.com/article/digital/ facebook-admits-organic-reach-brand-posts-dipping/245530.

3. Stacy Fisher, "The Top 10 Most Popular Sites of 2021," *Lifewire*, updated January 22 2022, https://www.lifewire.com/most-popular-sites-3483140.

4. Shannon Greenwood, Andrew Perrin, and Maeve Duggan, "Social Media Update 2016," Pew Research Center, November 11, 2016, https://www.pewresearch.org/ internet/2016/11/11/social-media-update-2016/.

5. *2021 Recruiter Nation Report*, Jobvite, 2021, https://www.jobvite.com/lp/2021-recruiter-nation-report/.

6. Chris Forman, "Programmatic Job Advertising: Powering the Next Wave of Recruitment," SourceCon, July 19, 2016, https://www.sourcecon.com/ programmatic-job-advertising-powering-the-next-wave-of-recruitment/.

7. "Alumni Services," Bain & Company, accessed May 9, 2022, https://www.bain. com/about/alumni-services/.

8. "Citi Alumni Network," Citi, accessed May 9, 2022, https://alumni.citi.com/.

CHAPTER 8. MAKING DIGITAL RECRUITING ACCESSIBLE AND INCLUSIVE

1. "Persons with a Disability: Labor Force Characteristics," Bureau of Labor Statistics, updated February 24, 2022, https://www.bls.gov/news.release/disabl.toc.htm.
2. "Digital Accessibility," PEAT, accessed May 9, 2022, https://www.peatworks.org/futureofwork/a11y/.
3. Sylvia Ann Hewlett, Melinda Marshall, and Laura Sherbin, "How Diversity Can Drive Innovation," *Harvard Business Review*, December 2013, https://hbr.org/2013/12/how-diversity-can-drive-innovation.
4. "Diversity & Inclusion Workplace Survey," Glassdoor for Employers, September 30, 2020, https://www.glassdoor.com/employers/blog/diversity-inclusion-workplace-survey/.
5. *The Bottom Line: Connecting Corporate Performance and Gender Diversity*, Catalyst, 2004, https://www.catalyst.org/wp-content/uploads/2019/01/The_Bottom_Line_Connecting_Corporate_Performance_and_Gender_Diversity.pdf.
6. *Waiter, Is That Inclusion in My Soup? A New Recipe to Improve Business Performance*, Deloitte, May 2013, https://www2.deloitte.com/content/dam/Deloitte/au/Documents/human-capital/deloitte-au-hc-diversity-inclusion-soup-0513.pdf.
7. Jessica Miller-Merrell, "27 Companies Who Hire Adults with Autism," *Workology* (blog), April 12, 2016, https://workology.com/companies-hiring-adults-with-autism/.
8. *The 2021 Edelman Trust Barometer*, Edelman, 2021, https://www.edelman.com/trust/2021-trust-barometer.
9. Massachusetts Association for the Blind and Visibly Impaired, www.mabvi.org.
10. "Create an Inclusive Apprenticeship Program," PEAT, accessed May 9, 2022, https://www.peatworks.org/policy-workforce-development/inclusive-apprenticeship-programs/create-an-inclusive-apprenticeship-program/.
11. "eRecruiting & Accessibility: Is HR Technology Hurting Your Bottom Line?" PEAT, November 30, 2015, https://www.peatworks.org/erecruiting-accessibility-is-hr-technology-hurting-your-bottom-line/.
12. Lisa Kaplan (@lisackaplan), "THREAD: Today I went to the public library for the first time in a long time," Twitter, June 24, 2019, https://twitter.com/lisackaplan/status/1143275350777978880.
13. Alethea Group, https://www.aletheagroup.com/.
14. Monica Torres, "This Simple Job Hiring Requirement Can Reinforce Poverty," *HuffPost*, July 11, 2019, https://www.huffpost.com/entry/phone-verification-barrier-get-a-job_l_5d1cfc59e4b0f312567e1316.
15. Emily A. Vogels, "Digital Divide Persists Even as Americans with Lower Incomes Make Gains in Tech Adoption," Pew Research Center, June 22, 2021, https://www.pewresearch.org/fact-tank/2021/06/22/digital-divide-persists-even-as-americans-with-lower-incomes-make-gains-in-tech-adoption/.

16. "eRecruiting & Accessibility: Is HR Technology Hurting Your Bottom Line?" PEAT, November 30, 2015, https://www.peatworks.org/erecruiting-accessibility-is-hr-technology-hurting-your-bottom-line/.
17. "DOJ Settlements and Website Accessibility," PEAT, accessed May 9, 2022, https://www.peatworks.org/policy-workforce-development/doj-settlements-and-website-accessibility/.
18. "Information and Technical Assistance on the Americans with Disabilities Act," Department of Justice, accessed May 9, 2022, www.ADA.gov.
19. "WCAG 2 Overview," Web Accessibility Initiative, updated March 18, 2022, https://www.w3.org/WAI/standards-guidelines/wcag/.
20. "Accessibility Principles for Images," PEAT, November 23, 2016, https://www.peatworks.org/accessibility-principles-for-website-images/.
21. *TechCheck*, PEAT, accessed May 9, 2022, https://www.peatworks.org/digital-accessibility-toolkits/techcheck/.
22. "WCAG 2 Overview," Web Accessibility Initiative, updated March 18, 2022, https://www.w3.org/WAI/standards-guidelines/wcag/.
23. "Section 508," General Services Administration, section508.gov; "DOJ Settlements and Website Accessibility," PEAT, accessed May 9, 2022, https://www.peatworks.org/policy-workforce-development/doj-settlements-and-website-accessibility/; *ETSI EN 301 549:V1.1.2: Accessibility Requirements Suitable for Public Procurement of ICT Products and Services in Europe*, European Telecommunications Standards Institute, 2015, https://www.etsi.org/deliver/etsi_en/301500_301599/301549/01.01.02_60/en_301549v010102p.pdf.
24. "WCAG 2 Overview," Web Accessibility Initiative, updated March 18, 2022, https://www.w3.org/WAI/standards-guidelines/wcag/.
25. "Using Plain Language to Enhance eRecruiting," PEAT, accessed May 9, 2022, https://www.peatworks.org/digital-accessibility-toolkits/talentworks/make-your-erecruiting-tools-accessible/talent-sourcing/using-plain-language-to-enhance-erecruiting/.
26. "Buy IT!—Your Guide for Purchasing Accessible Technology," PEAT, accessed May 9, 2022, https://www.peatworks.org/digital-accessibility-toolkits/buy-it/.
27. "Staff Training Resources," PEAT, accessed May 9, 2022, https://www.peatworks.org/digital-accessibility-toolkits/staff-training-resources/.

CHAPTER 9. COMPLIANCE, DIVERSITY, PRIVACY AND RISK

1. "Executive Order 11246," Wikipedia, updated October 20, 2021, https://en.wikipedia.org/wiki/Executive_Order_11246.
2. "Rehabilitation Act of 1973," Wikipedia, updated May 6, 2022, https://en.wikipedia.org/wiki/Rehabilitation_Act_of_1973.
3. "Vietnam Era Veterans' Readjustment Assistance Act," Wikipedia, updated May 7, 2022, https://en.wikipedia.org/wiki/Vietnam_Era_Veterans%27_Readjustment_Assistance_Act.

4. Vivian Hunt, Lareina Yee, Sara Prince, and Sundiatu Dixon-Fyle, "Delivering through Diversity," McKinsey & Company, January 18, 2018, https://www.mckinsey.com/business-functions/people-and-organizational-performance/our-insights/delivering-through-diversity.

5. "VEVRAA Hiring Benchmark," US Department of Labor, accessed May 9, 2022, https://www.dol.gov/agencies/ofccp/vevraa/hiring-benchmark.

6. "Information and Technical Assistance on the Americans with Disabilities Act," Department of Justice, accessed May 9, 2022, www.ADA.gov.

7. L. Kraus, E. Lauer, R. Coleman, and A. Houtenville, *2017 Disability Statistics Annual Report: A Publication of the Rehabilitation Research and Training Center on Disability Statistics and Demographics*, University of New Hampshire, 2018, https://eric.ed.gov/?id=ED583258.

8. "On the Job," Understood, accessed May 9, 2022, https://www.understood.org/topics/en/on-the-job.

9. Aleksandra, "63 Fascinating Google Search Statistics," Seo Tribunal, September 26, 2018, https://seotribunal.com/blog/google-stats-and-facts/.

10. Matthieu Manant, Serge Pajak, and Nicolas Soulié, "Can Social Media Lead to Labor Market Discrimination? Evidence from a Field Experiment," *Journal of Economics & Management Strategy* 28, no. 2 (2019): 225–246, https://doi.org/10.1111/jems.12291.

11. Jay Shambaugh, Ryan Nunn, and Lauren Bauer, "Independent Workers and the Modern Labor Market," *Brookings*, June 7, 2018, https://www.brookings.edu/blog/up-front/2018/06/07/independent-workers-and-the-modern-labor-market/.

12. Liane Hornsey, "Measuring What Matters: Diversity at Uber," Uber Newsroom, March 28, 2017, https://www.uber.com/newsroom/diversity-report/.

13. Bo Young Lee, *Uber Diversity & Inclusion*, Uber, 2019, https://uber.app.box.com/s/sbftlylmmi018wwq5gyplnwu8wntazxx?uclick_id=afa4a615-7b0f-4baf-bf98-bc2530c91863.

14. Jessica Miller-Merrell, "Episode 146: Workplace Elephant: Tackling Age Discrimination," August 8, 2018, in *Workology Podcast*, https://workology.com/ep-146-workplace-elephant-tackling-age-discrimination/.

15. Jo Weech, "Over 40 and Interviewing? Have These Things Happened to You?" LinkedIn, July 19, 2018, https://www.linkedin.com/pulse/over-40-interviewing-have-things-happened-you-jo-weech.

16. Peter Gosselin, "If You're over 50, Chances Are the Decision to Leave a Job Won't Be Yours," *ProPublica*, December 28, 2018, https://www.propublica.org/article/older-workers-united-states-pushed-out-of-work-forced-retirement.

17. Patricia Cohen, "New Evidence of Age Bias in Hiring, and a Push to Fight It," *New York Times*, June 7, 2019, https://www.nytimes.com/2019/06/07/business/economy/age-discrimination-jobs-hiring.html.

18. Jake Frankenfield, "General Data Protection Regulation (GDPR)," *Investopedia*, November 11, 2020, https://www.investopedia.com/terms/g/general-data-protection-regulation-gdpr.asp.

19. Amy Ann Forni and Rob van der Meulen, "Gartner Says Organizations Are Unprepared for the 2018 European Data Protection Regulation," Gartner, May 3,

2017, https://www.gartner.com/en/newsroom/press-releases/2017-05-03-gartner-says-organizations-are-unprepared-for-the-2018-european-data-protection-regulation.

20. Alexa Lardieri, "First Robot Granted Citizenship in Saudi Arabia," *US News & World Report*, October 27, 2017, https://www.usnews.com/news/world/articles/2017-10-27/first-robot-granted-citizenship-in-saudi-arabia.

21. Mike Snider and Jessica Guynn, "'Facebook Is Discriminating against People,' in Housing Ads, Trump Administration, HUD Charge," *USA Today*, March 28, 2019, https://www.usatoday.com/story/money/business/2019/03/28/facebook-advertising-discriminatory-trump-administration-charges/3296995002/.

22. Kevin Granville, "Facebook and Cambridge Analytica: What You Need to Know as Fallout Widens," *New York Times*, March 19, 2018, https://www.nytimes.com/2018/03/19/technology/facebook-cambridge-analytica-explained.html.

23. "Social Media Fact Sheet," Pew Research Center, April 7, 2021, https://www.pewresearch.org/internet/fact-sheet/social-media/.

24. Mary Madden, "Public Perceptions of Privacy and Security in the Post-Snowden Era," Pew Research Center, November 12, 2014, https://www.pewresearch.org/internet/2014/11/12/public-privacy-perceptions/.

25. "Health Information Privacy," US Department of Health and Human Services, accessed May 9, 2022, https://www.hhs.gov/hipaa/index.html.

26. *Cost of a Data Breach Report 2020*, IBM Corporation, July 2020, https://www.ibm.com/security/digital-assets/cost-data-breach-report/1Cost%20of%20a%20Data%20Breach%20Report%202020.pdf.

27. Asaf Cidon, "Threat Spotlight: Lateral Phishing," *Barracuda* (blog), July 18, 2019, https://blog.barracuda.com/2019/07/18/threat-spotlight-lateral-phishing/.

28. 2018 SHRM Employment Law & Legislative Conference, Society for Human Resource Management, March 12–14, 2018. https://www.shrm.org/resourcesandtools/legal-and-compliance/employment-law/pages/6-ways-hr-can-help-prevent-a-data-breach.aspx

29. Jessica Miller-Merrell, "Disparate Impact & Disparate Treatment in the Workplace," *Workology* (blog), April 7, 2011, https://workology.com/part-3-the-era-of-corp-social-media-discrimination/.

30. Chai R. Feldblum and Victoria A. Lipnic, *Select Task Force on the Study of Harassment in the Workplace*, US Equal Employment Opportunity Commission, June 2016, https://www.eeoc.gov/select-task-force-study-harassment-workplace.

CHAPTER 10. BUSINESS OUTCOMES AND SUCCESS

1. Jessica Miller-Merrell, "Episode 145: Recruiting Metrics Drive Business Processes," August 1, 2018, in *Workology Podcast*, https://workology.com/ep-145-recruiting-metrics-drive-business-processes/.

2. Kevin W. Grossman, "Survey Says: What Candidates Want from Employers during the Application Process," Talent Board, July 25, 2019, https://www.thetalentboard.

org/article/survey-says-what-candidates-want-from-employers-during-the-application-process/.

3. Tallulah David, "23 Surprising Stats on Candidate Experience—Infographic," CareerArc, June 14, 2016, https://www.careerarc.com/blog/candidate-experience-study-infographic/.

4. Jessica Miller-Merrell, "Episode 195: How to Use Net Promoter Scores in Recruiting," August 28, 2019, in *Workology Podcast*, https://workology.com/ep-195-how-to-use-net-promoter-scores-in-recruiting/.

5. "How Employee Referrals Impact Retention," iCIMS, October 19, 2018, https://www.icims.com/blog/how-employee-referrals-impact-retention/.

6. Haiyan Zhang and Sheri Feinzig, *The Far-Reaching Impact of Candidate Experience*, IBM, 2017, https://www.ibm.com/downloads/cas/YMOARJJG.

CHAPTER 11. ARTIFICIAL INTELLIGENCE AND OTHER NEW RECRUITING TECHNOLOGY

1. Aaron Smith, "Searching for Work in the Digital Era," Pew Research Center, November 19, 2015, https://www.pewresearch.org/internet/2015/11/19/searching-for-work-in-the-digital-era/.

2. Steve Sharpe and Jen Garcia, "Intuit Forecast: 7.6 Million People in On-Demand Economy by 2020," Business Wire, August 13, 2015, https://www.businesswire.com/news/home/20150813005317/en/Intuit-Forecast-7.6-Million-People-in-On-Demand-Economy-by-2020.

3. Maria Ignatova, "New Report Reveals the Trends That Will Define Recruiting in 2017," *LinkedIn Talent Blog*, October 3, 2016, https://www.linkedin.com/business/talent/blog/talent-strategy/trends-that-will-define-recruiting.

4. Paul Petrone, "Here Is Why Employee Referrals Are the Best Way to Hire," *LinkedIn Talent Blog*, August 3, 2015, https://www.linkedin.com/business/talent/blog/talent-acquisition/reasons-employee-referrals-are-best-way-to-hire.

5. *The Ultimate List of Employer Brand Statistics for Hiring Managers, HR Professionals, and Recruiters*, LinkedIn Talent Solutions, accessed May 9, 2022, https://business.linkedin.com/content/dam/business/talent-solutions/global/en_us/c/pdfs/ultimate-list-of-employer-brand-stats.pdf.

6. "40+ Stats for Companies to Keep in Mind for 2021," Glassdoor for Employers, accessed May 9, 2022, https://www.glassdoor.com/employers/resources/hr-and-recruiting-stats/.

7. Glarocque, "Q2 2019 Global HR Tech Venture Capital Review," WorkTech, July 2, 2019, https://larocqueinc.com/q2-2019-global-hr-tech-venture-capital-review/.

8. Jessica Miller-Merrell, "#HRTechConf: How HR Buys Their Human Resource Technology," *Workology* (blog), September 11, 2018, https://workology.com/hr-buys-human-resource-technology/.

9. Lin Grensing-Pophal, "Chatbots Expedite Recruiting, Save HR Time," *SHRM Magazine*, February 13, 2018, https://www.shrm.org/ResourcesAndTools/hr-

topics/talent-acquisition/Pages/Chatbots-Expedite-Recruiting-Save-HR-Time.aspx.

10. "Best Recruitment Marketing Platforms," G2, accessed May 9, 2022, https://www.g2.com/categories/recruitment-marketing.

11. Jessica Miller-Merrell, "Episode 176: Sourcing Technology You Can't Live Without," April 10, 2019, in *Workology Podcast*, https://workology.com/ep-176-sourcing-technology-you-cant-live-without/.

12. "US Programmatic Digital Display Ad Spending, 2019–2023," Insider Intelligence, accessed May 9, 2022, https://www.emarketer.com/chart/252300/us-programmatic-digital-display-ad-spending-2019-2023-billions-change.

CONCLUSION: WORKPLACE 2040

1. *Closing the STEM Gap: Why STEM Classes and Careers Still Lack Girls and What We Can Do about It*, Microsoft, 2018, https://query.prod.cms.rt.microsoft.com/cms/api/am/binary/RE1UMWz.

2. Peter Weddle, *Circa 2118: What Humans Will Do When Machines Take Over* (TAtech, 2018).

3. Jessica Miller-Merrell, "Episode 168: How Robots & Artificial Intelligence Will Change Our Workplace," February 6, 2019, in *Workology Podcast*, https://workology.com/ep-168-how-robots-artificial-intelligence-will-change-our-workplace/.

4. Amy Elisa Jackson, "Popular Companies Using AI to Interview & Hire You," Glassdoor, December 31, 2018, https://www.glassdoor.com/blog/popular-companies-using-ai-to-interview-hire-you/.

5. *Freelance Forward 2020*, Upwork, September 2020, https://assets-global.website-files.om/5ece60393f5cbb1b2f25ef60/5f60b48411b19fb49de5f664_Upwork_2020_Freelance_Forward%20(1).pdf.

6. "PRO Unlimited Announces Top Market Trends in the White-Collar Gig Economy," Cision, December 1, 2020, https://www.prnewswire.com/news-releases/pro-unlimited-announces-top-market-trends-in-the-white-collar-gig-economy-301182197.html.

7. Rachel Pelta, "15 Top Career Fields for Freelance Jobs in 2021," December 2020, FlexJobs, https://www.flexjobs.com/blog/post/top-freelance-career-fields/.

8. "What Kinds of Work Are Done through Gigs?" Gig Economy Data Hub, accessed May 9, 2022, https://www.gigeconomydata.org/basics/what-kinds-work-are-done-through-gigs.

Index

importance of 192
keyword search 206
measuring success on 58
metrics 57
setting up 203
time on site 204
traffic sources 204–205
web traffic 205
gossip 181
government 24
distrust of 24
Government Accountability Office
(GAO) 157
The Great Resignation 250
growth market 34

H

hacking 182–183. *See also* data breach
happy hour 212
harassment 188. *See also* workplace
harassment
Harvard Business Review 26, 137
hashtag 50, 120
health care 164, 179–181
health insurance 40
high school 258
high-volume hiring 213
high-volume positions 213
HIPAA 178
does not protect 180
Family Medical Leave Act
(FMLA) 179
HIPAA Privacy Rule 179
Occupational Health Records 180
protects 178
resources 181
state-specific 180
Wellness Program Information 180

hiring benchmarks 141, 163
federal contractor 159–160
nonfederal contractor 161–162
hiring button 60
hiring discrimination
age 169
country of origin 165
Facebook 165
in the gig economy 166–169
medical conditions 164, 181
pregnancy 164, 181
Uber 167–169
hiring funnel 193
hiring manager 164, 211, 215
expectations of 211
recommendations 133
video with 104
working with 31
Honeywell 74
Hopkins, Jason 197
HR and Recruiting Buyer Survey 223–224
HR certification exams 50
HRetreat xiii
HR metrics 17–19, 193–194, 199
candidate acceptance rate 214
candidate-to-hire ratio 81, 194
cost-per-hire 17, 126, 141, 211, 244
external source-of-hire 114
internal rate of return 196
internal source-of-hire 114
interview-to-hire ratio 214–216
lost productivity 82, 194
payback period 196
profitability index 196
qualified candidates-per-hire 213–214
quality-of-hire 82, 194, 245
recruitment 74
retention 74, 208, 257
revenue-per-employee 17

About the Author

Jessica **Miller-Merrell** is the founder and chief innovation officer of Workology.com, a workplace resource destination for HR, recruiting professionals, and business leaders, and host of the *Workology Podcast*. The site was twice listed as a "Top 75" career resource by *Forbes*.

Jessica is an HR and recruiting process and optimization consultant, and her expertise is sought after and sourced by publications including *Economist*, *Forbes*, *CIO Magazine*, CBS, *Entrepreneur Magazine*, and SHRM's *HR Magazine*.

Jessica earned a SPHR designation in 2008, SHRM-SCP in 2015, and a Master Neuro-Linguistic Programming (NLP) certification in 2021. She holds a bachelor's degree in anthropology and business from Kansas State University and a master's degree in business administration from Webster University. Jessica is from a small town in Kansas and currently lives in Austin, Texas, with her husband, Greg, and daughter, Ryleigh.

About SHRM Books

SHRM Books develops and publishes insights, ideas, strategies, and solutions on the topics that matter most to human resource professionals, people managers, and students.

The strength of our program lies in the expertise and thought leadership of our authors to educate, empower, elevate, and inspire readers around the world.

Each year SHRM Books publishes new titles covering contemporary human resource management issues, as well as general workplace topics. With more than one hundred titles available in print, digital, and audio formats, SHRM's books can be purchased through SHRMStore.org and a variety of book retailers.

Learn more at SHRMBooks.org.